MENSWEAR REVOLUTION

MENSWEAR REVOLUTION

The Transformation of Contemporary Men's Fashion

JAY MCCAULEY BOWSTEAD

BLOOMSBURY VISUAL ARTS
LONDON • NEW YORK • OXFORD • NEW DELHI • SYDNEY

BLOOMSBURY VISUAL ARTS
Bloomsbury Publishing Plc
50 Bedford Square, London, WC1B 3DP, UK

BLOOMSBURY, BLOOMSBURY VISUAL ARTS and the Diana logo are trademarks of
Bloomsbury Publishing Plc

First published in Great Britain 2018
Paperback reprinted 2022

© Jay McCauley Bowstead, 2018

Jay McCauley Bowstead has asserted his right under the Copyright,
Designs and Patents Act, 1988, to be identified as Author of this work.

For legal purposes the Acknowledgements on p. xii constitute an extension of this
copyright page.

Cover design by Holly Bell
Cover image © Victor VIRGILE / Getty Images

All rights reserved. No part of this publication may be reproduced or transmitted in
any form or by any means, electronic or mechanical, including photocopying,
recording, or any information storage or retrieval system, without prior
permission in writing from the publishers.

Bloomsbury Publishing Plc does not have any control over, or responsibility for, any
third-party websites referred to or in this book. All internet addresses given in this
book were correct at the time of going to press. The author and publisher regret any
inconvenience caused if addresses have changed or sites have ceased
to exist, but can accept no responsibility for any such changes.

A catalogue record for this book is available from the British Library.

Library of Congress Cataloging-in-Publication Data
Names: Bowstead, Jay McCauley, author.
Title: Menswear revolution : the transformation of contemporary men's fashion /
Jay McCauley Bowstead.
Description: New York : Bloomsbury Academic, An imprint of Bloomsbury
Publishing Plc, 2018. | Includes bibliographical references.
Identifiers: LCCN 2017046799 | ISBN 9781474289009 (hardback)
Subjects: LCSH: Men's clothing–History–21st century. |
Fashion–History–21st century.
Classification: LCC TT617 .B67 2018 | DDC 646.4/02–dc23
LC record available at https://lccn.loc.gov/2017046799

ISBN:	HB:	978-1-4742-8900-9
	PB:	978-1-4742-8901-6
	ePDF:	978-1-4742-8902-3
	ePub:	978-1-4742-8899-6

Typeset by Integra Software Services Pvt. Ltd.
Printed and bound in Great Britain

To find out more about our authors and books visit www.bloomsbury.com
and sign up for our newsletters.

To **Christine McCauley** and **Jim Gleeson**, with love.

CONTENTS

List of Figures ix
Acknowledgements xii

Introduction 1

1 Disciplinary Discourses 7
   New markets 8
   (A)historical continuities 9
   New men? 12
   Hipster hate 14
   Performance anxiety 17
   Fearing femininity 19
   Reverse discourse 20
   Contested masculinities 25
   Disciplinary discourses 28

2 Historical Resonances 31
   Fashion and modernity 32
   The birth of consumer culture 38
   The 1980s 54
   Suited and booted 62
   Authenticity and irony 65

3 Body Language: Toward a Phenomenology of Masculinity 71
   Embodied and disembodied masculinities: The male body in the twentieth century 72
   The liberated body 77
   Holding out for a hero 83
   The 1990s and its legacy 92
   The fourth sex: Androgyny and objectification 99

4 Millennial Men 111
Subculture, music, and fashion 120
Queering men's fashion 123
Millennial men 124

5 The Shock of the New 129
The state of the art: Menswear since 2010 131
Androgyny in contemporary menswear 146
Workers of the world unite 154
Athleisure 157
Deconstructing tailoring 160
The new monasticism 164
The shock of the new 168

Conclusion 171

Notes 177
References 187
Index 203

LIST OF FIGURES

Number	Title	Artist/Source	Date	Page No
1.1	Outfit with asymmetric vest and jacket with bottle tops. Helmut Lang Spring/Summer 2004	Pierre Verdy/AFP/Getty Images	2003	23
2.1	Advertisement for His Clothes	His Clothes/John Stephen	1962	34
2.2	"sun…sand…sea…Simpson!" Advertisement	Simpson of Piccadilly	1966	37
2.3	Peter Chatel	*L'Uomo Vogue*/Oliviero Toscani	1969	41
2.4	Di giorno o di sera, con ironia	*L'Uomo Vogue*/Oliviero Toscani	1969	42
2.5	Di Sera una Moda Sdrammatizzata	*L'Uomo Vogue*/Oliviero Toscani	1969	43
2.6	Paris	*Tailor & Cutter*/World Textile Information Network	1970	46
2.7	Paris	*Tailor & Cutter*/World Textile Information Network	1970	47
2.8	Outfit by "Young Club" Norway	*Tailor & Cutter*/World Textile Information Network	1971	48
2.9	Outfit by Miguel Diaz	*Tailor & Cutter*/World Textile Information Network	1972	49
2.10	Presenting the alternative IMBEX (The Alternative Pant)	*Tailor & Cutter*/World Textile Information Network	1972	51
2.11	Shirts with a view	Conde Nast/Jerry Salvati	1973	53
2.12	"The New Glitterati"	*The Face*/Jill Furmanovsky and Fiona Russell Powell	1984	57
2.13	"British Menswear Takes Flight"	*The Face*/Stephen Linard and Eamonn McCabe	1986	58
2.14	Strange Tales! Depeche Mode	*Smash Hits*/Eric Watson	1984	60
2.15	"Desk Set"	Conde Nast/*Gentlemen's Quarterly*	1988	63
2.16	"Chevignon Advertisement"	*Arena Homme+*	1994	67
2.17	Overtones	*Arena Homme+*/David Bradshaw and Tim Richmond	1994	69
3.1	Mayogaine Paris Advertisement	*L'Uomo Vogue*	1971	79
3.2	La Moda a Roma si recita a Soggetto	*L'Uomo Vogue*/Elisabetta Catalano	1969	81
3.3	*Gentlemen's Quarterly*	*L'Uomo Vogue*/Anon	1988	86

LIST OF FIGURES

Number	Title	Artist/Source	Date	Page No
3.4	Grease Monkeys	*The Face*/Herb Ritts and Michael Roberts	1984	90
3.5	"Snip it, rip it, colour it or patch it"	*The Face*/David Sims and Adam Howe	1990	100
3.6	"Wah Wah"	*The Face*/Corinne Day and Melanie Ward	1993	101
3.7	*Raf Simons Spring/Summer 1998—Black Palms*	Yoko Takahashi	1997	103
3.8	Dior Homme Spring/Summer 2007 by Hedi Slimane	*Collezioni Uomo*	2007	105
4.1	A+ Collections: Yves Saint Laurent Rive Gauche	*Arena Homme+*/Tabitha Simmons and Tom Munroe	2001	117
4.2	A+ Collections: Yves Saint Laurent Rive Gauche	*Arena Homme+*/Tabitha Simmons and Tom Munroe	2001	118
4.3	*Clubber at Trash*	Author's Collection/Jay McCauley Bowstead	2002	122
4.4	Jil Sander Spring/Summer 2009 by Raf Simons	Marcio Madeira/Getty/(Photo by Venturelli/WireImage)	2008	125
4.5	Costume National Spring/Summer 2005 by Ennio Capasa	*Collezioni Uomo*	2005	127
5.1	*Craig Green Spring/Summer 2015*	Getty/Photo by Tristan Fewings	2014	130
5.2	*Lanvin Spring/Summer 2012 by Lucas Ossendrijver*	Nathalie Lagneau/Photo by Victor VIRGILE/Gamma-Rapho (via Getty Images)	2011	133
5.3	*Lanvin Spring/Summer 2012 by Lucas Ossendrijver*	Nathalie Lagneau/Photo by Victor VIRGILE/Gamma-Rapho (via Getty Images)	2011	134
5.4	*Lanvin Spring/Summer 2012 by Lucas Ossendrijver*	Victor Virgile/Photo by Victor VIRGILE/Gamma-Rapho (via Getty Images)	2011	135
5.5	*Juun. J Spring/Summer 2014*	Victor Virgile/Photo by Victor VIRGILE/Gamma-Rapho (via Getty Images)	2013	137
5.6	*Juun. J Spring/Summer 2014*	Victor Virgile/Photo by Victor VIRGILE/Gamma-Rapho (via Getty Images)	2013	138
5.7	*Juun. J Spring/Summer 2014*	Victor Virgile/Photo by Victor VIRGILE/Gamma-Rapho (via Getty Images)	2013	139
5.8	*Juun. J Spring/Summer 2014*	Victor Virgile/Photo by Victor VIRGILE/Gamma-Rapho (via Getty Images)	2013	140
5.9	*Raf Simons Spring/Summer 2013*	Yanis Vlamos/Photo: FRANÇOIS GUILLOT/AFP/Getty Images	2012	142
5.10	*Raf Simons Spring/Summer 2013*	Yanis Vlamos/Getty/Photo by Antonio de Moraes Barros Filho/WireImage	2012	143
5.11	Grace Wales Bonner Spring/Summer 2017 by *Ezekiel*	Photo by Estrop/Getty Images	2016	149
5.12	Grace Wales Bonner Spring/Summer 2017 by *Ezekiel*	Photo by Estrop/Getty Images	2016	150

LIST OF FIGURES

Number	Title	Artist/Source	Date	Page No
5.13	Grace Wales Bonner Spring/Summer 2017 by *Ezekiel*	Photo by Estrop/Getty Images	2016	151
5.14	Grace Wales Bonner Spring/Summer 2017 by *Ezekiel*	Getty Images/Estrop/ Contributor	2016	152
5.15	"Fall/Winter Look Book"	Photo by Fahim Kassam	2013	155
5.16	*E. Tautz Spring/Summer 2017*	Photo by Estrop/Getty Images	2016	161
5.17	*E. Tautz Spring/Summer 2017*	Photo by Estrop/Getty Images	2016	162
5.18	Craig Green Spring/Summer 2017	Photo by Ben A. Pruchnie/Getty Images	2016	165
5.19	Mai Gidah Spring/Summer 2016	Ali Adulrahim and Thomas Sels	2015	167

ACKNOWLEDGEMENTS

This book is the culmination of many years of passionate engagement with men's fashion, and, as such, many people have been instrumental in its gestation and eventual emergence into the world. I would like to express my deep gratitude to the teaching team at the RCA's Critical Writing in Art & Design program, Brian Dillon, Nina Power, Jeremy Miller, and David Crowley for their encouragement and critique. Without David's support, in particular, it is unlikely that this monograph would have seen the light of day.

A number of practitioners, journalists, and academics have contributed selflessly to this text; their subject knowledge has proved invaluable. Special thanks are due to Frank Mort, Ike Rust, Charlie Porter, Ali Abdulrahim, Thomas Sels, Alex Needham, Sean Suen, and James Long. I would like to thank Shaun Cole of London College of Fashion for his continuing generosity: I am not the first (and doubt I shall be the last) young academic to benefit from his expertise at a critical point in their career. I am grateful to Andrew Reilly, editor of *Critical Studies in Men's Fashion*, for giving me a break in academic publishing and for his continued support and encouragement. I am also grateful to Bloomsbury Academic for placing their confidence in me and for giving me the opportunity to write this book. Thanks to Jeremy Atherton Lin for casting a critical eye over the manuscript, and in the process improving readability no end, and to Sonia Elks for her advice on the introduction and conclusion (it really helped). Conversations with friends and colleagues, including Frances Grahl, Fennella Hitchcock, and Charlie Athill, have influenced and informed the text: I am lucky to have such thoughtful and engaging interlocutors.

I would like to thank my mother, Christine McCauley, for teaching me to sew and knit and for fostering my love of fashion through our frequent trips to the Museum of Childhood (its beautiful collection of boys' clothes—including, memorably, a kimono and velvet suit—is now sadly hidden away). The wonderful dressing-up outfits my Mother made for me when I was a child were the stuff that dreams are made of, and it was this fascination for the transformative possibilities of clothing, which she enabled, that ultimately led me here.

My husband, Jim Gleeson, has supported me throughout the process of writing *Menswear Revolution* in more ways than I can possibly list, in sickness and in health, in happiness and in sorrow, for richer and, mostly, for poorer—I really couldn't have done it without him.

INTRODUCTION

In the showroom for Autumn/Winter 2016 London Fashion Week Men's, where buyers browse designers' stalls, exchange business cards—and hopefully place orders—the big story was one of stiff and spongy fabrications and complex origami-like construction in which layers of fabric were pleated and folded to cocoon the body.

Designer Wan Hung combined jewel-like tones with precisely engineered clothing that spoke of a glistening interstellar future—three-dimensional cubes of cloth creating textured panels and epaulets, yokes, pockets, and collars cut as nets to stand proud from the garment (Hung, 2016).

At Ali Abdulrahim's label Mai Gidah, cut and decoration were allied to produce pieces that alluded both to Van Eyck and to Ghanaian art: a palette of warm colors were brought together in intricately cut motifs seamed-in to form an integral part of the garment's construction. The silhouette was oversized—reminiscent of late seventies and early eighties avant-garde Japanese design, with pieces either abstractly draping or stiffly standing away from the body (Abdulrahim, 2016).

As I browsed, and handled these original, unusual, startlingly inventive garments, I reflected how much menswear, has changed since my formative years as a teenager in the 1990s. Then, in the years before men's fashion weeks, when only one men's fashion magazine was published in the UK, and long before the advent of fashion blogs, I had scoured niche zines like *Sleazenation, Dazed & Confused, and i-D* (themselves difficult to get hold of, and requiring a special trip into town) for any glimpse of interesting or unusual men's style. I emulated the looks I found using second hand and vintage shop finds and received, for my pains, the stares of strangers, their outright hostility and occasionally, frightening, unprovoked acts of violence.

Within a few years, over the course of the early and mid-2000s, under the influence of pioneering designers such as Hedi Slimane and Raf Simons, men's fashion had transformed—a metric, so it seemed, of the opening up of masculinity. New magazines like *Another Man, Fantastic Man*, and *10 Men* were launched; Lulu Kennedy and Topman began the MAN initiative to nurture menswear talent and to showcase new work; and high street shops Zara,

Topman, and H&M began selling skinny jeans, drapey knitwear, and patent leather shoes. Meanwhile, formerly rundown areas of big international cities such as Shoreditch, Williamsburg, Kreuzberg, and the Canal St Martin were suddenly populated with a new breed of fashionable male—nonchalant, dressed-up, and dandyish.

This renaissance in men's fashion paved the way for today's dynamic scene, in which it has become common for innovative, award-winning designers like Grace Wales Bonner and J. W. Anderson to emerge from menswear rather than from women's fashion (something unthinkable in the 1990s, when radical fashion was taken, a priori, to be womenswear).

As I shall explore, this transformation of men's fashion is not without its precursors, most notably the mod and peacock styles of the 1960s and 1970s and the avant-garde subcultural aesthetics of the 1980s. But the changes that have taken place in menswear since the turn of the millennium—while sharing aesthetic properties of some of these earlier moments of innovation—are also in some ways quite distinct. Crucially, the institutional support for creative menswear has changed radically: since Hedi Slimane launched the inventive and highly successful Dior Homme label, accruing enormous profits for Maison Christian Dior, luxury fashion houses have woken up to the economic potential for men's fashion. As a result, designers like Alessandro Michele of Gucci, Lucas Ossendrijver of Lanvin, and Jonathon Anderson of Loewe are given considerable resources and creative freedom to develop and promote their menswear lines.

Equally significant has been the emergence of new models of gender. Notwithstanding periodic reactionary backlashes, today, the "homophobia, misogyny, violence and homosocial separation associated with orthodox masculinity is increasingly unfashionable" (Anderson, 2009: 153), and there is growing empirical evidence of men's dissatisfaction with "hegemonic" forms of gender expression (Bridges, 2013; Christensen and Jensen, 2014; Barry and Phillips, 2016; Dahlgreen, 2016). In this way, sustained by investment from the luxury sector and from the high street and in dialog with inclusive forms of masculinity, men's fashion continues to develop, to explore new terrains, new aesthetic and formal tendencies, and new approaches to embodiment.

At 9 am on Monday, January 11, 2016, sitting in a basement in Holborn I waited for Sean Suen's Autumn/Winter 2017 catwalk show to commence. Having awoken to the news of David Bowie's death, there was something strangely moving in seeing the models emerge clad in silver trousers, or full-flowing flares—their cheekbones glittering with makeup. It seemed to me a fitting homage to a figure so central to reimagining male dress. These poignant references to Bowie, an inspiration to countless designers, reflected the fact that he (like the other twenty first century boys—Marc Bolan, Iggy Pop, designers John Stephen, Freddie Burretti, and Mr Fish, as well as countless anonymous fashion consumers) was instrumental in pushing back the boundaries of men's dress in the 1970s in a way that was to prove hugely important to more recent reinventions of the male wardrobe.

Along with the glitter, there were allusions to the military in the form of gunflaps, greatcoats, and utilitarian reflective tape which were combined with a seventies glamor—wide lapels, blouson jackets gathered at the waist, silver leather, lurex and jacquard weaves in orange, red, and brown (Suen, 2016). Here, as at the McQueen collection that had shown earlier in the week, the models' faces appeared to be pierced with oversized safety pins—their makeup and jewellery recalling Lee Bowery's collaborator and muse Trojan.

This *bricolé* approach in which the iconic motifs of hegemonic masculinity were combined—anomalously—with seventies and eighties counter-cultural androgyny was also seen at the James Long show that I had attended the previous Sunday. Long had designed a tie-dyed camouflage of jungle green and vivid manganese blue which he had made up as cargo pants and denim jackets. And he had teamed these garments, variously, with striped lurex knits, sequined T-shirts, jogging bottoms, oversized down jackets, sparkling-striped boots, and poppy-printed dressing gowns. It was as if Ziggy Stardust and his spiders had joined a militia (Long, 2016).

In this way, Long and Suen's collections were about reconciling more traditional elements of the menswear wardrobe, be they tailoring or casualwear, with those which—if not feminine precisely—upset and overturned the normal expectations of menswear. This sort of formal and semiotic experimentation was also seen in various ways at Alexander McQueen, Xander Zhou, E. Tautz, and Topman Design that same season. A very modern approach to designing clothing for men and one, as I shall unpick in the following chapters, that speaks to significant changes in the structures of twenty first century masculinity.

As 2016 progressed and as the Italian tailoring label Brioni announced falling profits and planned job cuts—followed by the panicky, short-lived tenure of new, controversial creative director Justin O'Shea—many column inches were spent on the rumored death of the suit (Collard, 2016: 24–25; Hadis, 2016; Stern, 2016). It seemed, to paraphrase Nik Cohn's 1972 refrain, that today there truly were no gentlemen: or to put it in other terms, that men's fashion in late modernity had rejected the petit bourgeois, orthodox masculinities of old, to embrace something much more plural, diverse, and strange.

No doubt the alleged death of the suit has been announced prematurely. After all, in the great revolutionary transformation of womenswear of the 1920s, women didn't give up wearing dresses; rather the look, feel, construction, and meaning of those dresses changed, and as the twentieth century progressed, a much broader range of garments—often borrowed from menswear—were integrated into women's vocabularies of gender expression. Since the turn of the millennium, men's fashion has seen its own revolution, one predicated upon the achievements of earlier decades, and one that is yet to touch all corners of men's sartorial expression. But this radical set of changes has, nevertheless, seen the sector grow at more than twice the rate of womenswear (Milligan, 2011) as a profusion of new men's fashion labels, fashion weeks, magazines, and blogs have been founded, and as menswear has expanded to encompass a much greater range of possibilities, aesthetics, and subjectivities.

In researching this text, I have undertaken interviews with a variety of fashion professionals, designers, journalists, and academics drawing on their insights and experiences, as well as attending and observing fashion shows and trade events. The ideas that I explore in this book have been developed through close engagement with men's fashion over many years, including by working in the field. This auto-ethnographic approach has influenced the way in which I frame my investigation of menswear by foregrounding issues of power, agency, and control.

Informed by this background, my dominant mode of research has been the close reading of garments and images. My approach to the textual analysis[1] of men's fashion is one founded in a desire to tease out the connections between cultural practices and social and political processes. But it is also one that attempts to be attentive to the affective, emotional, aesthetic power of fashion. Which is to say, the way that great works of design both express and simultaneously transcend their sociocultural milieu: the heart speeding up, the shortness of breath, the excitement that viewing a new collection can provoke. Beauty, desire, and enchantment—the messiness and corporeality of the human response—are all too easily obscured by the hard, rational prose sometimes mandated within the academy. In attempting to capture the tactility of fashion, I have looked to writers such as Christopher Breward who so vividly evokes the texture of *fin de siècle* modernity in "Ambiguous Role Models" (2005: 101–118), and to Angela Carter with her lush, expressive, over-ripe evocations of material culture, the body, and place (1979).

It is hardly original, in discussing textual analysis, to draw on the work of Roland Barthes, but his writing—particularly as collected in *Mythologies* (1972)—remains a compelling guide to conducting semiotically influenced readings of popular culture. In this book I not only draw on the structuralist, semiological aspects of Barthes' work, but also upon his intuitive, aesthetic, and emotive reading of popular taste, as captured in his essay on "Ornamental Cookery" (1972: 78–80) in which the sumptuous silliness of Elle's recipes are felt as strongly as their class contradictions.

As well as engaging closely with designers, stylists, and photographers and their work, this book has also developed in dialog with other voices that have spoken eloquently and thoughtfully about menswear both in an academic context—such as Frank Mort, Shaun Cole, Christopher Breward, and Ben Barry—and in the world of fashion journalism like Charlie Porter and Adrian Clark. It strikes me that to appreciate why these writers have spent so much time exploring, discussing, defending, and asserting the importance of men's fashion, one has to understand both the experience of being a man who falls

INTRODUCTION

outside the rules of normative masculinity and also the way that men's fashion, as a discipline, has so often been pushed to the periphery and rendered invisible.

For me, as a slim, androgynous, gay teenager in the late 1990s and early 2000s—someone who found himself reflected almost nowhere in popular culture—it was to fashion that I turned for positive, affirmative representations to which I could relate. In this way, the niche titles of the style press, and the indie club nights like *Nag, Nag, Nag* and *Trash* that they promoted, represented for me wonderful moments of approval and acknowledgement: spaces in which qualities that were elsewhere stigmatized instead became cool and desirable. The transformational qualities of clothing and the practices of customizing, styling, and making garments felt like freedom, agency, and the right to define myself. But wearing flares, seventies Italian shoes and purple angora (sourced from flea markets and thrift shops) also came with risks. On various occasions I was chased down train carriages, shoved up against walls, followed down the street … and finally, and most frighteningly, surrounded by a gang of young men—in the mid-afternoon on a public thoroughfare—and stabbed in the face.

These formative experiences continue to inform my understanding of men's dress, not only because they are etched indelibly onto my body and psyche, but also because they revealed to me—in a way that theory alone could not have—that men's fashion exists as a profoundly political and contested set of practices: a form of resistance to orthodox ideologies of gender so potent that others will try violently to suppress it. My work—like that of Mort, Cole, Porter, Breward, and Barry—articulates the importance of menswear as a form of expression and identity formation. And like those writers, I am not only seeking to reflect observable, empirical realities in my work, but also to actively intervene in a set of discourses (in academia, in the museum, and in the media) that have so often marginalized and obscured men's fashion: discourses that have declared the fashion practices and representations that have been so crucial in the formation of my identity to be silly, effete, and of no consequence. Fashion, for all its limitations and frustrations, has been one of the spaces in which non-normative gender identities have been most accepted, and in which new ways of inhabiting and performing masculinity have been most enthusiastically explored.

Invested as I am in men's fashion, my perspective is not a "view from nowhere" (Nagel, 1986)—mine is not a disinterested perspective uncolored by subject position. In the humanities and social sciences, the subjective and emotional cannot be neatly bracketed off from the rational: as researchers, we not only gain insight through observation and analysis, but also by making sense of our own experiences. In investigating empirical data, I am always an "I" as well as an "eye." Acknowledging my subjectivity is essential because I am not somehow outside or above the historical and cultural processes I describe, I am immersed in them and a product of them. Sociologists Jill McCorkel and Kristin Myers (2003) have noted the ways in which scholars can use their personal experiences to enrich their studies "in the field" and whether explicitly, like bell hooks (1994), or implicitly, like Judith Butler (2011) and Stuart Hall (Akomfrah, 2013), the knowledge one accrues from everyday interactions can inform and enliven one's critical work.

The fact that fashionable men's clothing has changed very rapidly at the level of silhouette, fabrication, and form from the beginning of the millennium onwards is a matter of historical record. So too is the proliferation of menswear labels, fashion weeks, and new men's designers that have accompanied this present decade. But the meaning of this set of events and their connections to our wider culture—as we shall see in the next chapter—is much more fugitive and contested.

In this book, drawing upon diverse visual and material sources, on interview data and on my own experiences, I hope to make sense of the truly radical transformations that have occurred in men's fashion over the past two decades. This menswear revolution has not only resulted in the innovative, playful, irrepressible designs that so impressed me at London Fashion Week Men's and which I explore in more detail in Chapter 5: it also connects to a broader set of shifts in masculinity which men's fashion both reflects and actively contributes to.

1
DISCIPLINARY DISCOURSES

On a packed train from Croydon to London Victoria the other day, I found myself standing a little way from two young men who were in the midst of a lively and good-natured conversation. It seemed that there was going to be a party, or perhaps a big night out, and the pair were discussing what they planned to wear, "You know the blazer I wore to my cousin's wedding?," asked one. "I've got those black jeans with zips, and I'm going to wear those and my high tops with it." "With a shirt?," asked the other. "No." He was thinking more along the lines of a T-shirt, possibly a long one, he explained, but had to find it first. His friend, though, was thinking of not wearing a jacket—it was summer after all—but just the "collarless shirt he'd got in Hugo Boss," possibly to be styled with a "pair of Tiempo Vettas" or "maybe dress it up a bit smarter with loafers." "Sick bruv," replied his mate.

For the whole twenty minutes of the journey, the friends talked about various iterations of outfits, their respective merits and demerits, a mutual friend who had just had his hair braided into thick corn rows, and why balding men ought to just shave it off. "Like, what are you hanging onto?" Easy to ask when you're 21! But what most struck me about this conversation was the sheer pleasure and enjoyment the two friends took in imagining, contemplating, and discussing clothing; how they were going to look; what other friends might wear; and the kind of impression they hoped to make. The joy, camaraderie, and personal meaning that people—including men—find in fashion is so often absent from sociological accounts of dress. Similarly, journalistic discussions of men's fashion often strike a note of disapproval: articles declare that *men are now subject to the tyranny of fashion* or to its *whims and caprices,* as if a lack of sartorial choice was synonymous with freedom.

At various points in history, throughout the "peacock revolution" of the 1960s and 1970s, during punk and new romanticism, and indeed today, men's fashion—the discipline of designing clothing for men and the practice of styling, customizing, and wearing it—has been particularly fruitful and alive. At other times, fashion for men has been widely disparaged, and attempts have been made to suppress it.

When we speak of fashion we speak of a complex network of interlinking fields of endeavor and social relationships. Fashion is a phenomenon made up of a set of connections between a design discipline; a manufacturing industry; a communications industry; various dynamic social groupings, subcultures, and demographics; a range of ideological forces; and factors in the wider economy. None of these relationships are one-directional, nor are the aesthetic, political, or economic interests of the various players necessarily in harmony with one another—indeed, they are frequently in conflict. For this reason, Carol Tulloch (2010) and Susan Kaiser (2012: 6) have spoken of style-fashion-trend as "articulated" hyphenated interlinking terms: it is impossible to meaningfully distinguish "style" from "fashion," since a style, even an individual's style, must have emerged at a particular historical point and in relation to a set of mutually understood symbols and meanings. Fashion as a word encompasses a sense of change, of *zeitgeist,* of a relationship to a historical moment—and indeed, fashion is often used as a metaphor to describe shifting styles in fields other than clothing. But we should also hear in the word fashion its use as a verb: *façonner (facere),* meaning to fashion, shape, or create.

To deny men the right *de se façonner,* to shape or make themselves anew, is to hold them within an unshifting masculinity not of their choosing: this conservatism, like all conservatisms, is one that implicitly favors the status quo, an existing set of power relations. Perhaps relatedly, like the two lower-middle-class, suburban black men on the train from Croydon, men's fashion has often emerged not from the élite, but from marginal, aspirant groups—from Jewish tailors like Cecil G and Mr. Fish, who left such a mark on twentieth century menswear, from working-class subcultures like the teds and the mods, from the gay style innovators like Vince and John Stephen of Carnaby Street, and from black British, Caribbean, and African-American style.

Fashion's etymological link to making, creating and producing connects it to the word "poem" – a corruption of the Greek *Poēma* or *Poiēma*— which is similarly derived from the verb to make or create. In this linguistic link, there is a truth about the beauty and significance of making: the power to make and remake, to fashion oneself.

New markets

In 2015, the market research company Euromonitor stated that menswear spending had grown by 4.5 percent in the previous year, well outstripping womenswear growth (Homma et al., 2015); market researchers IbisWorld found that online sales of men's fashion had grown at a faster rate over the past five years than any other product category (Davidson, 2015: 3), and—looking into the future—Mintel predicted a 27 percent growth rate in men's fashion over the next five years (PR Newswire, 2014).

In this present decade, there has been an amplification of discourse surrounding men's fashion as journalists, marketers, trend prediction agencies, and others have woken up to the increasing commercial significance of fashion for men (Davidson, 2015: 3; Marriott, 2015; Sigee, 2015: 13; Friede, 2016: 3). This expansion of the sector, as I shall go on to argue, owes much to the pioneering designers of the 2000s—Raf Simons, Hedi Slimane, Ennio Capasa, and Lucas Ossendrijver—who demonstrated that creative menswear design, if properly supported and marketed, could prove a lucrative proposition. At the same time, digital and print media focused on menswear has proliferated, disseminating images of fashionable men and fashionable menswear, of various sorts, to an ever-wider audience, exposing men to a broader range of representations of masculinity, and thus to new masculine subjectivities.

In commenting upon and analyzing these phenomena, a common question has been "Why now?" Why is men's fashion enjoying this renaissance, and what does this mean for men and masculinity more generally? I shall attempt to address these crucial questions in the course of this book; but in addition to investigating the factors that have contributed to contemporary menswear's creativity and commercial success, it is equally important to ask what has impinged upon it hitherto.

Even a cursory exploration of historical men's dress prior to the nineteenth century, into the vestimentary cultures of non-Western societies, or into the youth and subcultures of the twentieth century, would demonstrate that men are no way intrinsically less interested in clothing than women. Indeed, as indicated by the young men I observed on the train from Croydon, men, when given permission to dress up and to play with their appearance, often relish the opportunity. So what forces have acted to prevent men from enjoying sartorial self-expression? And why does men's fashion continue to provoke hostility, or even anger?

(A)historical continuities

The 1970s and early 1980s were characterized by formal experimentation in menswear that was the legacy of the sixties' "peacock revolution," the spirit of modernity that accompanied "the affluent society" (Galbraith, 1958), and latterly the shock tactics of punk and new romanticism. By the late 1980s and early 1990s, however, something of a counter-revolution was underway: youth culture, with the rise of acid casuals, grunge, and indie, was both less ostentatious and less fashion-orientated than in the early 1980s. The often-experimental menswear of the 1960s and 1970s had come to be recollected with faint embarrassment, condemned for its synthetic fibers, leisure suits, and clashing colorways.

The 1980s, as Stuart Hall describes, was a period in which the progressive postwar consensus was swiftly unraveling (1988a: 20–27; 1988b: 20–21), and while in the earlier part of the decade punk's nihilism and sixties "permissiveness" lived on in avant-garde and subcultural style, by the late 1980s and early 1990s, culture had taken a decidedly nostalgic turn: family values, reinstated dado rails, and Cary Grant suits were all in the ascendant. As part of this pervasive nostalgia, a new menswear discourse emerged, both in style magazines such as *GQ, Arena*, and *Esquire*, as well as in men's style manuals, in which commentators argued for a return to "classic," "timeless" sartorial standards.

Paul Keers, writing in *A Gentleman's Wardrobe* of 1987, characterizes menswear as a form governed by a continuity that reflects "timeless" masculine archetypes:

> Classic men's clothes were not born from a designer's drawing board, or from the seasonal whim of a couturier. They have come down to us on the backs of practical men, whether sportsmen or soldiers, wealthy or working men. Classic menswear is not about designer names; it commemorates, among others, the Duke of Wellington, the Prince of Wales, Lord Raglan, the Earl of Cardigan the Duke of Norfolk and the Earl of Chesterfield. Its history is as much about common sense as dress sense. (Keers, 1987: 8)

In 1989, Richard Martin and Harold Koda published the influential *Jocks and Nerds*, a book generously illustrated with tasteful black and white images of famously well-dressed, stylish men of the early and mid-twentieth century. More recent fashion photographs joined these historical images, but they too had a nostalgic feel. Martin and Koda's text turned out to be a much-copied format, and bookshop shelves still groan under the weight of near identical imitations to this day. In 1989, this characterization of menswear as composed of archetypal forms had some currency, seeming to articulate a longing in the fashion and culture of the period to return to a solid, "authentic" masculinity. But as its imagery and discourses were endlessly repeated by style guides and potted histories throughout the 1990s into the 2000s, their relevance steadily decreased. As late as 1999, Bernhard Roetzel in his book *Gentleman: A Timeless Guide to Fashion* advances a sartorial philosophy ossified in the standards of the early twentieth century:

> All over the world pale grey flannels are regarded as ideal with a navy blue blazer. A necktie should be worn with the outfit. Striped ties are often recommended, but dark blue neckties with small motifs, ties in single colors, or Hermès ties look good too. (Roetzel, 1999: 148)

Throughout the 1990s and early 2000s, a new genre of specialist books aimed at a new men's fashion consumer emerged. These titles sat somewhere between costume history, dress manual, and coffee table book and frequently featured longer essays alongside more journalistic reportage and numerous photographs. These publications were clearly a response to an increased commercial, scholarly, and journalistic engagement in menswear, but they also acted to codify a widely held understanding of menswear as characterized by classicism, archetype, and a series of key iconic garments.

Various titles in this vein include *Gentleman: A Timeless Fashion* (Roetzel, 1999), *Material Man* (Malossi, 2000), *Man About Town* (Hayward and Dunn, 2001), *Dressing the Man: Mastering the Art of Permanent Fashion* (Flusser, 2001), and *Dressing in the Dark: Lessons in Men's Style from the Movies* (Maneker, 2002). And while these books undoubtedly represented an intensification of interest in men's fashion, they did not constitute an increased plurality of discourse. With few exceptions, the books reproduced a set of tropes, images, and characterizations—jocks, military types, proletarians, "English eccentrics," and aristocrats engaged in country pursuits—that soon become relentless in their predictability. No less repetitive were the classical menswear forms: military uniforms, formal tailoring, casual tailoring, jeans, and sportswear which, again, were used to hammer home a message of durability and iconicity in men's dress. Typically, these iconic garments were accompanied by celebrity and filmic idols of the late 1930s, 1940s, and early 1950s: the Duke of Windsor, Fred Astaire, Cary Grant, Gary Cooper, Marlon Brando, and James Dean, along with assorted athletes and soldiers.

Whether a paean to the coarse twill of khaki or an ode to the perfect Windsor knot, these texts frequently had something curiously pedantic in their portrayal of menswear as a set of infinitesimally specific and subtle rules:

> I was musing about shoes in general and loafers in particular. In my estimation, there are a handful of versions that transcend fashion and speak volumes about the wearer [...] In England there is the Harrow by Edward Green. An elegant and refined shoe dating back to the 1930s, the Harrow is distinct by butted seam at the toe [...] And let's not forget New and Lingwood [...] it is, after all, the loafer of choice for old Etonians. (Hackett and Tang, 2006: 22)

And despite their claims to timelessness (one book going as far as to adopt the subtitle *A Timeless Fashion*), these texts were, in fact, quite deliberately situated in a specific time and place: their images unmistakably evoking an Anglocentric world of early-twentieth century masculinity.

Indeed, there is something distinctly odd in the temporality of these accounts; they not only iron out the complexity and change which actually occurred in menswear of the early and mid-twentieth century, but also collapse together contemporary photographs with much earlier images: nostalgically attired models implying an unbroken line of sartorial continuity between the late 1940s and the turn of the millennium. Notably absent are images from the 1960s and 1970s, periods in which color, print, exaggerated detailing, and new forms of fabrication challenged traditional tailoring. Nor does the experimental design of the 1980s feature: such figures as Issey Miyake, Michiko Koshino, Workers for Freedom, Jean Paul Gaultier, Kenzo, and John Galliano, with their asymmetric, oversized, pleated, and playful menswear are all neglected. Thus these accounts of perennial, immutable—and in the words of Alan Flusser—"permanent fashion" clearly involve a degree of ahistoricism.

By the turn of the millennium, the accounts of menswear provided by Roetzel (1999), Flusser (2001), Engel (2004), Maneker (2002), and Hackett and Tang (2006) describe a set of relationships between historic and contemporary men's fashion that, in the wake of a new generation of creative designers, is decisively breaking down. In this sense, these accounts should be read less as descriptive (as attempting to capture the reality of how men relate to clothing) than as prescriptive, restrictive, and normative (as attempting to shape and guide these attitudes). Indeed, in their universal statements about men and in their distrust of modishness, change, or flux, they suggest that there is only one correct way to dress as a man—and perhaps only one way to be a man as well.

These claims for menswear, then, act as proxy claims around gender, the apparent timelessness of sartorial forms acting to affirm the unchanging nature of male identity. In this writing—with its emphasis on appropriateness, subtlety, strictly defined codes, and conformity—the suit comes to symbolize a set of decidedly Victorian values: an emblem of a confident, unshowy, patrician masculinity. It is possible, as Christopher Breward (2016) has done, to read men's tailoring quite differently—as an expression of hybridity and flux, as the materialization of a particular historical moment, or as a point of confluence between opposing dialectical forces (of democracy and elitism for instance). But to apply these more nuanced and historically accurate readings, risks opening up the possibility that the assuredness, self-confidence and apparent fixity of the masculinity celebrated by Roetzel (1999), Flusser (2001), Engel (2004), Maneker (2002) and Hackett (2006) might itself be in question.

New men?

It is perhaps unsurprising to find the affirmation of an orthodox, normative masculinity from conservative male voices (whose investment in the continuation of the status quo might be expected), but it is more surprising to find claims for the immutability of masculinity from within ostensibly feminist discourses. Nevertheless, during the 1980s in particular, feminist writers expressed hostility towards the emergence of more expressive forms of men's fashion and incredulity at the notion that masculinity was undergoing (or perhaps could ever undergo) a process of reform. This position might seem paradoxical—since the success of any feminist project is predicated on challenging and changing gender norms—but it relates to a strand of second-wave feminist thinking that tended, rather problematically, to associate the *trappings of femininity* with inauthenticity, falsity, and patriarchal power while seeing "masculine" behaviors as the authentic expression of male will, agency, and desire.

This skepticism towards the possibility of reforming masculinities expressed itself with particular force in the discourses that emerged around the New Man[1] amongst writers such as Judith Williamson (1986: 25), Polly Toynbee (1987: 10), and Rowena Chapman (1988: 225–248). Chapman's characterization of the New Man is perhaps particularly telling: not only does she accuse him of being narcissistic, consumerist, and image obsessed, she also ascribes to him—and his alleged co-creators in the media and advertising—a low cunning, suggesting that beneath his appealing, well-groomed, and lightly fragranced exterior lurks an old patriarchal man. "Men change" she states, "but only to hold on to their power, not to relinquish it" (1988: 235). Chapman's distrust of New Mannism focuses not only on representation, fashion, and grooming but also on other "feminine" qualities of nurture and emotional literacy that the New Man—"the great pretender"—supposedly affects in order to hoodwink unsuspecting women. Toynbee (1987: 10), citing research by Lewis and O'Brien (1987), concludes that the New Man is a chimera: she argues "men are no better than they were, fathers are as absent and as useless as ever."[2]

According to this way of thinking, men dress and behave as they do not because they are socialized, disciplined, or coerced into doing so, but as an assertion of privilege and power. Thus, men who attempt to overturn conventional masculine modes and mores, especially by adopting "feminized" practices, are seen either as self-deluded and inauthentic or as a threat—wolves in sheep's clothing trespassing into female domains not to challenge patriarchy but to extend it.

Needless to say, the assumptions that underpin such readings are both essentialist and empirically flawed since they fail to recognize the disciplinary regimes, violence, and hierarchy intrinsic to the maintenance of hegemonic masculinity. And by reifying this hegemony they foreclose the possibility of reforming male identities that must (almost by definition) take on behaviors and subjectivities that have been historically coded feminine. Nor were Chapman and Toynbee unique: their attitudes echo activists like Carol Hanisch (1975), who combines a profound distrust of male consciousness-raising efforts with some rather startling homophobia, and authors such as Doris Lessing (1962; 1985) with her insistence upon "real men" and disdain for "men who are little boys and homosexuals and [...] half-homosexuals" (1962: 205). Not only are these discourses obviously sexist, and often homophobic, but they are also strategically puzzling since they inevitably alienate men with aspirations of gender equality.[3]

Of course, there were also feminist voices such as Barbara Ehrenreich (1984) who saw the New Man in broadly positive terms as a genuinely new and more liberated social type: a figure who had emerged in response to shifts in family life and consumer culture to break from the stifling conformity of fifties masculinity.

Similarly, theorist Lynne Segal in her 1987 text *Is the Future Female?* is highly critical of the separatist, essentialist dogmas evident in much feminist thought of the time—she has in mind such figures as Mary Daly, Andrea Dworkin, and Dale Spender—whom she argued underplayed the historically contingent nature of gender and underemphasized the way in which masculinity is socially structured. Following in Segal's footsteps, more recent feminist commentators and activists have increasingly engaged in more fruitful debates around masculinity, from bell hooks' *The Will to Change* (2004), which deals with the numbing, oppressive effect of patriarchal values on men, to Jennifer Siebel Newsom's film *The Mask You Live In* (2015), both representing examples of feminist discourse that neither reinforce normative masculine values nor uncritically collapse together men and patriarchy as if they were equivalent terms.

Nevertheless, notions of masculinity as essentially unchanging, along with a profound suspicion of non-hegemonic expressions of masculinity, were loudly articulated by both conservative and notionally progressive voices during the 1970s and 1980s. And, as I shall argue, such prejudices continue to hold considerable sway in media discussions of men's fashion, hipsterism, and grooming to this day.

In response to these critiques, by the 1990s the New Man had fallen increasingly out of favor, becoming something of a figure of fun, and by the middle of the decade, marketers, journalists, and, perhaps most of all, editors of a new breed of "irreverent" men's magazines like *Loaded* and *FHM,* had identified an emerging demographic they branded the "New Lads" (Crewe, 2003). Scornful of sophistication, sexual politics, and metropolitan style, the New Lad was interested in "football, booze, bonking and babes" (Birch, 1994: 26). *Loaded* editor James Brown went so far as to claim his magazine was for men that "have accepted what we are and have given up trying to improve ourselves" (Brown, 1994 cited in Birch, 1994: 26), a triumph for immutable, perennial, and unchangeable masculinity, perhaps, except that the New Lads were so clearly a response to the cultural and gender discourses of their period: self-consciously, performatively, even "ironically" retrograde in their behavior and attitudes.

Hipster hate

In a North American and specifically New York context, the term "hipster"—as associated with fashionable scenesters and trendy hangouts in gentrifying areas—was already in use by the early 2000s (McKinley, 2002: 1). But it is in the mid-to-late 2000s that hipster reentered the mainstream lexicon to describe a style and lifestyle that might previously have been described as "indie" (Lorentzen, 2007). Hipsters were the young, arty-looking, vintage-clad inhabitants of down-at-heel but now regenerating urban areas (Hackney in East London, Kreuzberg in Berlin, Williamsburg in New York), and the term held a generally pejorative set of connotations—particularly of inauthenticity and superficiality. The naming of hipsterism (along with the volume of discourse about hipsters generated between 2007 and 2014) gestured to the economic, creative, and geographic significance of this expanding demographic. But significantly, the nomenclature "hipster" was most often applied from without rather than from within the subculture, and generally as a term of abuse.

The hipster subculture emerged from a scene of warehouse parties, clubs, minor galleries, and independent businesses (particularly cafés) that began to colonize deprived areas of major Western cities (New York City, Berlin, London) during the early 2000s as part of a process geographers have termed "the great inversion," the movement of people back into inner cities after the middle-class flight of the mid-twentieth century (Ehrenhalt, 2012).

Within the indie scenes that emerged in these cities, there was a noticeable tendency towards camp and kitsch: the discarded flotsam and jetsam of consumer culture of the past—old crockery, mohair jumpers, cassette tapes—reappropriated to become precious, beautiful, or worthy. It was a strategy that relied on an inversion of conventional consumer and social values—a celebration of redundancy, silliness, and bad taste; of the optimism and naïveté of postwar mass-manufactured products—in much the same manner as described by Susan Sontag (2009 [1966]) in her seminal essay "Notes On Camp." At the level of gender and sexuality, too, hipsters and proto-hipsters (in the grand tradition of youth cultures) broke from normativity by valuing nerdiness, weirdness and androgyny, and hipster hangouts were often mixed gay, lesbian, and straight.

A huge volume of popular discourse from magazine articles to blogs has emerged around hipsterism since 2007, some of it celebratory, but the vast majority arch, critical, or downright hostile. And while some writers have sought to rehabilitate the hipster, the highly gendered, effemiphobic[4] nature of hipster critiques and their impact on cultures of masculinity are rarely discussed or acknowledged.

In the blogs that arose during the late 2000s, including *Hackney Hipster Hate* and *Look at This Fucking Hipster*, the majority of posts featured androgynously or extravagantly dressed men sporting pendants, short-shorts, low-cut T-shirts, big-glasses, tight trousers, or similar apparel. The image conjured up by the term "hipster," at least in popular consciousness, is almost always male and some 80 percent of the results generated by a Google Image search are of men. Female hipsters are less likely to be the focus of debate, attention, or stigma since their fashionability is less likely to be deemed transgressive, and because female hipsterism is difficult to distinguish from other forms of fashionable femininity. While fashionability amongst men is often mocked or problematized, both in the press and elsewhere in popular discourse, to be female and fashionable is considered normal, desirable, nigh on compulsory.

An example of the way in which notions of masculinity inform critiques of hipsterism is found in a 2010 post from *Hackney Hipster Hate* featuring a photograph of a rather forlorn young man sitting on the pavement beside the closed grill of a shop. The blog's author writes:

> All crashed out, mewing like a sick kitten and clearly wrecked after a night on the boutique lagers and face powders! Look at his silly pink socks! Check out the crayon-blue skinnys [jeans]! What an irredeemable, spluttering twat! No wonder he feels the need to dowse himself in other people's piss down there on the paving. It's the essential punishment for being a ridiculously-dressed wreck … You might feel it's cruel to expose someone so vulnerable on a blog like this. He might have had his iPhone snaffled … or his earnings swiped. I'M GLAD HE'S A MESS. I HOPE HE GOES TO PRISON. I HATE HIM BY SIGHT ALONE. (Anon, 2010)

There is an obvious violence to *Hackney Hipster Hate's* contempt for this unfortunate stranger, but the precise terms in which this anger is expressed are also informative. The hipster's clothing, of course, is singled out for critique, but there is also a sense in which his fragility—with its attendant cultural associations of effeminacy and immaturity—has provoked the blogger's ire. This is reflected in the terminology used to describe the young man: "mewing," "kitten," "pink," "boutique," "twat," and "vulnerable" which, troublingly, seem to justify the authors' wish to see him debased, as forcefully expressed in the nouns "piss," "punishment," and "hate."

There is a similarly gendered quality to the "irreverent" website *Encyclopedia Dramatica's* description of hipsters as "narcissistic douchebags" and "faggots" (Encyclopediadramatica.se, 2011). And, less offensively, in Reuben Dangoor's 2010 video *Being a Dickhead's Cool*, which is predominantly made up of clips of ostentatiously dressed young men of, in his words, "indeterminate sexual preference" (Dangoor, 2010). Similarly, Polly Vernon in *The Times* (2011) states "hipster boys are effete and incredibly thin; you wouldn't want to rely on them in a fight."

It is notable that all these critiques are explicitly predicated on male hipsters' failure to conform to orthodox masculinity, but it is also significant that accusations leveled at hipsters are so frequently centered upon narcissism, inauthenticity, and pretention. As Dan Fox (2016) suggests, to call someone pretentious is to refuse their right to define their own identity, to claim that their way of inhabiting the world is false or illegitimate. An insistence on authenticity, in this sense, acts as a means of surveillance and as a claim to authority. Accusations of pretentiousness are also charged with class and gender politics. From Georgian fops and Regency Dandies to the moral panics of the twentieth century, the alleged deviancy, effeminacy, and affectation of aristocratic, bohemian, or subcultural masculinities is contrasted against the "authenticity," normalcy, and "naturalness" of respectable working-class and petit bourgeois identities. This set of associations continues to be felt in the charge that hipsters are agents of gentrification (accusations that suggest that, rather than a lack of public housing, restrictive planning and zoning, or an overall increase in demand, gentrification is driven by people having too many tattoos and drinking cocktails out of jam jars).

At least partially in response to these critiques and anxieties, new forms of male hipsterism developed during the late 2000s that favored nostalgic, late-nineteenth and early twentieth century aesthetics signaling a more "authentic" and traditional masculinity. I describe these developments in fashionable dress in greater detail in Chapter 5. Indeed, this bearded, plaid shirt-wearing, workwear-clad figure has become the dominant stereotype of hipster in recent years (though these changes have done little to diminish hipster hate).

Performance anxiety

As theorists such as Judith Butler (1990) and Erving Goffman (1956; 1986 [1963]) affirm, identities—including masculine identities—are performative; which is to say they are continually produced and reproduced through social practice. For Butler, the ways that we act, appear, and interact with others create and reaffirm our gender identities. It is through these performative social practices—what we wear, how we speak, how we move in social spaces—that sex/gender remains legible and through which coherent identities are maintained. As both Butler and, earlier, Michel Foucault have suggested, these ways of acting and being are policed or "disciplined" by the codes, ideas, and expectations that shape society. They call this shared knowledge of appropriate behaviors (in turn reinforced through the performance of identity) "discourse." And since gender has been performed in very different ways at different times and in different places and since, for Butler, there is no gender outside of discourse, her theory of performativity implies the possibility of radically changing gender subjectivities.

For Goffman, the performance of social interaction is similarly implicated in the production of identity, and he explicitly uses the metaphor of the stage to describe the social world (1956). In Goffman's model, identity is maintained dramaturgically; roles, masks, and performances are assumed according to a set of conventions as a way of managing and mediating external power structures and the responses of others.

Nevertheless, despite the well-established nature of these theories and their considerable acceptance within the academy, in much popular discussion masculinity continues to be viewed as a unitary, coherent, and relatively immutable identity. As we have seen, both adherents of traditional menswear and critics of New Mannism lean heavily on notions of an unchanging, essential masculinity in their prescriptions of "acceptable" masculine dress and comportment. While "common sense" understandings of gender often acknowledge the performativity, the play-acting, the smoke and mirrors of femininity, masculinity is assumed to be real, authentic, and intrinsic. This, I would argue, is why male pretentiousness represents such a profound challenge for normative masculinity: using irony or playfulness in the construction of a male identity (as, for example, hipsters do) or otherwise drawing attention to its *constructedness* threatens the whole edifice of masculinity. It implies that men can or could be other, and that men's subjectivities are contingent and open to question.

The degree to which *disciplinary discourses* surrounding men's fashion and appearance police men's expressions and understandings of their own identities can be felt in the empirical work conducted by Rosalind Gill, Karen Henwood, and Carl McLean (2005). In their qualitative research focusing on men's attitudes to their bodies, the importance of "not taking yourself too seriously," and of not being "fake," "false or posy" (45–54) emerged as a strong theme. And the researchers found that their respondents studiously avoided describing such practices as attending the gym or wearing a tattoo or piercing in terms that implied the desire to cultivate a particular appearance or of wanting to look attractive. The researchers state that "being thought vain or narcissistic was something profoundly feared by the vast majority of the men we interviewed" (2005: 50). In this way, discourses surrounding narcissism place men in a double bind, under pressure to look good but unable to show an interest in their appearance. Perhaps more importantly, the taboo nature of male vanity has the effect of delegitimizing self-expression and bodily autonomy by enforcing conformity.

Proscriptions against male "pretension," "narcissism" and against modish dress are predicated on a sexism that holds men and women to fundamentally different standards of behavior. These taboos against men's self-expression police gender by enforcing a single, hegemonic, orthodox form of masculinity and by militating against the emergence of plural masculinities. The stigmatization of fashionable male identities acts to sure up the position of those men whose power and authority is based on their allegiance to orthodox masculinity (and to relatively secure markers of status such as social class, occupation, and educational attainment). Conversely, these discourses devalue emergent, subcultural, and avant-garde forms of masculine identity—which are often based on more diffuse forms of (sub)cultural capital including appearance and fashionability.

Fearing femininity

What is striking in the hipster and New Man discussions I have reviewed, as well as in others I shall discuss later in the chapter, is their profound distrust, fear, and hostility towards effeminacy, however innocuous its expression. This is felt in Chapman's (1988) suggestion that men appropriate femininity in order to extend patriarchy, as well as in the more aggressively phobic hipster discourses. More generally, it is notable that, while women's appearances are obsessively scrutinized, policed, and judged in popular culture, women and girls who adopt "masculine" dress and behavior are much less stigmatized and disdained than boys and men who adopt feminine behaviors or modes of presentation. Emily Kane (2006: 149–176) in her qualitative, experiential work on parents' attitudes to gender amongst preschool children found that parents were much more likely to respond positively to gender nonconforming traits they perceived in their daughters than in their sons. She found that fathers, in particular, policed and discouraged feminine behaviors amongst boys, and that while certain domestically orientated forms of play historically coded feminine, such as cooking and playing house, might be tolerated, feminine clothing and presentation—along with activities like ballet—were almost universally discouraged or forbidden to boys.

As writers as diverse as Stephen Ducat (2005), Klaus Theweleit (1989), and David Plummer (1999) have affirmed, normative, orthodox masculinity is maintained through a pathologization of effeminacy in which men deny and reject those qualities within themselves—fragility, emotionalism, nurturance—that are coded feminine, insisting upon unambiguous and impermeable boundaries between masculinity and femininity (Ducat, 2004: 5). This disparagement of femininity is obviously profoundly misogynistic, but it also has an enormous effect on the regulation of men and boy's behavior. Indeed, the vast majority of insults that boys and men experience—including those found in the discourses reviewed in this chapter—are predicated on the inferiority and abjection of femininity. For this reason, even the most minor infraction against normative masculine dress (Serano, 2007: 286–287; Bitterman, 2016: 37–39) can provoke stigma, hostility, and worse.

Happily, however, theorists such as Anderson (2009) and Christensen and Jensen (2014) have suggested that these patriarchal orthodox forms of masculinity are ceasing to be hegemonic and are gradually being replaced by more inclusive forms of masculinity (at least amongst some groups).

Effemiphobia's close relation is, of course, homophobia.[5] David Plummer has suggested that, "In men's spheres, the yardstick for what is acceptable is hegemonic masculinity and what is unacceptable is marked by homophobia and enforced by homophobia" (1999: 289). In this sense, the primary function of homophobia is to demarcate the boundaries of acceptable heterosexual masculinity rather than to police homosexuality per se. Similarly, while effemiphobia impacts most violently on conspicuously gender non-conforming males, its influence is felt much more widely in inhibiting the growth of more diverse, plural, and progressive masculinities in general. Indeed, Eric Anderson (2009) who has written on the emergence of what he terms "inclusive masculinities" describes how these new forms of gender expression and identity are predicated on the rejection of misogynistic and effemiphobic discourses.

Activist and writer Julia Serano accounts for widespread effemiphobia (or what she calls effemimania) by distinguishing between unilateral and "oppositional sexism" (2007: 307). Serano states that "oppositional sexism favors those with typical gender inclinations over those with exceptional ones" (2007: 307), so that the violence, anger, and distrust provoked by effeminacy in men and boys has a dual etiology—it results both from the devaluation of femininity in general and from an antipathy towards atypical gender expression in particular. Like Connell's theory of hegemonic and subordinate masculinities, the concept of oppositional sexism complicates the notion of male privilege by highlighting the multiple sources (and intersections) of privilege and oppression. While male privilege remains a useful frame for understanding the endurance of patriarchy, effemiphobia, oppositional sexism, and subordinated masculinities demonstrate that neither men nor women have a monopoly on either privilege or subordination.

Reverse discourse

In spite of the continued prevalence of media discourse stigmatizing men's engagement with fashion, in the run-up to the millennium designers such as Raf Simons, Hedi Slimane, Ennio Capasa, Tom Ford, and Helmut Lang were proposing a new menswear aesthetic with ever greater confidence: it was a look characterized by a close-cleaving silhouette, translucent fabrics, dandyish tailoring, and bare skin. The significance of this shift in menswear was felt in the journalism that responded to these designers' collections. As Amy Spindler for *The New York Times* put it, designers like Ford, "instead of gearing designer suits to make men look successful, powerful and established," were making them seem "younger, thinner and sexier" (Spindler, 1997: 14). Meanwhile, Raf Simons' punk references, cobweb sweaters and skinny, wan teenage models garnered attention by presenting a vision of menswear that radically diverged from the tanned, muscular, commercial look that had dominated the previous decade. Indeed, his edgy, androgynous aesthetic unnerved some; Alix Sharkey, in *The Guardian*, branded Simons' Spring/Summer 1998 collection "sardonic" and his models "ghoulish" (1997). In this way, Ford and Simon's divergence from a set of menswear codes that had dominated from the late 1980s onward not only signaled a change in style but also provided a compelling counter-narrative

DISCIPLINARY DISCOURSES

to the notion of men's fashion (and masculinity) as rule-bound, unchanging, and conformist.

Though Simons, Lang, and Ford all attracted column inches (Spindler, 1997: 14; Menkes, 1998: 11; Clark, 1999: 10a) at the turn of the millennium, it was Slimane's bold intervention in men's fashion—first at Yves Saint Laurent from 1996 and subsequently at Dior Homme—that most emphatically signaled a repudiation of those normative discourses outlined previously in this chapter— and from the narrow model of men's fashion that had gained hegemony over the course of the 1990s. Charlie Porter, writing in *The Guardian* in 2001, declared:

> Nothing exciting is meant to happen in men's fashion. Yet in Paris right now, the talk is all of Hedi Slimane, the designer whose work at the newly established Dior Homme is provoking a radical rethink in the stagnating ateliers of menswear. (Porter, 2001: 62)

This sense of a brewing rebellion against the suffocating strictures of menswear and masculinity is also felt in Adrian Clark's writing for *The Guardian* which asked: "Does menswear really have to be so boring? What it has lacked, for over a decade, is some drive, some guts, some wider choice" (1999: 10b). And perhaps most significantly, Slimane himself—speaking here in an interview for *L'Officiel*—explicitly refers to masculinity as a set of arcane rules and arbitrary constraints that he attempts to push against, resist (and perhaps ultimately reform). He states:

> There is a psychology to the masculine: we're told don't touch it; it's ritual, sacred, taboo. It's difficult but I'm making headway, I'm trying to find a new approach. A men's collection can be creative, desirable, enlivened … Menswear can become fashion too. I don't think this should be forbidden for men. I'm looking for a way through. I want to create something with a closeness, a sense of intimacy, a directness. (Slimane, 2001 cited by Cabasset, 2001: 70)

Here, and elsewhere in his championing of the slim male body as "real" and authentic (Healy, 2001: 163), there is an appeal to a kind of strategic essentialism: an attempt to strip away the accumulated values and constraints mandated by orthodox masculinity—including dominance, conformity, muscularity, physical strength, and reserve—and to replace them with something more "natural" "desirable" and "enlivened."

Mike Featherstone, in *Consumer Culture and Postmodernism* (2007) draws upon Pierre Bourdieu's *Distinction* ([1979] 1984) to suggest that cultural intermediaries,[6] particularly in what he refers to as "para-intellectual fields like design," occupy an ambiguous class position in which they are less invested in the status quo and are instead reliant upon more diffuse forms of cultural capital (2007: 19). According to Bourdieu, such groups engage in tacit attempts to overturn hierarchies of taste through the promotion of progressive or outré forms: in his words, "the canonization of not-yet-legitimate or minor, marginal forms" (1984: 326). Central to an understanding of Slimane's and Simons' work, then, is this desire to disrupt hierarchies of taste—particularly those associated with hegemonic bourgeois masculinity. Not for nothing did Slimane transform the fusty "Christian Dior Monsieur" into "Dior Homme."

To this extent, the outsiderness of both Simons and Slimane—one compounded by queerness, gender nonconformity, working or lower-middle-class backgrounds (and, in Simons' case, provincial origins), are key to understanding the edgy, rebellious aesthetics they develop. Significantly, both designers have spoken of finding points of identification in musicians such as David Bowie and Kraftwerk, with their weird, otherworldly allure (Limnander, 2006: 47; Yahoo Style, 2015).

For Lang, too, it was an alienated, working-class youth, and a feeling of otherness that led him to create an alternative identity through his clothing, and ultimately to become a designer (Seabrook, 2000: 114). In his collections from the late 1990s to the mid-2000s, there is a sense of, quite literally, deconstructing conventional menswear. In his Spring/Summer 2004 collection, apertures and cut-out sections bisect shirts and jackets, and unfurl across vests—exposing here a midriff, there a nipple, here an arm. These curious, asymmetric garments disrupt and unsettle expectations and are about as far away as one can imagine from the pedantic sartorial codes mandated by Keers (1987), Roetzel (1999) and their ilk (Figure 1.1).

In the work of Lang, Slimane, and Simons, then, there is a concerted effort to overturn the standards, assumptions, and aesthetics of normative masculinity, to reject and replace them with something else: a celebration not of strength, dominance, and conformity, but of a much more ambiguous, liminal gender identity.

Slimane's radical approach to menswear during the early and mid-2000s—androgynous, glamorous, and sported by rangy indie musicians—can be read as a kind of reverse discourse, in which fashion as a "matrix of transformation" (Foucault, 1978) acts to celebrate and legitimize forms of masculinity that had previously been stigmatized. In order to achieve this goal, the ideas and assumptions surrounding masculine appearance along with the mechanisms through which these ideas were communicated and inculcated (techniques of knowledge if you like) had to be challenged. These discursive processes—the reframing and reimagining of men's fashion—can also be seen in the writing of journalists such as Charlie Porter, Adrian Clark, and Suzie Menkes,

Figure 1.1 Lang, H. and Verdy, P. (2003) Spring/Summer 2004 Collection. Paris. Asymmetric vest and jacket with bottle tops, photographed by Pierre Verdy.

whose celebration of these pioneering designers expressed a desire to open up and reform menswear—to make space for "some wider choice" (Clark, 1999: 10b).

As I shall go on to describe in Chapter 4, the 2000s saw a period of rapid expansion in designer menswear, accompanied by an amplification of journalistic discourse surrounding men's fashion. It also saw significant shifts on the high street as mainstream menswear retailers introduced more varied and trend-based collections. In 2012, London founded the first stand-alone men's fashion week, London Collections: Men, subsequently followed by men's fashion weeks in New York and Toronto, in this way cementing and institutionalizing the newfound commercial and creative status of menswear (Milligan, 2011; Gallagher, 2012; Fashion United, 2014).

To borrow a term from Foucault, I would argue that men's fashion—at the level of design, as image, as worn, in written discussion, and as an industry—can be best understood as a "discursive formation" ([1972] 1989). By this I mean a set of heterogeneous and sometimes competing disciplinary approaches that produce individual statements—in the form of a designer's collection, or an advertising campaign—and also create new forms of identity or subjectivity (the fashionisto, the hipster, the metrosexual).

The importance of fashion in activating, opening up, and making space for new subjectivities is evident in the qualitative work of scholars Ben Barry and Barbara Phillips (2016: 17–34), who found that engaging with images of fashionably dressed male models enabled their participants to "express new masculine identities" (2016: 30). Similarly, Matthew Hall (2015) characterizes fashion and grooming practices (and their discussion in online forums) as practices of metrosexual identity formation that challenge the fixity of traditional masculinity. Masafumi Monden (2012: 227–313; 2015), undertaking textual rather than experiential research, describes the ways in which young Japanese men adopt elegant, dandyish, and "cute" modes of dress as a rejection of conformist salaryman and Euro-American identities, highlighting the manner in which Japanese cultures of fashion have anticipated many of the shifts recently seen in menswear in the West.

The newfound importance of men's fashion in exploring identity is also felt in the work of designers themselves. In 2013, Ike Rust, then head of the Royal College of Art's influential Menswear Master's program, stated:

Menswear certainly has gained a particular currency today. [… Menswear] designers [are] not only creating something which is about a particular time or place; but also expressing something of themselves. And this self-expression is something menswear designers have begun to do more of, which is something in the past we had typically associated with womenswear. (Rust, 2013 [interviewed in] McCauley Bowstead, 2013)

Similarly, Lucas Ossendrijver, head menswear designer at Lanvin, suggested:

> What we try to do with the menswear [...] is actually to make clothes that are special, that are different, that are not a uniform [...] For me clothes are a means to express your personality, to underline the personality of somebody. And I think also clothes are a means to have fun. (Ossendrijver, 2013, cited in Barneys New York, 2013)

For Foucault, discourse represents a group of statements, propositions or ideas, especially those associated with an institution or discipline, that express certain values and exert power. Discourse, like power, is productive: it produces and reproduces knowledge as well as producing subjects and subjectivities. We can see men's fashion as constituted of a series of discourses: statements about what men might, could, or should be, and about beauty and aspiration. In this way, the power of fashion should be understood less in terms of coercion (as it sometimes has been traditionally) and more in terms of activating a range of competing propositions or ideas. To this extent, the discourses, ideas, and propositions from which menswear, as a discursive formation, is composed have shifted substantially since the turn of the millennium, in turn freeing up men's fashion to become a medium of expression, creativity, and self-actualization. On the other hand, as we have seen, those discourses that seek to constrain, shape, and *discipline* menswear and masculinity within an essentialist, nostalgic, normative model of gender have not suddenly disappeared, but remain prominent in various sectors of the media, publishing, and comment.

Contested masculinities

In the wake of Christian Dior Monsieur's rebranding as Dior Homme under Hedi Slimane, big Parisian fashion houses like Lanvin and Balenciaga founded or relaunched men's lines under named designers; numerous men's fashion magazines (*10 Men* in 2004, *Another Man and Fantastic Man* in 2005, and *Numéro Homme* in 2007) were launched; and high street retailers like Topman and Zara began to take their menswear offerings much more seriously. Topman pioneered the use of designer collaborations in menswear in the early 2000s and in 2005 established the MAN initiative[7] to incubate menswear talent and to provide a platform within London Fashion Week for new designers. By 2012, as London founded the first Men's Fashion Week and as menswear sales boomed, journalists, marketers, and fashion professionals heralded the dawning of a new era for the sector (Fashion United, 2012; Gallagher, 2012).

Nevertheless, as might be expected from the hipster discourses reviewed earlier in the chapter, the response of the press to these developments was decidedly mixed. Fashion journalists often reacted with uninhibited enthusiasm to the newfound dynamism of the sector, but other commentators demonstrated a greater sense of ambivalence or hostility to the expansion of men's fashion, styling, and grooming.

These ambivalences were felt in articles that satirized contemporary men's fashion, positioning it as variously unwearable, ridiculous, or as representing a failed and invalid form of masculinity. At *The Guardian*, the music journalist Alexis Petridis and style commentator Hadley Freeman eyed developments in menswear with a combination of feigned horror and glee, taking turns to deliver well-crafted pot shots at the latest trends. Petridis' regular feature involved donning an unlikely combination of contemporary designer pieces to "humorous" effect. He declared a trend for leggings "disturbing," claiming they made him look "like a cross between Timothy Claypole and something off the sex offenders register" (2007) and described the wearing of leather caps as "cartoonishly linked to the desire to, as the [Village] People put it, hang out with the boys" (2009). Freeman took aim at vests—worn by nerds who want to look like a "sexy macho dude" (2006a), jewelry worn by "wannabe gangsters," and men who "think they're Byron" (2006b), while low-cut tops were allegedly "caused by the hipster virus" (2010).

Writing more recently in 2013, Judith Woods at *The Daily Telegraph* focused her critiques more broadly on men's increased interest in fashion. She described metrosexuals as "she-men," "insufferable sissies," "needy and vain," and as "petulant as princesses," declaring:

> [They] know their way around the Clarins counter considerably better than they do any B&Q ... Welcome to modern men—the metrosexual monsters we have created. According to a new survey, a horrifying one in five women claims their partner is so high-maintenance that he spends longer in the bathroom than they do ... their sissification has gone too far. There's something very disturbing about going out with a chap who is prettier than you are ... Frankly, I couldn't care about lipstick on his collar. But the day he comes home with a shea butter lip balm in his pocket is the day I move out. (2013: 35)

Clive Martin (2014), writing for a very different publication in the shape of *Vice* magazine, strikes a strange note of nostalgia for the "fearless, beacons of Northern European masculinity" of yore. In criticizing a generation of image-obsessed young men, he states that where once they would have "waged shitty wars in foreign countries" and "defended the honours of other people's wives" they now "look dreadful and bizarre [...] they are the modern British douchebag— pumped, primed, terrifyingly sexualised high-street gigolos [...] gym bunny wankers, patrolling their turf in T-shirts that looked like they'd been torn down the middle by a big angry dog."

In these discussions of men's fashion, appearance and grooming, predictably, the specter of effeminacy is raised, particularly in Woods' piece that employs feminizing language like "princess," "sissy," and indeed "she-man" as a way of delegitimizing metrosexual identities. Meanwhile, practices considered quite normal for women are claimed as evidence of pathological male narcissism: a rather crude example of oppositional sexism and effemiphobia. Less expectedly—though relatedly—there is a palpable sense of unease around male sexuality and the male body that runs across several of the articles: this is reflected in Petridis' allusions to homosexuality and mention of sex offenders, in Freeman's references to Byron, and most of all Martin's critique of "wankers" and "terrifyingly sexualised high street gigolos." There is a strong sense of anxiety—terror, even—about the ways in which revealing clothing and new exercise and cosmetic regimes have increasingly recentered the male body as a focus of the gaze. And there is also, in Woods' article, a fear that this process amounts to an unwelcome trespass into a feminine sphere that represents a challenge to heterosexual power dynamics. A patina of irony and humor allows these commentators license to say some rather extreme and unpleasant things: most notably, Martin's suggestion that waging "shitty wars in foreign countries"—is a less problematic way for young men to spend their time than going to the gym and wearing low-cut T-shirts.

As Foucault suggests, discourse should be understood as a set of competing regimes of truth and power relations and therefore "the media," like "fashion," should be seen as a space in which multiple actors with frequently opposing interests and beliefs are simultaneously active. Despite this plurality of voices, certain themes and ideas circulate and are frequently repeated.

The discussions of men's fashion and style that emerged during the 2000s and 2010s, in response to the dynamism and flux of the field, reflect divergent, frequently opposing, competing claims to truth. These claims, in turn, are enmeshed in power relations, identity politics, and economics: there are fashion professionals who see new creative possibilities in the expansion of menswear; there are those who see shifts in men's fashion as part of a process of opening up and pluralizing masculinity (perhaps thereby finding newfound acceptance for themselves); and there are those who recognize the commercial possibilities of a dynamic, creative menswear market. Simultaneously, there are some—perhaps particularly on the traditional left—who view the commercialization of masculinity as an alienating force reinforcing the primacy of capitalism; there are socially conservative discourses that fear challenges to orthodox forms of masculinity; and there are men (and women) who sense that emergent forms of fashionable masculinity may challenge their own claims to power and authenticity.

Disciplinary discourses

Despite flowerings of innovative men's fashion in the 1960s, 1970s, and in the early 1980s, for much of the twentieth century, discourses surrounding fashion have focused almost exclusively on clothes designed for and worn by women. Such accounts not only marginalized men's fashion but claimed it hardly existed at all: women wore fashion, while men simply wore clothes. In the 1990s, in particular, a number of writers attempted to dispel this notion, documenting the ways in which men had adopted fashionable dress as a means of individual and group expression. Accounts including Shaun Cole's *Don We Now Our Gay Apparel* (2000), Christopher Breward's *The Hidden Consumer* (1999), Tim Edwards' *Men in the Mirror* (1997), Frank Mort's *Cultures of Consumption* (1996), and Sean Nixon's *Hard Looks* (1996) revealed the complexity, diversity, and significance of fashion created for and worn by men and critiqued the assumptions underlying conventional accounts of men's dress. These books were immensely important in demonstrating that men's fashion existed, was meaningful and could be analyzed, and made sense of as a gendered text: I have drawn extensively from them in researching this piece of work. But since these writers were unable to read the future (or to travel forward in time) as we near 20 years since the publication of their respective key texts, such accounts are no longer able to explain the dramatic changes to menswear that have occurred over the past two decades.

The paucity of journalistic and academic discourse around men's fashion compared with that of womenswear prior to the mid-1990s could be justified by a claim that there was simply less of it about, that it was of a lower quality, or that few men were interested in it. But such claims ignore the evident importance that fashions of various sorts clearly played in constructing subcultural and counter-cultural male identities in the latter part of the twentieth century, from teddy boys and zazous, to mods, hippies, and punks. Crucially, the late 1970s witnessed a growing legitimatization of scholarly engagement in subcultural aesthetics, not least in Hebdige's *Subculture: The Meaning of Style,* published in 1979. And the period was also characterized by the growing popularity of feminist and gender-based analyses of culture within the academy. Meanwhile, in the early 1980s, subcultural and youth fashions were increasingly communicated through a growing industry of style magazines—*BLITZ, The Face*, and *i-D*—which acted to connect subculture to strands of high-end fashion.

For a generation of theorists who came of age in the 1970s and 1980s, including Breward, Edwards, Nixon, and Mort, these tendencies came together in a nineties literature that captured contemporary men's fashion as a manifestation of masculinity in flux. It is easy to see how the dynamism of subcultural men's fashion in the late 1970s and early 1980s might have influenced the thinking of these writers by demonstrating fashion's capacity to challenge hegemonic masculinity. Perhaps the sense of urgency in their writing was a response not only to the comparative dynamism of men's fashion towards the end of the 1970s and at the beginning of the 1980s but also in response to a set of problematically essentialist discourses around masculinity that, as I have suggested, were resurgent during the 1980s and early 1990s. To this extent, these writers were attempting to intervene in cultures of masculinity as well as to describe them.

The insistence that menswear was an inherently conservative form did not suddenly dissipate or collapse under academic critique: indeed, having flourished in the late 1980s, it persisted throughout the 1990s and into the early 2000s, serving a function that was less descriptive than prescriptive. A culture that considered fashion the "natural" realm of women demanded that men, if they were involved at all, should author women's fashion rather than subject themselves to its desiring gaze.

In this chapter, I have described how the normative imperative that men's clothing should not "go too far" and that it should remain confined within an essentially nostalgic model of masculinity still persists. It is a form of reaction concealing itself within accepted opinion, general statements, and an insistence on a status quo that irons out plurality of expression. Menswear, these voices insist, should echo the archetypes of an unchanging hegemonic masculinity: classic tailoring, jeans and workwear, and garments of military origin (though not showy dress uniforms). The partisans of progressive menswear designers, theorists, stylists, fashion journalists, and others have, over the past twenty years, been involved in a struggle to define menswear as fashion, to redefine men as potential fashion consumers,[8] and in various ways, explicitly and implicitly, to make the case for men's fashion as a site of radicalism and resistance.

2
HISTORICAL RESONANCES

In the last decades of the twentieth century, the vibrant, experimental, and optimistic men's fashions of the late 1960s and 1970s came to be treated as something of a gag: fodder for silly party costumes, Mike Myers films, and the punch line to "humorous" greeting cards. What made sixties and seventies menswear the butt of jokes, during the 1990s in particular, was not just that it contradicted contemporary axioms of good taste—womenswear of the seventies encompassed just as many synthetic fibers and loud prints—but that in doing so it transgressed the dominant aesthetic of masculinity: it seemed not just gauche but also contentious—too body-conscious, fey, and over the top.

The familiar trope of *femininity as performance* and the self-evidently radical shifts in the lives of women over the course of the twentieth century meant that, by its final decade, vintage women's fashions could confidently be presented as amusing, mildly sexy, exotic artifacts of the past. Vintage menswear, by contrast, was more problematic. In the 1990s, a period in which masculinity was frequently declared to be "in crisis" (Segal, 1990 [2007]: xviii; Beynon, 2002: 75–95), prevailing masculine culture was too brittle, defensive, and anxious to gaze with indulgence and equanimity at its past: Patricia Cunningham in an essay charting the rise and fall of that quintessentially seventies ensemble "the leisure suit" describes the stigma that still clung to the outfit well into the 1990s (2008: 99).

The emergence of men's fashion in the 1960s and 1970s, after the drab conformity of the early 1950s, certainly did sometimes result in naïve design. But this naïveté is far from the only story. The 1960s and 1970s were decades of immense creativity, dynamism, and moments of great formal and aesthetic sophistication in menswear. Moreover, at the very point that the styles of "the peacock revolution" and its aftermath were most maligned in mainstream culture—in the run-up to the millennium—they were being referenced, *bricolé*, and reclaimed by youth and avant-garde culture: by indie musicians like Brett Anderson and Jarvis Cocker, and by a new breed of menswear designers who were poised to revive men's fashion after a decade-long slumber. The style and silhouette of the 1960s and 1970s provided a paradigm for creative designers at the cusp of the millennium to follow by demonstrating that menswear could be fashionable, energetic, and exciting: they did so by borrowing liberally from subcultures as diverse as mod, punk, and glam, from the minimalism of Cardin to the unashamed maximalism of peacock pomp. Indeed, as I suggested in the introduction to this book, seventies fashion and subculture remains a key reference for contemporary menswear designers.

Fashion and modernity

In a British context, the mod (or modernist) look originated in the mid-to-late 1950s amongst an urban, often gay, bohemian crowd. Entrepreneur Bill Green opened *Vince's Man's Shop* on Newburgh Street in Soho in 1954 selling small runs of garments sometimes sourced from France and with a recognizably "continental look": shorter jackets, narrow trousers, and casual clothing including roll-neck sweaters, black jeans, hipster trousers, fitted jerseys, and vividly colored or patterned pieces (Cohn, 1971: 60–61; Cole, 2000: 71–74). Having initially appealed to a predominantly gay clientele, *Vince's* customer base widened to encompass straight artists, actors, and others looking for relief from the dreary conformity of 1950s mainstream fashion. Like Bill Green, the tailor Cecil Gee, who provided flash suits for bandleaders and jazz musicians, was a rare innovator of the 1950s. And like Green, he achieved innovation, to a great extent, through a flight from respectable Englishness, purveying "razzle-dazzle American styles" and from the mid-1950s, an Italian look influenced by Brioni consisting of short jackets, narrow trousers, pointed-toe shoes, narrow lapels, and skinny ties (Cohn, 1971: 44–45). In this way, mod culture emerged out of hybridity: a combination of Italian, French, and American influences all of which, ironically, cohered into a style that was to prove a major British cultural export.

By the early 1960s, *Vince's Man's Shop* had spawned competitors, including a string of shops owned by erstwhile employee John Stephen (Cohn, 1971: 66).[1] Meanwhile, the mod look was adopted by a broad demographic of young and frequently working-class men who popularized a close *Italianate* tailoring — again characterized by a shorter jacket, fitted trousers — and elements of casual wear. The look was assembled both from items of bespoke or made to measure tailoring (more affordable at the time than it would be today) and various off-the-peg items (Cole, 2000: 75). Although the mod aesthetic was strongly associated with youth, it went on to influence the cut of mainstream menswear during the mid- to late 1960s. And as youth culture developed over the decade, John Stephen's Carnaby Street shops were joined by other retailers around Soho, Portobello, and the Kings Road including *Mr Freedom, Hung on You*, and *I was Lord Kitchner's Valet,* specializing in foppish, neo-regency, brilliantly colored, and richly patterned garments with oversized or complex collars, cuffs, and finishings. The pared-back simplicity of the mod look had given way to splendor and elaboration, and increasingly as the decade wore on to the Orientalist fantasies of hippiedom and the "Peacock Revolution."

In his 1971 text *Today There Are No Gentlemen*, Nik Cohn—one of the first writers to reflect seriously on the changes that had taken place in menswear over the course of the 1960s—considers the shifts in gendered mores from the mid-1950s, when Bill Green's *Vince's Man's Shop* started trading, to the early 1960s, when Carnaby Street as shopping destination was born. Cohn writes that Vince's sold clothing that "could once have been worn by no one but queers and extremely blatant ones at that" but which by the early 1960s were "bought by heteros as well" (1971: 62). This, argues Cohn, represented a facet of the breakdown of rigid class and gender norms in the postwar period: "nothing seemed fixed any more—all the roles were blurring, and there was an evolving of the whole concept of what makes men attractive" (1971: 62). A lithe figure, a close-cleaving silhouette, colors, prints, and modes of comportment that would once have been considered effeminate all formed part of this transformation, so too did a growing acceptance of casual garments and leisure wear as fashion (Cohn, 1971: 63).

The lounge suit in its simplicity and uniformity has often been thought of as the ultimate symbol of modernity[2]—its uniformity was perhaps at its apotheosis in the immediate post–Second World War context of rationing, the demob suit, and the hegemony of large multiple tailors like Burtons, Hepworths, and Associated Tailors. It is in the 1960s, by contrast, that we see the beginnings of men's fashion as we understand it today—hybridized, ambiguous, and in flux—encompassing tailoring, but by no means limited to conventional sartorialism: a site of invention and a space in which masculinity could be interrogated and explored.

This opening up of menswear is felt in the influential men's magazine *Town* (formerly *Man About Town*) during the 1960s. In the November 1962 edition, an advert for John Stephen's "His Clothes" boutiques appears (by now with branches on Regent Street, the King's Road, and Carnaby Street). It features a moodily lit ingenu in a striped cotton roll-neck, his back and shoulder at three quarters to the camera, the thick, jaunty stripes of his matelot forming diagonal lines within the tightly cropped composition: these are echoed by striated light reflected onto the surface upon which the model sits—lending the image a distinctly modernist air, while, emerging from a shadowy background, the model's boyish features and lustrous hair are picked out in bright directional light. (Figure 2.1). This mod aesthetic also appears, albeit in a somewhat watered-down form, in an advert for Simpson of Piccadilly in the September 1962 edition of *Town* in which the figures (this time hand-rendered rather than photographed) are again positioned at dynamic diagonals. The foremost figure with his navy suit, thin turquoise tie, and white-framed sunglasses communicates a certain clean-cut modernity, but the message is somewhat undermined by the tweedy, muted tones of the brown-suited man in the background—his inclusion perhaps

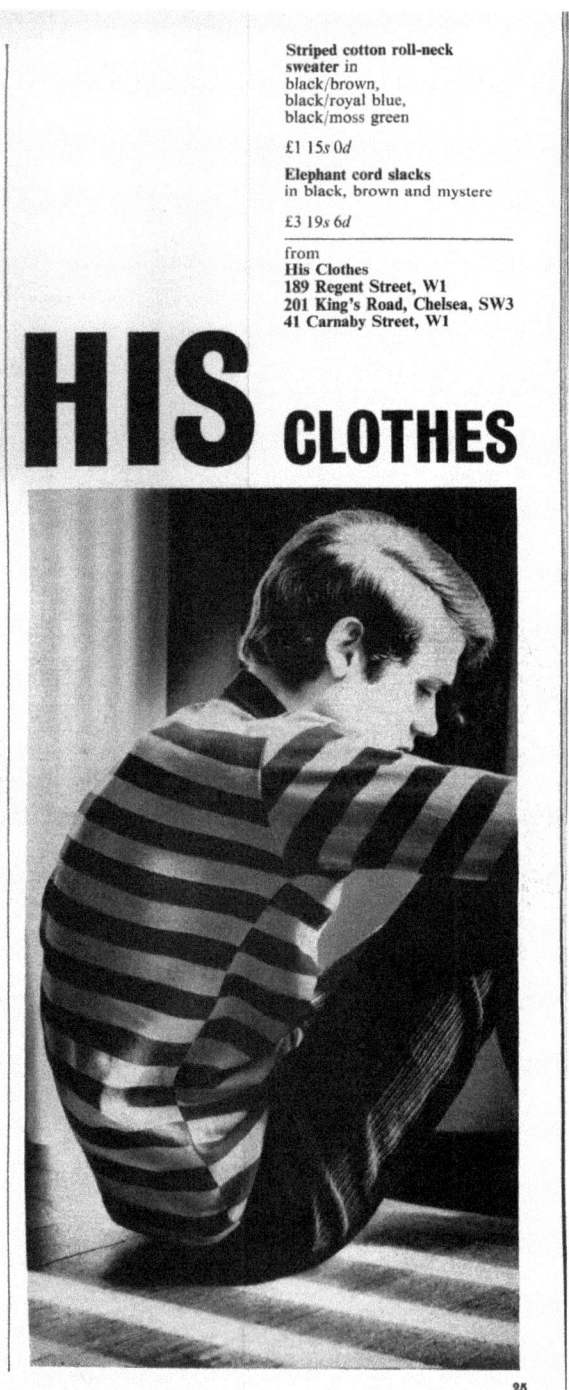

Figure 2.1 Stephen, J. (1962). His Clothes Advertisement. *Town* (11), p. 25.

representing a hedging of commercial bets—and the artist's drawing style, featuring craggy-faced models and fibrous lines seems already to belong to a slightly earlier era (Simpson Piccadilly Advertisement, 1962: 6).

It is significant that the slimmer line and feeling for color was, by 1962, infiltrating more mainstream outfitters such as Simpson as well as the more outré His Clothes. And the growing emphasis on youthfulness described by Cohn and gestured to in the John Stephen's advert is strongly felt in *Town* during the early 1960s, which features quasi-ethnographic studies of emerging youth cultures, not least in an article profiling a small group of North London mods (Barnsley, 1962: 48–53) that includes a certain 15-year-old Mark Feld, later to become the T. Rex frontman Marc Bolan. The article is rather lyrically entitled "Faces Without Shadows," with the semi-salacious standfirst "Young men who live for clothes and pleasure." It contends:

> Mark Feld, Peter Sugar and Michael Simmonds were brought up in Stoke Newington. The most important thing in the world to them is their clothes: they have cupboards and shelves bulging with suits and shirts often designed by themselves in bright, strange and violent colours. In their vocabulary they, and the few other contemporaries of whom they approve, are described as "faces"—the necessary ingredients are youth, a sharp eye for dressing, and a general lack of mercy toward the rest of the world. (1962: 48)

The article goes on to describe the trio's extremely discriminating approach to dress, the shops and boutiques and discotheques they frequent, and their difficulty in persuading tailors to make their suits *comme il faut*. It is significant to note that two assistant hairdressers Sugar and Simmonds and working-class schoolboy Feld/Bolan could, in 1962, afford to employ tailors and fund a lifestyle of going out, being seen, and dancing the twist: "nowadays everyone twists so we have a different twist" (Sugar, 1962 cited in Barnsley, 1962: 51). This emergence of youth culture was, of course, closely linked to the increasing prosperity and greater social mobility of the period.

Moreover, as Cohn (1971) suggests, discourses of gender, sexuality, and the contestation of normative masculinity are very evidently at work in the fashionable subcultures that emerged in the early 1960s. Barnsley quotes Sugar stating, "We're all a bit exhibitionist [...] I admit. Some of our clothes are a bit effeminate but they have to be. I mean you have to be a bit camp. I mean who cares" (Sugar, 1962 cited in Barnsley, 1962: 51). Feld/Bolan goes on to say, "You get a lot of jeers and shouts round our way [...] If you wear something that's a bit different it's 'Nancy' and 'Look at this queer'" (Feld, 1962 cited in Barnsley, 1962: 51). Despite this opprobrium, however, *the faces'* attitude to appearing queer is defiant, which is significant since the article is written some time before the decriminalization of homosexuality in England and Wales in 1967[3] and given the evident risk of violence associated with adopting this ambiguous look. Sugar's comment that their clothes "have to be a bit effeminate" is noteworthy—because it underlines the way that a perceived effeminacy is inextricably bound up with male difference and self-expression: that being seen as queer is a cost that *has to be* borne in order to transgress the normative standards of masculine dress. In this sense, Nik Cohn and *the faces'* ways of talking about being "queer" are much more about gender than they are about sexuality (if it is possible to tease apart those two closely related phenomena). I would argue that the lessening taboo around effeminacy in the 1960s was to prove significant to the blossoming of men's fashion and the opening up of masculine identities over the following two decades, allowing men to celebrate exhibitionism, nonconformity, and a more playful approach to dress.

In an optimistic article in the same 1962 edition of *Town* entitled "Bulge takes over," Ronald Bryden (1962: 40–45) discusses the demographic "bulge" of the postwar baby boomers now coming of age, identifying their difference from previous generations, and speculating on what it might mean for Britain. Bryden (presciently touching upon themes that would go on to animate the then nascent discipline of cultural studies) predicts the rise of greater individuality as new forms of popular culture and subculture, freed from traditional communal identities of class and geography, are relocated within emerging practices of consumption and commercial experience.

> The pseudo-sociologists [...] when they mourn over us as lonely exiles from the gregarious, cosy old days of pub and music-hall; what they're deploring is a flowering of individuals [...] the end of the warm, anonymous tribalism of slum and village whose "wisdom" was to think as everyone else thought. The new generation is thinking for itself [...] They're going to be classless. Their clothes already are. (Bryden, 1962: 43–44)

By the mid-1960s, the shift towards more disinhibited, youthful, and classless fashions described by Brydon seem increasingly to have taken root. Sabre "Waikiki Swimtrunks" are advertised in an abstracted, stylized illustration of two bronzed men in briefs against a vivid orange background (Sabre Helanca Advertisement, 1964: 31). A 1966 edition of *Town* features a variety of garments in velour which, having won "acceptance as a fashion fabric for casual wear" (Thomson, 1966: 12), is shown made up as a roll-neck jacket patterned with an oversized paisley motif and as a variety of jackets and pullovers in "brilliant reds, greens and blues."[4] By 1966, the textured fifties draftsmanship of Simpson's 1962 advert is replaced with an illustration of two male and two female figures rendered in a smooth, stylized sixties line, the two men wear very brief shorts (one with a striped roll-neck, the other with a polo shirt) and both have impossibly long, slim, and tanned legs (Figure 2.2). John Stephen had catered to a young

Figure 2.2 Simpson Guitare Beachwear Advertisement (1966). Town (7), p. 14.

clientele with limited funds, but increasingly the innovations of youth culture were bubbling up, and not only to Simpson of Piccadilly.

Menswear, as Cohn suggests, had become polychromatic, more fitted, and less formal, and now placed a much greater focus on the body than in the decades before. The "bright, strange and violent colours" of *the faces* that Barnsley had described were becoming less remarkable as the decade went on.

The birth of consumer culture

In the 1975 text *Resistance through Rituals*, John Clarke, Stuart Hall, Tony Jefferson, and Brian Roberts argued and that youth culture and subcultures of the postwar period, characterized by "hedonism, permissiveness, anti-authoritarianism, moral pluralism, and materialism," while diametrically opposed to dominant, traditional, bourgeois moral codes, nevertheless emerged out of the logic of advanced consumer capitalism and were central to its success and survival (1993 [1975]: 51). According to Clarke, Hall et al., the birth of a youth-oriented consumer culture in the 1960s, one closely allied to a more socially liberal set of values, acted both to guarantee and support Western capitalism while simultaneously representing a grave threat to the values of class, gender, and sexuality held dear by the system's dominant classes. As the authors put it:

> This was an altogether different—puzzling, contradictory—world for the traditional middle-classes, formed in and by an older, more "protestant" ethic. Advanced capitalism now required not thrift but consumption; not sobriety but style; not postponed gratifications but immediate satisfaction of needs; not goods that last but things that are expendable: the "swinging" rather than the sober life-style. […] The sexual repressiveness and ideals of domesticity enshrined in the middle-class family could not easily survive the growth of "permissiveness." (1993 [1975]: 51)

There is, perhaps, something problematically teleological in the account summarized above, and the authors' description of an economic "base" that *demands* or *causes* changes in the cultural "superstructure" is too neat and one-directional for my liking. Nevertheless, this analysis synthesizing Marxist, Gramscian, and Marcusian insights is compelling because it expresses the tensions and contradictions inherent in the development of youth cultures in the 1960s.

For example, the owners of large menswear businesses who might have been expected to enthusiastically celebrate the prospect of a new and dynamic menswear market were at first—as Cohn describes—somewhat slow to embrace it (1971: 107–111). What might have benefited these businessmen's bank balances nevertheless threatened their conceptions of decency, good taste, and masculinity. Instead, it was left to young entrepreneurs,[5] in the early part of the decade, to drive forward men's fashion.

The rapid and radical changes in popular culture during the 1960s and 1970s were often aggressively resisted by representatives of the old moral order both

HISTORICAL RESONANCES

from the right, as with the campaigner Mary Whitehouse, and on the left, its pundits viewing popular culture as an instrument of capitalist manipulation.

A less subtle mind than Stuart Hall's might have used Gramsci, with his theory of *hegemony* (the cultural means by which power is consolidated and popular consent achieved), and Marcuse, with his profound distrust of consumerism which he argued produced "false needs" quite differently. But Hall and his colleagues outline both the ways in which the consumer culture of the 1960s was "profoundly adaptive" to the needs of capitalism, and simultaneously the ways in which it activated resistance to and subversion of the dominant cultural forms of the establishment. For Hall et al., the new consumerism of the 1960s and 1970s, rather than being a corruption of the counter-culture was an intrinsic expression of it. Thus counter-culture, youth culture, and subculture—the progressive and radical formations of the period—expressed themselves through fashion, music, and dancing as much as they did via traditionally political means.

In many ways, the 1960s witnessed the invention of men's fashion as we know it today: a mass phenomenon, albeit one led from urban centers by initially quite small subcultural groups. This popularization of men's fashion in the 1960s and 1970s activated and made visible new forms of self-expression through increasingly diverse and differentiated forms of dress. The affluent society[6] and the advent of youth fashion meant that young men, including those from working and lower-middle-class backgrounds, were no longer obliged to dress like their fathers, but were able to formulate new and distinct forms of identity.

As the 1960s progressed, the neat, clean line of mod dress increasingly gave way to more elaborate, nostalgic, and Eastern influences as the hippie aesthetic emerged. Nic Cohn traces the look as far back as 1965, with the opening of Michael Rainey's store *Hung on You* "the first intimation of Hippie, of strangeness to come" as "Moroccan robes, Indian silks, Edwardian and Victorian remnants" came into vogue (1972: 119). By the summer of 1969, Mick Jagger was playing Hyde Park in a full skirted, flounced white voile dress—with ruffled collar and full sleeves—worn over white flared trousers, the ensemble created by menswear designer and provocateur Mr Fish.[7] Jagger's famous outfit (Gahr and Fish, 1969), its form reminiscent of Eastern European folk costume, gestured both to a desire to overturn the gender conventions of clothing, and to a neo-primitivist urge to access freer and more "authentic" modes of being that were frequently associated with a rejection of Western values.

Away from the British context, the Italian men's fashion magazine *L'Uomo Vogue* was launched in 1968, its early editions capturing the drama and dynamism of late sixties and early seventies menswear which was opening up not only at the level of color, pattern, and fabrication but also increasingly of form. A 1969 issue of the magazine features German actor Peter Chatel in an exquisite double-breasted white jacket by Costanzi for Fabiani: the jacket is made up in a soft flannel, with two covered buttons placed at the side seam to create an uncluttered, asymmetric front, while its shawl collar is finished with an unusual blunt ending recalling the closure of a traditional Chinese *hanfu*. It is an immensely skilled, assured, and elegant garment: in the apparent simplicity of its form and in the asymmetry of its folded front it feels distinctly Eastern, but the method of construction—the fit achieved through curving seams and darts, the set-in shaped sleeves and slightly padded shoulders—is distinctly European (Figure 2.3). Chatel sports the jacket with a silk shirt fastened at the neck with a foulard in the same fabric, the evening ensemble demonstrating how designers in the late 1960s were already reimagining formal menswear in quite fundamental ways.

This exciting moment of possibility is reflected in any number of images, features, interviews, and advertisements in *L'Uomo Vogue* during the late 1960s and early 1970s. Pared-back tailoring is seen in a photo story featuring actor Dino Mele wearing a series of double-breasted jackets that fasten to the collar like nineteenth century military uniforms (Dino Mele, 1968: 142), and in a photograph of director Lina Wertmuller whose husband, scenographer Enrico Job, sports a Nehru-like reversible, zip-fronted jacket with a stand-collar and matching trousers (Enrico Job, 1968: 109). More innovatively, a 1969 advert features a lapel-less, fitted double-breasted suit designed by Luigi Falco, which—in a gesture to modernity—transforms into an all-in-one by aid of a zip (Falco, 1969: 26)!

In addition to this feeling for pared back modernity, however, there is also an increasing flamboyance between the pages of the magazine that manifests itself in print, jewel-like color, silk scarves knotted raffishly at the neck, sheer fabrics, and exotic jewelry. A photo story featuring artist and director Antonello Aglioti from Autumn 1968 captures a feeling for a romantic neo-regency aesthetic as he poses in a striped cravat and shirt of his own devising, high-waisted trousers, a pocket-watch as a pendant and an ornate Indian chain in place of a belt (Mulas, 1968: 77).

A photoshoot in the 1969 special issue of the magazine presents "the bravest and most brazen fashions" (Toscani, 1969: 136–137). Model Victor Anelli[8] in a cheetah-patterned silk shirt, open to the mid-chest, gazes boldly back at the viewer from a dark background (Figure 2.4). This large image is surrounded by smaller photographs featuring gold jewelry, fur, leather and animal print designs—a lush Aladdin's cave of garments, while Anelli with his chin length, fringed, tousled haircut, along with a gold studded belt, folded arms, and direct gaze, embodies the "brazenness" the accompanying copy refers to, seeming to prophesize in his provocative stance and attire the coming of punk almost a decade hence. The previous pages feature the same model in a selection of glamorous, dishabillé evening wear, including a translucent cut-velvet shirt in black and gold, and a wide-lapelled, velvet dinner jacket worn with a black band at the shirt collar instead of a tie (Figure 2.5).

The connection between new forms of fashionable representation and new forms of masculinity is again made explicit in a 1971 edition of *L'Uomo Vogue* (Toscani, 1971: 102–104). An article and photoshoot (once more by Oliviero Toscani) entitled *The New Face of the New Dad*[9] features photographs of "Twenty-two dads and twenty-eight children" and we're told:

Figure 2.3 Toscani, O. (1969). Peter Chatel. *L'Uomo Vogue* (6), p. 118. Photographer Oliviero Toscani, who worked extensively for *L'Uomo Vogue* in the late 1960s and early 1970s, later became famous for his pioneering, avant-garde, sometimes controversial advertisements for Benetton. Perhaps some of this later radicalism can be felt in the new ways that he frames male fashion and the male body.

Figure 2.4 Toscani, O. (1969). Di giorno o di sera, con ironia. *L'Uomo Vogue* (6), p. 137.

Figure 2.5 Toscani, O. (1969). Di Sera una Moda Sdrammatizzata. *L'Uomo Vogue* (6), p. 135.

The new dad signifies a new way of life, a new way of living and behaving, a physical and visual symbol. [He is] demystifying the traditional formal-family hierarchy and creating another model—more fair, more true, and why not? more beautiful. [...] And where is this sort of long-haired dad found—these guys who, when they take their daughters to kindergarten, make the other kids cry because they want a dad like that too? They are photographers, graphic designers, industrialists, painters, art directors [...] They are real living people. (Toscani, 1971: 102)

Like Ronald Bryden's *Town* article of nine years earlier, *L'Uomo Vogue* is making a claim for a new demographic of young men increasingly liberated from the narrow, traditional identities of their parents' generation. But by the 1970s, under the influence of second-wave feminist discourses, this liberation was not only conceptualized at the level of class and geography but also in terms of gender. And an intriguing connection is made between fashion and fatherhood, caring for the self, and caring for others: the New Dads, we are told, are "men in Vogue" who represent "not only a cutting edge idea, but also a way of life" (Toscani, 1971: 102). Of course, this new father is hardly a mainstream representative of the early 1970s, but he does point to a hunger for new, radical forms of heterosexual masculinity that was characteristic of the period. In this way, the notions that surrounded the New Man of the 1980s—empathetic, antisexist, caring, and modish— are revealed to have much deeper historical roots. In 1970, Jack Sawyer had published an article entitled *On Male Liberation* which advocated a departure from dominant standards of masculinity (Goldrick-Jones, 2003: 32–33), and a series of pro-feminist men's liberation books arguing that the emotionally repressive "male sex role" was damaging to men were to follow (Bradley, 1971; Pleck and Sawyer, 1974; Fasteau, 1975; Nichols, 1975). In this sense, the 1971 *L'Uomo Vogue* article reflects a set of shifting discourses surrounding masculinity that were connected to broader notions of political and psychological emancipation.

Clearly, *L'Uomo Vogue* of this period is focused on a rather niche section of society; its pages are filled with celebrities and beautiful people: those for whom a permissive society, or at least much freer and more open one, had well and truly arrived. Clearly, it would be foolish to assume that these representations were typical of Italy as a whole. Nevertheless, such images do speak of the profound changes that had been wrought by the Italian *miracolo economico*, the postwar boom that had transformed defeated Italy—poor and mostly rural—into a major economic power: urbanized, educated, and with dramatically improved standards of living (Crafts and Toniolo, 1996). Italy's famous fashion and textile industries, the patrons of *L'Uomo Vogue*, played no small part in this process of economic expansion. And the fact that there was sufficient commercial and consumer demand to support a menswear publication with high production values and a strong focus on directional fashion demonstrates, by the late

1960s, the existence of a much wider demographic interested in consuming images of this aspirational lifestyle and in emulating its glamorous aesthetic.

Although the more radical developments in menswear of the 1960s were predominantly confined to a young, fashionable, & urban scene, by the 1970s a spirit of innovation began to influence the menswear market much more generally. For example, the trade magazine *Tailor & Cutter* remains surprisingly quiet on mod developments throughout the early to mid-1960s, but during the early 1970s, its illustrations and articles feature an increasingly wide range of experimentally cut menswear and examples of garments tailored from new fabrics including double-faced jerseys, elaborate jacquard weaves, and synthetic and mixed-fiber cloth of various constructions.

It is my view that the significance of innovations in menswear during the 1970s has been seriously undervalued and remains ripe for reassessment. Not only have the 1970s effectively been *written out* of a number of accounts of men's dress, but even in more un-biased costume histories, sixties and seventies menswear tends to presented as an isolated aberration from the norm: a narrative that ignores connections between the 1970s and recent developments in men's fashion.

Issues of the *Tailor & Cutter* magazine during the early 1970s represent particularly valuable documents because they offer an insight into contemporary attempts to formulate a men's wardrobe that responded to changes in contemporary mores and firmly situated menswear in the modern world. Moreover, as a trade journal, *Tailor & Cutter* was concerned with highlighting content of *commercial* interest to its readers, so the stylistic innovations it featured would have exercised a relevance beyond small youth or subcultural groups.

Two photographs accompanying an article entitled simply "Paris" update readers on the latest men's collections from the French capital: a model wears a "long coat in birds-eye wool worsted, worn over a high-necked tunic with vertical pockets slashed into the body" (Figure 2.6), and in the other photographs two different tailored jackets in strikingly graphic, jacquard weaves, as well as a caped ensemble with a blouson jacket, breeches, and high leather boots (Figure 2.7). The article goes on to suggest: "Compared with the excitement of a week or so before in Rome, the Paris Collections were relatively quiet" (Paris, 1970). It is noteworthy that these outfits, seeming quite bold today, were deemed insufficiently exciting in 1970, a sign of the desire for novelty and change within the industry at the time.

An image from April 1971 features, amongst other outfits, a fitted, boldly striped suit constructed from jersey (Figure 2.8). The jacket's zip-fastening, absence of lapels, and zipped patch pockets work together to denote modernity, and the model is photographed mid-stride (and in front of a sports car), the diagonal composition suggesting dynamism. Despite the outfit's casualness, it nevertheless retains some of the precision of more traditional tailoring. And it forms part of a number of features in *Tailor & Cutter* which reimagine the suit so as to become more flexible, lightweight, and modern. There are, of course, connections to Pierre

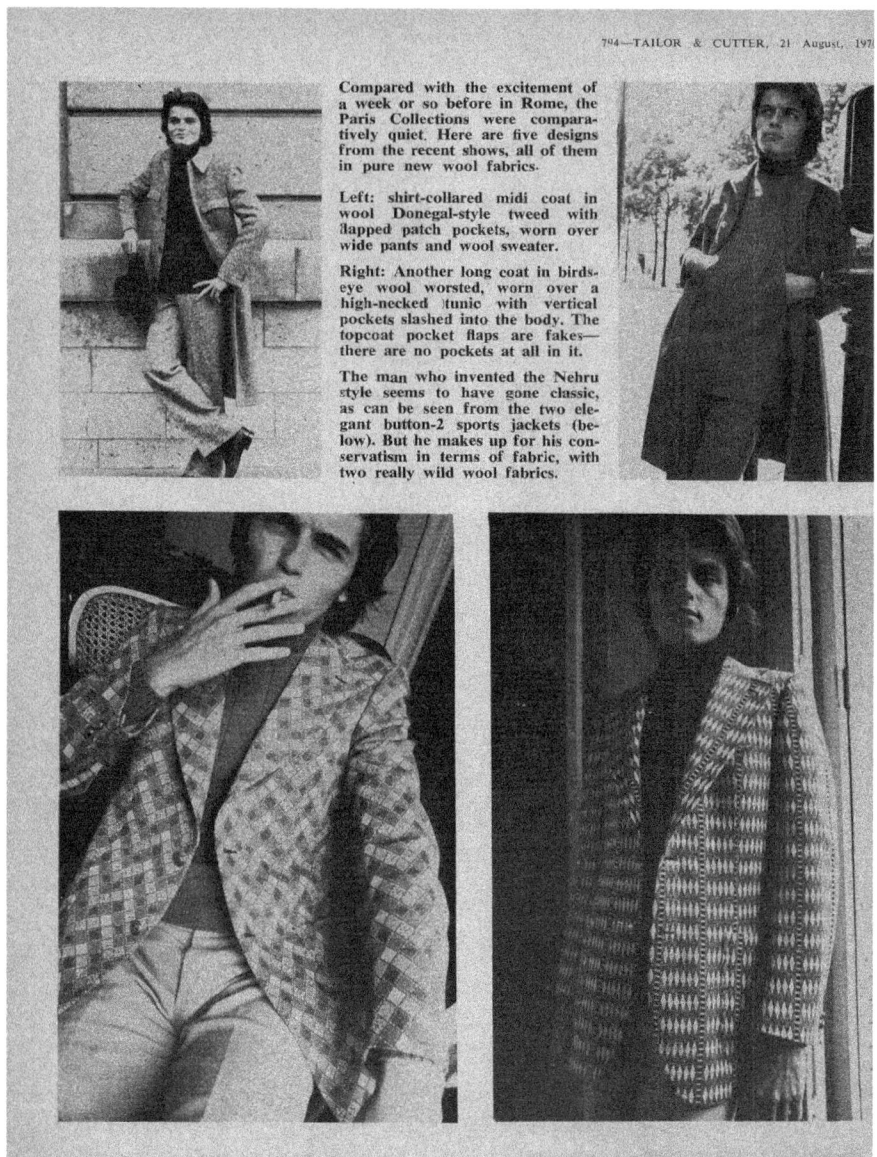

Figure 2.6 Paris. (1970). *Tailor & Cutter*, November 1970 (1153), p. 794.

Figure 2.7 Paris. (1970). *Tailor & Cutter*, November 1970 (1153), p. 795.

really counts) the emphasis has been quite different.

Though Horne Brothers will be combining both approaches in their re-styled Long Room which opened up in Oxford Street this week (see THE MONTH), most of the garments sold generally will be as conventional as the 20,000 Crimplene jackets which Hepworths plan to make this year. That, incidentally, is exactly 20,000 more than they made last year, though they have done well with Crimplene pants bought outside their own production facilities.

One problem has been that jersey, as such, has had very little appeal to the fashion end of the trade, which continues to be the main sector of growth. At a time when the emphasis there in fabrics is upon texture and other tactile qualities, synthetic and natural fibre jerseys alike have tended to have a bland, rather neutral impact upon the sense of touch.

fashionwise, this shininess could become a bonus point, of course.

One knitter is adding rabbit hair to improve the surface texture, and even cashmere is turning up in a jersey structure. So far, the problem of "pilling" has not been as great as might be expected.

Stroud Riley have produced a Dacron/cotton jersey which is a very cool cloth for summer wear, and which has been very successful on the American market. Like a number of knitters, they are working hard on pure new wool jerseys, which actually require very little development work to answer most of the objections to the knitted structure, apart from the high porosity which is common to all fibre. IWS have also made available a machine washable jersey, but this has tended to mar the aesthetic qualities, producing a rather harder feel. As Richard Stroud says, "People do not appear anxious to wash their suits."

This jump suit in COURTELLE single jersey by Tricot-France shows how plain and jacquard fabrics in co-ordinating shades complement each other. The trousers are in a single jersey rib in pillar box red, and the roll neck top is in a sand red/jacquard.
Left: made in 100 per cent DACRON jersey from Du Pont, this grey/red striped suit has a zip front and zipped breast pockets. One of the design details is the lack of pockets on the bottom part of the jacket. The suit is made by Young Club, Norway.

Figure 2.8 *Tailor & Cutter*. (1971). April 30, 1971, p. 7. The model on the left wears an outfit "Young Club" of Norway.

HISTORICAL RESONANCES

Figure 2.9 Prize-winning IFC Design. (1972). *Tailor & Cutter*, February (5457), p. 11. Design by Miguel Diaz.

Cardin's menswear experimentations of the 1960s: Cardin not only pioneered the minimal, revere-less "Cylinder Jacket" of 1960 but also introduced zip-fastened jersey styles in collections including "Cosmos" of 1967 (Blackman, 2009: 186; *Victoria and Albert Museum*, 2014). As the features from *Tailor & Cutter* suggest, by the early 1970s, some of these more avant-garde notions around men's fashion were increasingly being absorbed into the mainstream.

An image, again from *Tailor & Cutter*, here from February 1972, makes the point eloquently: A suit by Spanish tailor Miguel Diaz constructed from a textured wool (and polyester) jersey draws attention both to its manufacture and, subtly, to the figure beneath. The contrast topstitching, approximately 0.5 cm from the seam, highlights the inventive placement of style lines, and the wide spread of the lapel is cut to form a shallow arch, the notch at the collar just a narrow slit to avoid interrupting the line. The front of the jacket is formed of two pattern pieces, and the seam fitting the garment to the torso runs directly into the displaced seam of the sleeve, which in turn has been brought forward to create an elegant curved junction where the four pattern pieces meet. Finally, the pocket is created from an interaction of rounded rectangles and ellipses, the patch pocket and flap ingeniously interleaved between two lozenge-shaped, faced, and topstitched cut-outs (Figure 2.9). While it is easy to be distracted from the formal and creative significance of seventies fashion by the sometimes gauche photography through which it was recorded, the work of designers and tailors like Diaz is representative of a new spirit of innovation in menswear of the period, one characterized by a formally sophisticated approach to construction and silhouette deriving from but moving beyond traditional tailoring.

In a similar vein, an illustrated feature entitled "The alternative pant" in the April 1972 edition of *Tailor & Cutter* delineates a new technique for drafting trouser patterns to achieve an integrated yoke and side seam, in this way elongating the leg, emphasizing the thigh and buttock and, again, highlighting the elements of construction (Figure 2.10). It is indicative of the ways in which innovative menswear practitioners in the early 1970s found new ways to place the body at the center of their formal exploration through a play of structure and silhouette.

Further evidence that men's clothing and masculinity were being reimagined during the late 1960s and early 1970s can be found in science fiction films and programs of the period, such as *Star Trek* and *Space 1999*, which present a variety of futuristic possibilities for men's dress—often drawing on Pierre Cardin and Paco Rabanne in their construction. In this way, innovations at the level of form in late sixties and seventies menswear, and attempts to reimagine the future of men's fashion, should be seen very much in the context of a larger modernist project towards a freer, more liberated, classless male body, and there are obvious continuities between this formally reimagined, rationalized clothing and the dress reform movements of the first part of the twentieth century.[10] The formal, modernist approach to menswear of the late 1960s and early 1970s, with pared back, rever-less tailoring and geometric finishes, would reemerge in the new millennium, for example, in Raf Simons' work for Jil Sander (especially his Spring 2009 collection, with its references to the Bauhaus and de Stijl) and in the collections of Chris Van Asche for Dior Homme. In this sense, the inspiration that designers like Simons, Slimane, and Capasa drew from seventies

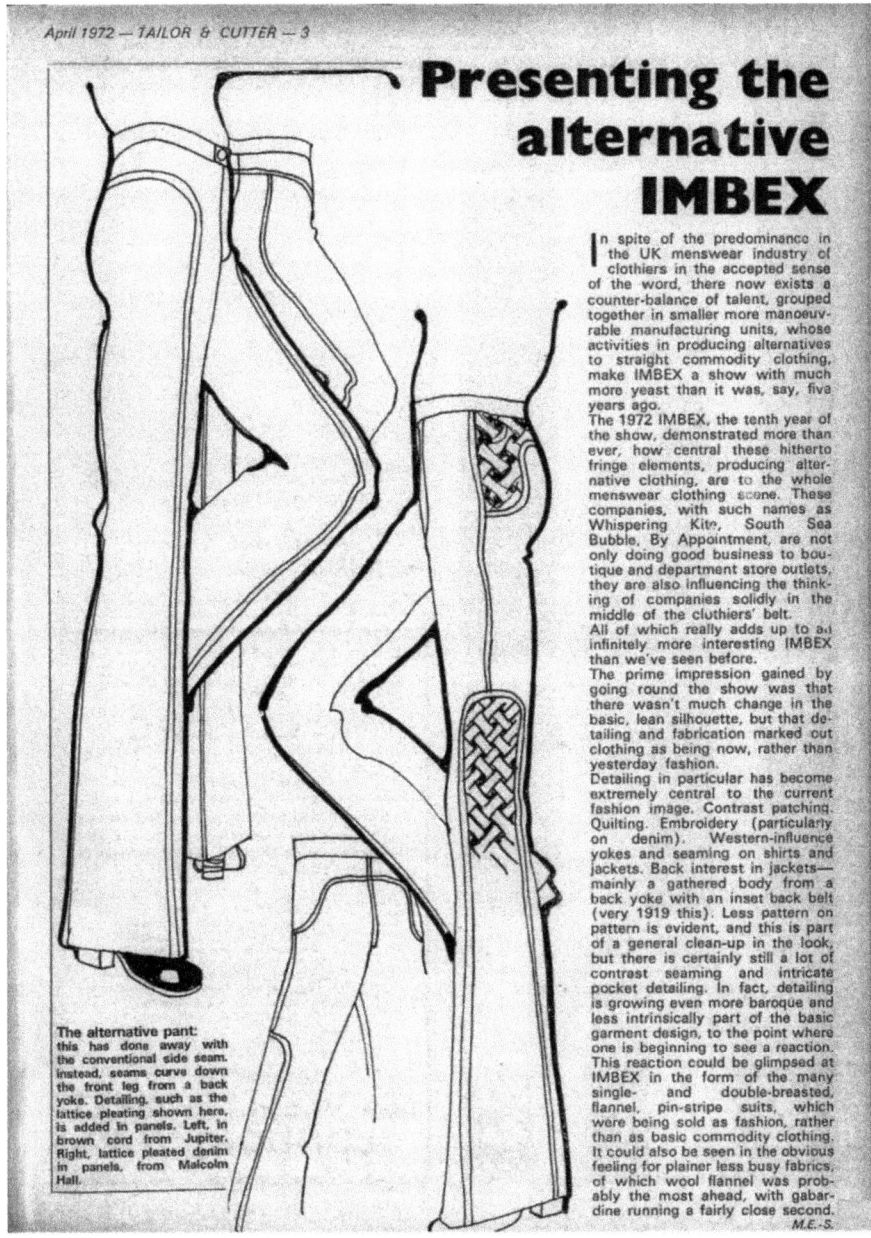

Figure 2.10 The Alternative Pant. (1972). *Tailor & Cutter*, April 1972 (5459), p. 3.

menswear connects men's fashion of the 2000s—with its inventive construction, soft draping cloth, low necklines, and attention to the body—to an earlier set of progressive reforms that stretch back beyond the 1960s and 1970s to an earlier moment of interwar innovation and *körperkultur*.[11]

Across the pond, American *GQ* magazine also captured the sexy, corporeal mood of menswear during the 1970s, promoting colorful fashions that drew attention to the male body through their fit and fabrication. The Summer 1973 edition of *GQ* features, variously, models in brief nylon swimming trunks with elaborate abstract prints, lounging on the veranda of a Tunisian nightclub in gauzy safari suits, and posing against a backdrop of North African ruins and brilliant blue skies (*Gentlemen's Quarterly*, 1973: 58–68, 96–99). Throughout the issue, vibrantly patterned fabrics, vivid colors, and an emphasis on fit, particularly at the waist, predominate (Burdine, 1973: 22). One shoot pictures a model in a short-sleeved Hawaiian shirt printed with turquoise and soft pink palm motifs against a black background. The shirt is cut short to hit the natural waist and hemmed with jersey ribbing to synch it in—the sun-kissed, smiling model sports this garment with a pair of high-waisted, pleated, dusty-pink trousers (Figure 2.11). It is an outfit—perhaps like many of the decade—that confounds our contemporary notions of "good taste": in its exuberance, its lack of restraint, its joyfulness, it resists what Bourdieu terms the *pure gaze*[12] and demands instead "facile involvement and vulgar enjoyment" (Bourdieu, 1984: 447). As I have suggested, in recent years there has been something of a rehabilitation of *the decade that taste forgot* and I was struck by the aesthetic similarities between this 1972 image and the Spring/Summer 2016 Louis Vuitton menswear collection—all revere collars, orientalist motifs, and vivid colors. In this sense, the importance of seventies menswear for contemporary designers is due to, rather than in spite of, its divergence from restrictive, conventional axioms of tasteful reserve.

This ludic feeling in men's fashion continues well into the middle of the 1970s: in the May and July/August 1976 editions of *Uomo Vogue*, a sense of play is apparent in the confident use of color and texture that characterize the various photoshoots. Models smile, dressed in exotically patterned clothing of warm, vivid, contrasting hues; everything is bathed in light and seems somehow innocent and joyful (Valentino a Vent'Anni, 1976: 163). In contrast to *Tailor & Cutter* of a few years earlier, here the emphasis is less on the modernization and transformation of cut and more on a varied palette of colors, prints, and fabrications. Nevertheless, as in those earlier examples, the overarching emotion communicated in the various features and fashion stories of the magazine is one of possibility, energy, optimism, and pleasure.

The 1970s undoubtedly produced some exciting menswear. At the more glamorous end of the spectrum were the playful but exquisitely cut suits and jumpsuits which tailor and designer Freddie Burretti made for David Bowie, along with the more commercially significant work of tailors Tommy Nutter and Edward

Figure 2.11 Salvati, J. (1973). Shirts with a view. *Gentlemen's Quarterly*, 4 (43), p. 82.

Sexton, who dressed Mick Jagger, Bowie, The Beatles, and many others (and who helped to define the silhouette of the decade). Away from this starry firmament, images from *Men's Wear, Tailor & Cutter, GQ* and *L'Uomo Vogue* demonstrate how innovative menswear design was practiced by less famous designers and tailors at various levels of the market: these were practitioners who explored new techniques and materials, adapting men's fashion to meet the needs and desires of modern men with frequently elegant results.

The dynamic during the 1960s and early 1970s was towards greater and greater freedom in menswear: innovative approaches to cut and fit, and a greater use of color and pattern. By the tail end of the 1970s, however, men's fashion—and fashion in general—takes on a much more muted, nostalgic, quietly romantic quality. Models are photographed strolling through rugged moorland with tousled hair, in Fair Isle knits and corduroy, or perhaps leaning against the flaking wall of an abandoned farmhouse to evoke a rustic *Arte Povera* style. Men's dress during the latter half of the decade—with its hippyish, folkloric elements, and distinctive close cut—retains a recognizable character that differentiates it from menswear of the post-Second World War period and from "traditional menswear" more generally, but some of the intense energy, color, and innovation that are so characteristic of the first half of the decade are on the wane during its latter years.

In addition to these developments in mainstream menswear, subculture in the 1970s was also on the move, most notably in the rise of proto-punk and punk styles that emerged on both sides of the Atlantic during the middle of the decade. Unlike the aspirational hedonism of the mods, with their cosmopolitan look, or the idealism of the hippies, punk cohered—at least at the level of style—around nihilism and negation: the rejection of mainstream straight society not as a utopian gesture but as an act of refusal and repudiation on behalf of a "blank generation" who could "take it or leave it each time" (Hell, 1977). Both the increasing quietness and nostalgia of late seventies menswear and, conversely, the rebellious *bricolé* aesthetic of punk seem to connect to the economic and political uncertainties of the period. After the economic boom of the 1960s, in the years following the 1973 oil crisis, high inflation and rising unemployment across the developed economies of Europe and America slowly dampened the optimism of popular culture. Stalling economic growth, strikes and labor unrest, the depopulation of British and American cities, and the increasing competitiveness of Far Eastern economies all played into narratives of national decline. Nevertheless, despite the economic shocks of the period, the 1970s in Britain and much of Europe was a period of unprecedented affluence and social and cultural freedom for most ordinary people (Baumol, 1986: 1075; Forster and Harper, 2010: 4–9; Office for National Statistics, 2013). It is this feeling of affluence and freedom that can be so powerfully felt in the inventive, colorful, sometimes gauche but rarely boring menswear of the decade.

The 1980s

Growing out of this period of uncertainty and responding to it, the 1980s (in the UK and America in particular) was a decade of hard oppositions between left and right; it was the period in which the Keynsian postwar consensus was decisively shattered; a period of financial deregulation, high unemployment, rapid deindustrialization, and the associated destruction of working-class communities.

It was also a decade characterized by a vibrant and dynamic youth and street culture, multiple style tribes, expanding markets, as well as a diverse set of politics of resistance organized both around threatened class identities and the politics of gender, sexuality, and ethnicity. As women entered the workforce in ever greater numbers (Office for National Statistics, 2013) and as traditionally male-dominated industries came under threat, a set of discourses—and anxieties—surrounding the changing face of masculinity emerged, coalescing around the much-contested figure of the New Man.

The consumer boom of the 1980s spanning the years 1982–1989 was shorter and shallower than the period of postwar affluence that stretched from the late 1950s to the early 1970s (Mort, 1996: 2). Nevertheless, its advent marked a series of enormous, and for some, cataclysmic shifts at the level of economics and politics, and in terms of intellectual thought. Modernist, Fordist paradigms gave way to postmodern ethics and aesthetics: newly deregulated finance boomed, and so too did the *image industries* of advertising, design, marketing, forecasting, and merchandising. This was the swirling rollercoaster of signs and symbols, flashing lights, and glossy surfaces foretold by Baudrillard ([1972] 1981; [1981] 2010) as the business of selling, consuming, and promoting increasingly eclipsed the business of making (especially in the UK and America).

These polyvalent, diverging, and intersecting discourses map onto the menswear styles of the period; they are present in the eroticized male bodies that become prevalent in eighties fashion imagery; in the broad-shouldered sharp suits and striped shirts of *GQ*; in the new arty, casual tailoring of Giorgio Armani and Yohji Yamamoto; and in the radical, outré, queered, and androgynous aesthetics of magazines like *The Face, Blitz*, and *i-D*. In this way, fashion was both an expression of the new economic liberalism of the time—communicating aspiration, wealth, and the need to sell oneself—and simultaneously, in its more youth cultural and avant-garde manifestations, a crucial site of resistance to Thatcherite and Reaganite politics.

Rifling through back-copies of *GQ,* one could be forgiven for assuming that there was little more to eighties men's fashion than shoulder-pad executive chic and brawny models working out. But, this impression belies a more complex reality: menswear had bifurcated. Understated forties-inspired tailoring was resurgent, as titles like *Esquire, L'Uomo Vogue,* and *GQ* promoted a much more monochrome, normatively masculine, and much less formatively innovative menswear than they had a decade before. Theirs was an aspirational but rather safe men's fashion, based around the revival of a series of archetypes—country gents in tweeds, expansively shouldered businessmen in sober suits, and sportswear or jeans-clad hunks in states of partial undress.

On the other hand, subcultural and youth cultural menswear during the early and mid-1980s was, arguably, more radical and transgressive than at any time before or since. This avant-garde menswear—originating in clubbing, street style, and from a range of stylists, designers,[13] musicians and demi-mondains who had emerged from the same subcultural scene – was championed by a new, experimental and irreverent "style press." Magazines like *The Face, Blitz, i-D,* and *Time Out* occupied a very different space in contemporary culture than the more established fashion and music magazines that preceded and coexisted with them: these were magazines that cataloged street style and youth culture with a playful but sophisticated sensibility, with cutting-edge graphic design, and with a mixture of high and lowculture references.

The typography of designer Neville Brody at *The Face*, freely combining Constructivist, Bauhaus, and Dadaist graphic languages along with corporate logos and hand-rendered elements, echoed the bricolage aesthetic of the fashion stories that sat within his layouts. In a shoot entitled "The New Glitterati" (Furmanovsky and Russell Powell, 1984: 47–49), two "faces on the London clubscene," Richard and Joshua, appear against a spray of peacock feathers and a dramatically lit backdrop. In two photographs—a black and white close-cropped shot of the Richard's torso and head (Figure 2.12) and a full-length color portrait (Furmanovsky and Russell Powell, 1984: 48)—the club kid is pictured in an extraordinary outfit of his own devising. He wears a clone-like motorcycle cap further subverted through the application of jewels; a zoot suit with a wide-lapelled jacket and deep-pleated trousers in clownish red, yellow, and black tartan (lined in silver); a PVC- paneled shirt—its fetish, punk aesthetic juxtaposed against lavish, paste jewelry at the collar and placket; homemade sequined braces; silver lurex socks; and spray-painted high-top trainers. He poses assertively, almost filmically, playing the role of the confident, seductive star.

This innovative approach to the styling and presentation of menswear is evident in any number of shoots in the style press of the early to mid-eighties. An article from *Blitz* magazine of May 1983 profiles designer Elmaz Huseyin featuring her hand-painted shirts and vests, sported—along with sailor cap and shorts—by a model who lounges on a floor decorated with similarly swirling patterns (Webb and Owen, 1983: 28). A year later, in a story entitled "Relax!"—again from *Blitz*—Fiorucci sportswear and Lonsdale boxing apparel are combined with leather harnesses, studs, and chains in a series of photographs in which bare-chested models grapple and pose together (Siwan and Brown, 1984: 34–35).

More iconically, September 1986 saw Stephen Linard's photo story "Hell's Angels: British Menswear takes flight" appear in *The Face* (Linard and McCabe, 1986: 44–51). Amongst photographs of models sporting crowns, cowboy hats, cod pieces, and rubber gloves comes an incredible image. A figure in profile strides dramatically across the frame clad entirely in gold: metallic leather trousers; a gilded, fringed leather jacket; stack-heeled cowboy boots; bedecked in a profusion of glittering costume jewelry, and with gold plastic wings bound to his head to resemble a latter-day Mercury. His back leg extended, head thrown back, the model emits a howl of pain while his left hand plunges a gold-hilted dagger into his heart—a supremely glamorous act of self-annihilation (Figure 2.13).

Figure 2.12 Furmanovsky, J. and Russell Powell, F. (1984) "The New Glitterati," *The Face*, p. 47.

Figure 2.13 Linard, S. and McCabe, E. (1986) "British Menswear Takes Flight: London Calling," *The Face*, p. 46.

Bringing together diverse forms of attire—fetish clothing, sportswear, contemporary men's fashion, toys, and trinkets—these images demonstrate the newfound importance of *styling,* a phenomenon and career that emerged in the 1980s to transform fashion photography. Stylists like Iain R. Webb, Simon Foxton, and Ray Petri brought practices of customizing and reappropriating garments that were associated with subculture into the context of fashion proper.[14] And like the contemporary clubbing scene, centered around nights like Blitz, Cha-Cha, Le Kilt, The Beatroute, WAG, and Taboo (Webb, 2015), avant-garde styling and fashion photography—with its dramatis personae of Midnight Cowboys, Querelles, Pink Narcissi, and assorted rough trade—often had a strongly queer subtext.

If the fashions of the 1960s were the result of hybridity, how much more hybrid and mixed were the eighties youth cultural fashions that drew eclectically on a variety of prior scenes and historical moments, while playfully contrasting and juxtaposing these elements? Unlike earlier subcultures, the members of the "New Glitterati" documented in *The Face* weren't aiming for synthesis in their style: the legacy of punk, as Dick Hebdige (1979) describes, was to legitimize an explicitly collaged DIY approach to appearance and identity. And in the garments, poses, photography, and fractured intersecting typographic elements that frame these images, there is a sense of deliberate performativity—a desire to expose the inherently dramaturgic nature of identity, an urge to revel in the mutability and contradictions of gender. Sixties and seventies menswear had subverted normative masculinity and innovated at the level of form and silhouette, but there is something distinctive in the way that magazines such as *The Face, Blitz*, and *i-D* deliberately used camp—"the love of the exaggerated, the 'off' of things not being what they are"—as part of a broader radical postmodern sensibility (Sontag, 2009 [1964]: 279).

Tim Edwards (1997: 43) suggests that the avant-garde styles showcased in magazines like *The Face* and emanating from a smallish clubbing scene were, in their pure form, worn only by a limited number of highly fashion-literate young men clustered around urban centers. Nevertheless, the androgynous and performative nature of subcultural men's fashion in the early and mid-1980s resonated far beyond the cool cognoscenti who haunted Soho and Covent Garden. The dressed-up New Romantic/Blitz Kid/New Wave scene that had emerged from clubs like Billy's and Blitz not only produced stylists and fashion designers but also bands including Spandau Ballet, Sigue Sigue Sputnik, and Visage. Moreover, the post-punk synth-based musicians of the late 1970s and 1980s including The Human League, Depeche Mode, Gary Newman, Soft Cell, and Japan, despite originating in geographically distinct scenes,[15] brought together a set of visual and aural references—David Bowie, Roxy Music, Kraftwerk, the energy of punk, Weimar loucheness, and Bauhaus high-modernism—that were very similar to those of the Blitz, and that defined the look and feel of the period. As a result, you didn't have to go to an obscure hangout to see men with lipstick and backcombed hair in the 1980s, you just had to switch on the television and tune in to "Top of the Pops" or buy a copy of the teen music magazine *Smash Hits*! A cover photo from December 1984 features Depeche Mode's Martin Gore—all rouged lips, kohl rimmed eyes and a teased-out peroxide hairdo—spotlit against a crimson background. He wears a black lace negligée pulled down to expose his shoulders, chest and one nipple

Figure 2.14 Watson, E. (1984) "Front Cover," *Smash Hits*, p. 1.

with a leather miniskirt accessorized with handcuffs, striking a sultry fashion pose while his band mates behind are caught in an eerie red glow (Figure 2.14).

Despite the entrepreneurial nous of fashion and music's new wave (with their homemade clothing and hand-soldered synthesizers), this wasn't the image of Britain's economic resurgence that the Conservative government had in mind. The antipathy was mutual; Depeche Mode penned a critique of contemporary capitalism with the memorable line "the grabbing hands grab all they can" (Gore, 1983). In fashion, stylist Iain R. Webb (Webb and Lewis, 1986) scrawled anti-consumerist messages on his model's clothes, while Ray Petri celebrated an edgy and multicultural aesthetic or, as Frank Mort put it "Dole-style clothes for hanging around street corners" (1987: 193). In this sense, the self-conscious mixedness, fluidity, and cosmopolitanism of new wave/New Romantic fashion and music—along with its DIY ethos—represented a fundamental rejection of the social conservatism and jingoism that was resurgent in British (and American) politics during the 1980s (as well as a creative response to the high levels of youth unemployment that persisted throughout Margaret Thatcher's time in office).

Edwards is right to point out that relatively few people read the new style press—*The Face, Blitz*, and *i-D*—but their influence on cultural intermediaries and producers (journalists, media workers, and designers) was huge. As a result, the new wave/New Romantic look was widely diffused—albeit in a watered-down form. The mass-market high street retailer C&A, for example, introduced *Avanti* "a new label for fast dressers [...] Don't get left behind" in 1985. It was advertised with a photograph of a chain-wielding male model clad in pink that draws heavily on the aesthetic of *The Face* and *Blitz* (1985: 9). More generally, young men's style during the 1980s, with its distinctive blouson silhouette, bright casual wear, and big hair, was becoming increasingly popular and commercialized. In a personal interview, Frank Mort, one of the first theorists to pay serious attention to contemporary men's fashion, described the arrival of a new eighties menswear consumer as follows:

> I first noticed that something new was going on in when I was in Norwich. Young men were presenting themselves in a new way, dressed, styled and with hair like George Michael. This change wasn't being picked up in an academic literature, but it was there in the marketing literature which, like me, saw this as a phenomenon that went beyond image: there was something distinctly new in the way that the male body was being used in marketing, as well as the way in which companies were using much more sophisticated market segmentation and demographic information to target male consumers. (Mort, 2016 [interviewed in] McCauley Bowstead, 2016))

The 1960s and 1970s had been periods of sartorial innovation at the level of form, construction, and fabrication, and, in this sense, the aesthetic shifts of the 1980s can be seen as growing out of these earlier developments. As Mort has argued, however, what was distinctive about men's style and fashion in the 1980s was the way in which it was marketed, popularized, and communicated through an increasingly sophisticated, differentiated media, as well as in the newfound focus on the male body in advertising and fashion photography of the period.

As I shall explore in more detail in the following chapter, it was in the 1980s that the male physique explicitly and unapologetically became the subject of the female and homospectatorial[16] gaze in mainstream fashion imagery. Late sixties and seventies apparel, and fashion photography, often drew attention to the male form in eroticizing ways, so the origin of the eighties shift towards a sexualized masculine body lies in much earlier media practices. But there is a big difference between a photograph of a scantily clad model in the pages of *L'Uomo Vogue* (the sorts of representations that appear in men's fashion magazines from the late 1960s onward) and a massive billboard of pole-vaulter Tom Hintnaus wearing only briefs in the middle of Time Square: the latter a distinctively eighties phenomenon (Weber, 1982). Unlike the 1970s, when advertising foregrounded a sexualized masculinity often featuring male and female models cavorting together (Jobling, 2014: 155), it was in the 1980s that the disrobed lone male model appears, his body presented as the object of a desiring look in a way that had previously been associated exclusively with images of women.

In a sense, this recentering of the male body as an object of desire represents a return to Renaissance, Baroque, and Neoclassical forms of representation in which, as Germaine Greer suggested in her book *The Boy,* the male body was often highly eroticized. But whereas Neoclassical sculpture and painting used myth, classicism and piety as its alibi for nudity, eighties advertising adopted the symbols of normative, strong, proletarian masculinity in order to neutralize some of the subversiveness of these forms of representation.

Suited and booted

The flipside of the avant-gardism of *The Face, Blitz*, and *i-D* and of the extreme subcultural style of the 1980s was a self-conscious conservatism, especially evident in the menswear featured in magazines like GQ, *L'Uomo Vogue,* and *Esquire*. Amongst these titles, and amongst aspirational brands such as Valentino, Ermenegildo Zegna, and Ralph Lauren, forties nostalgia reigned supreme. A hand-illustrated advertisement for Valentino by N. Backes for Autumn 1983 positively revels in nostalgia: an anonymous heartthrob of the Hollywood Golden Age sports a wide-shouldered, peak lapel jacket of a forties cut, while the pastel and pencil used to render the image—along with the slightly Art Deco treatment of the face and Leyendecker pose—underline this wistful recollection of the past[17] (Backes, 1983: 231). This return to a conservative, understated tailoring—after the innovative cuts and fabrications of the 1970s—didn't always wear its retro-credentials so explicitly. In an image drawn from *L' Uomo Vogue* of July 1982, an outfit by that key figure of eighties menswear, Giorgio Armani, subtly evokes a 1940s classicism in the model's lantern jaw, padded shoulder, and wide lapel. Nevertheless, the boxy unstructured fit for which Armani became famous and use of highly textured fabrics firmly situate the image towards the end of the twentieth century (Metropolitan Look, 1982). Six years later, a double-page spread for *GQ* references the 1940s in a more literal fashion: a Humphrey Bogart lookalike in trench coat and fedora reenacts a final farewell with an anachronistically short-skirted Ingrid Bergman stand-in (Casablanca, 1988: 164–165).

Not only do these periodicals differ markedly from the innovative style press of the same period, their nostalgic aesthetics also contrast sharply with earlier iterations of their own titles. Indeed, looking through back issues of periodicals like *GQ* and *L'Uomo Vogue*—which during the 1970s had featured bright and inventive styles—this change is startling and relatively sudden. When compared with issues of only a few years previously, the fashions seem leached of the color and joy of the previous decade.

A feeling for classicism is also felt in another set of representations emblematic of the 1980s: the sharply suited captains of industry—apparently fresh from a hostile takeover—featured in many fashion shoots and advertisements of the era. *GQ* of September 1983, for example, offers a single-breasted Giorgio Armani

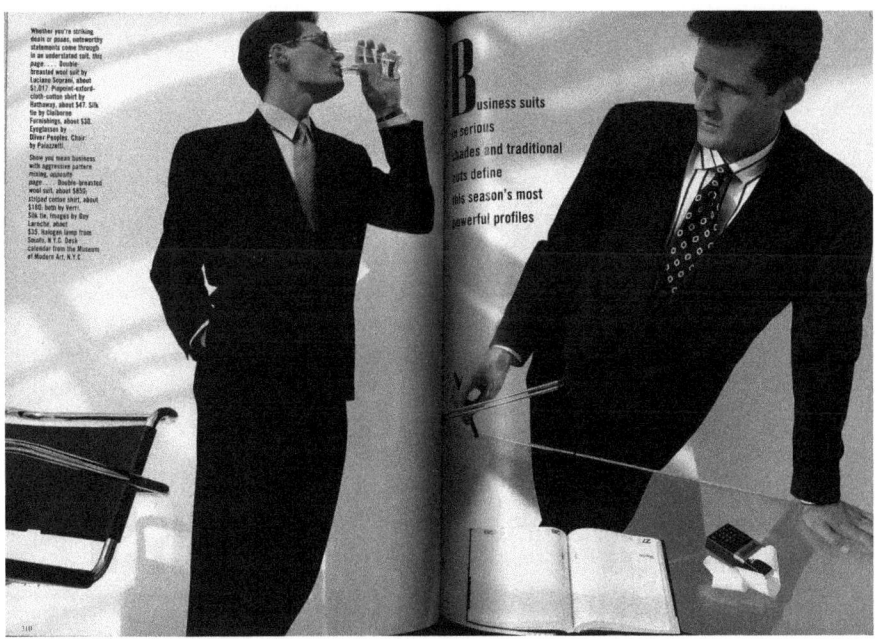

Figure 2.15 "Desk Set" (1988) *Gentlemen's Quarterly*, pp. 310–311.

suit in a textured "autumn weave" accessorized with a boldly striped shirt, silk tie, and copy of the *Wall Street Journal*—all sported by a mature and serious-looking executive. Across the page, a high-flier holding a lit cigar wears a wool tweed suit by Robert Stock—"an all American tradition" (Texture and pattern, 1983: 278–279). And in the same issue, designer Jeff Banks advertises business-like pinstripes and overcoats on two statuesque models who gaze purposefully into the distance from a starkly Modernist set (Banks, 1983). A photoshoot from *GQ* March 1988 also adopts a Modernist aesthetic, all Maholy-Nagy diagonals, and Le Corbusier furniture. The broad-shouldered, double-breasted suits the models sport; their clean-cut styling; and the photographer's sharply angled compositions lend the images a taught energy and a sense of frozen dynamism: the accompanying copy declares, "Business suits in serious shades and traditional cuts define this season's most powerful profiles" (Figure 2.15).

This tendency towards a muted color palette and iconic, classic menswear was linked to the expansion of the mainstream men's lifestyle press as it sought to move beyond readers with a specialist interest in fashion and towards a more general male consumer. As Sean Nixon (1996: 136–143) and Frank Mort (1996: 73–76) describe, the 1980s was a period of ambition and expansion for men's magazines.

Just as crucial, however, were a broader set of changing consumer aspirations, particularly those of the upwardly mobile, young professional "yuppie" who emerged out of the financialization of the US and UK economy, and a rebalancing towards the service sector. This consumer certainly wanted to look sharp—and was willing to spend on high-end goods—but most of all he wanted to look professional and successful, thus the resurgence of the "serious shades and traditional cuts" prescribed by *GQ* (perhaps enlivened by a striped or contrast collar shirt). Sociologist Tim Edwards dubbed this yuppie aesthetic "the corporate power look," suggesting that it signified "a return to traditionally masculine values of money, work, and success" (1997: 42).

Thatcherism and its brother creed Reaganism represented a strange mixture of revolutionary economics, nostalgia for fifties social mores, nihilism[18] and authoritarianism that, in their syncretic nature, were profoundly postmodern. Thatcherite and Reaganite politics weren't only marked by a repudiation of Keynesianism (and a shifting of the economy away from manufacturing and extractive industries). They also signaled a rejection of many of the social developments of the 1960s and 1970s—"the permissive society" of popular imagination. The cultural politics of the period were therefore deeply contested, with sharp divisions between progressive and conservative, left and right. The rise of the New Man, along with an energetic, subversive youth culture, were in this way contrasted against a more general shift within hegemonic culture towards a rhetoric of social conservatism, "traditional" gender roles, and what by the early 1990s came to be known as "family values." This shift in hegemonic values can be perceived in the moral panics of the conservative press of the period—combining a newfound salaciousness with affected moral outrage—

but it also shows up in attitudinal data. The British Social Values Survey reveals increasing support for the proposition "a man's job is to earn money; a woman's job is to look after the home and family" between 1984 and 1987 (Scott and Clery, 2013). And the same survey demonstrates a hardening of attitudes towards homosexuality over the course of the 1980s[19] (Park and Rhead, 2013).

It is perhaps unsurprising, then, that a longing for a traditional, "authentic" masculinity is reflected in the fashions of the decade. And this tendency manifests itself not only in conservative tailoring but also—especially during the late 1980s and early 1990s—in an increasingly nostalgic casual wear. An advert for Levi's "regulation chinos" from 1989, for example, takes the form of a pull-out facsimile magazine in the style of *Picture Post*. Black and white photographs show a chino-clad young man strolling through a cavernous Victorian railway station and in the midst of a blurry cityscape: the graphic framing of these images is clearly intended to evoke the 1940s (though the model's swept-back hair and leather jacket recall the 1950s). The front cover reads, "Levi Strauss regulation chinos. In 1944, you couldn't buy them. You had to earn them"—a tagline repeated again several pages later next to a reportage photograph of an aviator about to leap from a distressed plane (Watson, Bradshaw and Tango Design, 1989: 5). In this sense, the advert indicates the way in which menswear in the late 1980s and early 1990s increasingly drew upon a set of reassuringly familiar masculine archetypes: derring-do, military, and proletarian muscle. In the context of the commodification of masculinity, the rapid increase of women in the workforce, the decline of traditionally masculine manufacturing, and a general mood of social conservatism mainstream fashion and marketing responded with an active, muscular, "authentic" masculinity.

Authenticity and irony

By the first years of the 1990s, tax giveaways and financial deregulation were no longer enough to stimulate the flagging economy and a recession hit many parts of the world. As Coco Chanel once contended, "hard times arouse an instinctive desire for authenticity" (Chanel, 1932 cited in Bott, 2007: 94). In this way, the tendency towards a quieter, nostalgic, and much less inventive menswear, which has its origins in the 1980s, became even more pronounced in nineties men's fashion.

But it wasn't the economy alone that led to stagnation in menswear. The fashion industry, with its high concentration of gay and bisexual men, was hit heavily by the AIDS epidemic (with deaths peaking in Western Europe and America in the first years of the 1990s, before the introduction of antiretroviral drugs). In an interview I conducted with the menswear journalist and commentator Charlie

Porter, he underlined the devastating impact AIDS had exerted on men's fashion in the late 1980s and early 1990s.

> In New York but also in London, leading up to the AIDS crisis, there was a boom in menswear. And then AIDS hit. Lots of designers—Perry Ellis, Lee Wright and Willi Smith of Willi Wear—died. But as well as the demise of designers, there were also the stylists—Ray Petri in London—the hairdressers, the people who worked in the stores, the shop fitters, and a good chunk of the customers. When a large portion of an industry disappears, almost overnight, the infrastructure, contacts, knowledge and legacy that went along with them can't be replaced easily. (Porter, 2016 [interviewed in] McCauley Bowstead, 2016)

As well as hitting the more established New York fashion industry, AIDS also had a significant effect on the New Romantic subculture from which much of the energy of British fashion had emanated during the 1980s. The DJ, artist, and former club kid Jeffery Hinton states:

> AIDS was particularly devastating to a creative force [like fashion] not only in this country but in New York and globally. I'd say about 80% of my friends died during this period. (Hinton, 2013, cited in *Crane TV*, 2013)

Scarlett Canon, who ran the famous club night Cha-Cha and modeled for *i-D*, *Blitz*, and the fashion label Body Map, likened the experience of living through the AIDS pandemic to war: "you shouldn't be watching your friends die when you're in your 20s" (Canon, 2013, cited in *Crane TV*, 2013).

As Porter has argued, it wasn't until the turn of the millennium, as a new generation of designers and fashion professionals emerged, that men's fashion began to regain some of its former energy and dynamism. As well as the direct impact of the virus, the anxiety provoked by AIDS fed into a more general feeling of cultural conservatism—one associated with the increasing the stigmatization of homosexuality in the late 1980s and early 1990s (Park and Rhead, 2013). This conservative mood tended to discourage transgressive and queered representations of masculinity from encroaching as far into mainstream popular culture as they had during the early 1980s.[20]

In the midst of this subdued and anxious mood, men's fashion in the early and mid-1990s often fell back on a set of orthodox signifiers, often subtly undermined with a light sprinkling of irony. The popularity of orthodox masculine modes of presentation is apparent in the Spring/Summer 1994 edition of *Arena Homme+,* which references combat uniforms. A story entitled "Military precision"— perhaps a reference to the recent Gulf War—features models in a variety of rumpled pseudo-utility garments ("Military Precision," 1994: 64–65), the editorial text adding:

HISTORICAL RESONANCES

Figure 2.16 "Chevignon Advertisement" (1994) *Arena Homme+*, p. 137. Showing the influence of early nineties youth and subculture.

> This year's action man is primarily a creature of the desert, with shades of sand, gunmetal and stone [...] Combat trousers are a particular favourite, with chunky thigh pockets [...] in which to stash those all-important maps, secret codes and poison pellets. ("Military Precision," 1994: 64)

Ben Crewe (2003), in his analysis of the men's magazine market, draws attention to the pervasive sense of uncertainty surrounding male identities in the 1990s: this "crisis" in masculinity, a crisis of meaning, authenticity, and subjectivity had been identified by commentators and academics like Lynne Segal (1990) and Roger Horrocks (1994), but it was one that also concerned advertisers as they struggled to target male consumers. Crewe draws on the industry journal *Marketing* to illustrate this sense of confusion and ambivalence:

> What appears to be happening is that the conventional stereotype of men has died, but nothing has emerged to replace it ... marketers have run out of shorthand ways to talk about men. (Batstone, 1994: 20–21 cited in Crewe, 2003: 5–6)

Out of the decline of the eighties New Man paradigm, and in response to this gap in masculine representation, the figure of the "new lad" emerges: "unashamedly heterosexual, irreverent, often self-mocking, laced with innuendo, culturally referential and generally 'blokeish'" (Crewe, 2003: 6). Some of the most visible manifestations of this phenomenon were the new "lad's mags" *Loaded*, *FHM*, and *Maxim* which burst onto the men's magazine market from the mid-1990s onward (achieving enviable circulations). Distancing themselves from more serious, established titles like *GQ* and *Esquire*, "lad's mags" instead adopted a lowbrow and ironic tone focusing on football, sex, clubbing, and working-class celebrities—as well as more typical lifestyle topics (Beynon, 2002; Crewe, 2003). Crucial to the rhetoric of these magazines was their irreverence, jokiness, and horror at anything that could be perceived as "pretentious." And, in this sense, I would argue, the figure of the new lad developed in response to a crisis of authenticity in nineties masculinity. In the context of rapid industrial change and the shifting dynamics of heterosexual relationships, men sought to construct a masculine identity in the absence of the economic and familial structures that had previously underpinned it: the new lad, as subjectivity and as marketing tool, provided an access point to new modes of consumption and forms of identity construction at the same time as assuaging anxieties around effeminacy and pretention that had come to the fore, once more, in the 1990s.

Loaded, *FHM*, and *Maxim* were more known for their scantily clad female cover stars than they were for their fashion content, but the cultural influence of laddism was felt in representations of men's fashion in the style press. For example, *Arena Homme+* of Autumn/Winter 1994 includes a shoot entitled

Figure 2.17 Bradshaw, D. and Richmond, T. (1994) "Overtones," *Arena Homme+*, p. 151.

"Overtones." Five models, posed to resemble standing spectators on a football terrace, appear in a selection of parka jackets by Prada, Fred Perry, Armani Jeans, and Copperwheat Blundel, styled along with argyle knitwear, polo shirts, and button-down Ben Sherman Shirts that reference football casual, mod, and skinhead subcultures. The model's faces—shouting, frowning and clearly without makeup—along with their boisterous gestures, deliberately subvert our expectations of a fashion shoot. The image is unglamorous, unconcerned with sexiness, and but for the studio background, more like reportage photography (Figure 2.17).

Both the referential nature of "new lad" discourses and the concern for a certain sort of authenticity are clearly present in this image (despite its obviously constructed nature). Irony, humor, and bravado were also central components of laddism, and a 1999 advertisement for Ben Sherman, a brand associated both with the new lad and with 1980s casual culture, typifies the combination of knowingly retrograde gender politics and humor of the period. A silver-colored male mannequin, clad in a checked, untucked, Ben Sherman shirt and unfitted trousers, stands in a shop window in an aggressive stance—legs widely spaced, fists clenched, and arms folded. To the left, a more traditional shop dummy, its fine features contrasted against the impassive, semi-abstract face of the silver mannequin, lies in a state of collapse, partially dismembered (Ben Sherman Advertisement, 1999: 27). The implied narrative works on two levels: the implication of violence (the first dummy has attacked and laid low the second) and simultaneously one of redundancy: the more traditional mannequin in his respectable suit has been superseded by a tougher and more working-class "real man."

3
BODY LANGUAGE: TOWARD A PHENOMENOLOGY OF MASCULINITY

Men's fashion during the 2000s, and to the present day, has served as a space in which masculinities are explored through tactility, sensuality, the erotic display of the body, and in an "ideal" physique that differs markedly to that which dominated during the 1980s and 1990s. In short, the male body has been at the center—both literally and figuratively—of redefining and reinventing men's fashion from the turn of the millennium onward.

Integral to the new slim silhouette which Capasa, Simons, and particularly Slimane pioneered in the late 1990s and early 2000s were the models they cast for their catwalk shows and advertising campaigns. In an Autumn/Winter 2001 edition of *Arena Homme+*, an article entitled "Adam's ribs" asked:

> Who puts the slim into Slimane's shows? It's a transformation to confound Darwin […] the male model has transformed into a much sleeker animal. Gone are the grinning, pumped-up, all-American-types that dominated the Eighties […] In their place we have the less burly, more surly European skinny-boy. (Healy, 2001: 163)

In contemporary men's fashion, the body retains this central position: for Spring/Summer 2016, Alessandro Michele at Gucci revealed the torso through diaphanous chiffon shirts, lace, and crochet; long slim legs were bared in Juun. J's radically abbreviated shorts; while for Autumn/Winter 2017 Nasir Mazhar's models wore strange, sporty harnesses over bare chests. At Givenchy, Riccardo Tisci's athletic, muscular models embodied a casual, sporting aesthetic in oversized tunics and kilts, while at Lanvin Lucas Ossendrijver wrapped his wan, slender models in swathes of draping fabric.

The film theorist Laura Mulvey in her seminal essay *Visual Pleasure and Narrative Cinema* of 1973 wrote:

> In a world ordered by sexual imbalance, pleasure in looking has been split between active/male and passive/female. The determining male gaze projects its phantasy onto the female figure which is styled accordingly [...] the male figure cannot bear the burden of sexual objectification. Man is reluctant to gaze at his exhibitionist like. (1985 [1973]: 808–810)

And yet, the male figure in contemporary fashion from the catwalk to the advertising hoarding has certainly come to connote "to-be-looked-at-ness" in Mulvey's memorable phrase. How and why has the fashionable male body increasingly subjected itself to the gaze? What visual and embodied pleasures has this permitted men? And to what extent does the newfound body-consciousness of men's fashion bring with it a burden of sexual objectification?

Embodied and disembodied masculinities: The male body in the twentieth century

> Fascism, then, waged its battle against human desires by encoding them with a particular set of attributes: with effeminacy, unhealthiness, criminality, Jewishness (Theweleit, 1989 [1978]: 13)

The male body is conspicuous in the iconography of the 1930s and early 1940s. In both socialist and nationalist propaganda in the decades running up to the Second World War, powerful male figures—stripped to the waist—rend chains, wield hammers, clasp bayonets, or brandish flags; so too in sporting images, in which athletes in neoclassical attitudes hold javelins aloft, clench their biceps, or leap diagonally across the frame. But in fashion—from the fluid bias-cut gowns of the late 1930s to the exaggerated hourglass of Dior's 1947 new look—it is the female body much more than the male that is the locus of the desiring gaze.

There is a long and ignoble history, from the Classical thought of Plato and Aristotle to the Enlightenment philosophy of René Descartes, of associating man with rationality and woman with the body and nature. Feminist philosophers from Olympe de Gouges (1789) and Mary Wollstonecraft (1792) to Simone de Beauvoir (1949) worked to reclaim the right to education, knowledge, thought, and rationality to women. Later, second-wave feminists such as Hélène Cixous and Iris Marion Young argued for new forms of female-oriented philosophy and rhetoric that collapse artificial divisions between mind and body. As Elizabeth Grosz describes:

> Patriarchal oppression [...] justifies itself by connecting women much more closely than men to the body and, through this identification, restricting women's social and economic roles to (pseudo) biological terms. Relying on essentialism, naturalism and biologism, misogynist thought confines women to the biological requirements of reproduction on the assumption that [...] women are somehow more biological, more corporeal, and more natural than men. (1994: 14)

Both Grosz and Laura Mulvey rightly underline the ways in which the female body has been presented as a sexualized, passive object of the male gaze. But, of course, it would be quite wrong to assume that the male body has been somehow insignificant in the iconography of modernity. Indeed, as I shall argue, shifting ideologies have written and rewritten themselves onto the male body throughout the twentieth century and into our own. But since embodiment implies both vulnerability and the potential for sensual experience—both of which are marked as dangerously feminine in orthodox Western systems of gender—the male physique, at the level of symbol, has often played a peculiarly ambivalent role.

Thus, the masculine body in the early twentieth century representations to which I have alluded is frequently transformed into steely carapace, or sublimated into a mass of uniformed soldiers. By becoming a machine, it denies its own corporeality, as Klaus Theweleit describes in his analysis of the German militarist writer Ernst Jünger:

> Jünger's imaginary man is portrayed as a physical type devoid of drives and psyche; he has no need of either since all his instinctual energies have been smoothly and frictionlessly transformed into functions of his steel body [...] In the body-machine the interior of the man is dominated and transformed in the same way as are the components of the macromachine of the troop. For Jünger, then, the fascination of the machine lies in its capacity to show how the man might 'live' (move, kill, give expression) without emotion. Each and every feeling is tightly locked in steel armour. (Theweleit, 1989 [1978]: 159 cites Jünger, 1922)

The mechanized man the "body-machine" so vividly described by Theweleit is a figure who could only have emerged from the processes of modernity. And as Francesca Cancian (1987) underlines, these processes had profound implications for gender norms. The rapid industrialization of the nineteenth century led to a polarization of gender roles as manufacture shifted towards large-scale sites of production, becoming increasingly gender segregated[1] — women's work increasingly clustered in differentiated (low status) roles, in low paid sweated industries, and in the home.

As Michel Foucault (1995 [1975]; Bartky, 1990: 93–95) suggests, in modernity "rational" systems of organization, control, and scrutiny came to govern institutions, especially male-dominated institutions such as factories, prisons, the military, and asylums. In this sense, Jünger's man-machine — his ideal masculinity — that emerges in the 1920s and becomes dominant in the 1930s and 1940s is the human embodiment of both Taylorism and of Bentham's panopticon. The "ideal man" of the period's collective imagination is a figure for whom external control and authority have become internalized, for whom cog-like functionality and lack of subjectivity is not only idealized but inscribed upon his hard, affectless body. Thus, representations of the 1930s and 1940s rely on the female body to signal glamor, eroticism, and desire[2] while the hegemonic male body symbolizes strength, rationality, self-control, and power.

Nevertheless, the profound cultural and artistic changes — the chaos unleashed during the post–First World War period — did indeed make space for alternative, transgressive, radical expressions of masculinity that differ markedly from those idealized by Jünger. In the avant-garde sculpture, choreography, painting, and literature that emanated from Paris, New York, and Berlin during the 1920s (as well as in popular culture), the male body is aestheticized and eroticized, especially when framed as *exotic* and *primitive*. This exoticism forms a central part of the fascination commanded by the bejeweled, scantily clad figures of Vaslav Nijinsky and Léonid Massine in the orientalist fantasies of the Ballets Russes, as well as the allure of silent film star Rudolph Valentino, famed for his brooding physicality. But perhaps most of all, black music, dance, and art in the 1920s symbolize the exciting cosmopolitanism and taboo sexuality of Modernism closely allied to an imagined atavism: Senegalese dancer François Féral Benga became famous for his sensual "carnal choreography" at the Folies Bergère (Smalls, 2013) while the syncopated beat of jazz music animated European and American dance floors alike. And as Harlem Renaissance poet Langston Hughes described (with something of an exoticizing gaze): "Sleek black boys in a cabaret. Jazz-band, jazz-band, — Play, PLAY, PLAY! [...] White girls' eyes call gay black boys. Black boys' lips grin jungle joys" (Hughes, 1926 cited in Chinitz, 1997).

In this sense, the articulation of an aggressive, martial, and highly physical masculinity in the run-up to the Second World War was a reaction to the fusion and flux of the immediate interwar period. As Theweleit states, fascism (and indeed nationalism and Stalinism) waged their "battle against human desires by encoding them with a particular set of attributes": those of "effeminacy, unhealthiness, criminality [and] Jewishness" (1989 [1978]: 13). A sensual and louche form of male embodiment — in which the lines between African and European, Oriental and Occidental, "civilized" and "primitive," masculine and feminine become blurred — was fundamentally antithetical to nationalist and patriarchal ideals. Nationalism, associating the male body with the nation state, is fundamentally reliant on clearly demarcated borders that are threatened by hybridity and mixedness.

Moreover, the ideal male body of the 1930s and 1940s—strong, impenetrable, indivisible, and whole—not only served as an over-obvious metaphor for the nation, but also stood in stark contrast to the wounded soldiers who returned from the First World War. The cognitive dissonance implicit in propagandist representations of the ideal man is more strongly felt when compared to the disfigured bodies depicted by the likes of Otto Dix and George Grosz in their images of veterans of the "Great War" whose bodies had proved all too vulnerable, divisible, and human.

This affirmation of a muscular, instrumentalized, affectless form of embodiment also relates to a set of economic shifts that occurred during the 1920s and 1930s. Josep Armengol has argued that the financial collapse and subsequent depression engendered by the 1929 Wall Street crash "forced many men to give up their faith in the marketplace as a proof of their manhood" (2013: 33). He suggests that "one of the most obvious remasculinization strategies" at the level of politics, art, and indeed of the self "consisted in (re-)turning to the male body and, in particular, the strong, muscular, brawny body of the working-class male" (2013: 33). For Armengol, then, this cultural turn towards "images of hard bodies at work" (2013: 31) that manifested itself in the New Deal public murals of the Roosevelt administration[3] was an attempt to "remasculanize America" that related both to a profound disenchantment with the economic status quo, and simultaneously a dichotomization "between hard/masculine/working-class" and "soft/effete/upper-class" bodies (2013: 31). And so, despite their ideological divergence, Stalinist socialist realist, fascist, and New Deal social democratic propaganda all schematize national rebirth and salvation through hard, masculine, instrumentalized bodies.

In the post–Second World War context of the late 1940s and early 1950s, there is an increasingly domestic inflection to representations of masculinity in Europe and America.[4] The heroic male figures of the interwar period are replaced by the image of the salaryman, breadwinner, and father as head of the family. And since fascism, militarism, and the imagery of the Great Depression had placed the brawny male body so firmly at the center of their propagandist efforts, peace and long-hoped-for prosperity were to look profoundly different. Indeed, even where the athletic male figure does appear, as in a 1954 Lyle and Scott advert for Y-front underpants described by Paul Jobling (Sprøgøe, 1954 in Jobling, 2014: 6 and 22) he is a domesticated and substantially de-eroticized figure associated with consumer products. Mercè Cuenca (2013) has suggested that the male body disappears as a signifier of hegemonic masculinity in the popular culture of the 1950s (2013: 50), arguing that the new ideal of white-collar masculinity that emerged during this period was predicated on the de-emphasis of corporeality and sexuality. Nik Cohn, writing in a specifically UK context, strikes a similar note, eloquently summing up the drabness, sexlessness, and lack of *élan* of 1950s British menswear:

> During the early fifties the double breasted suit went out of favour and left the field to the single-breasted, button-three in dark grey: the classic High Street suit. It was very ugly indeed. It had no shape and no life, no sense of movement. In fact it was anti-clothing, a denial of attraction [… Customers] wanted to be respectable, businesslike, anonymous. They wanted their clothes to hide them. (1973: 39–40)

The cultural conservatism of the early 1950s can be understood as a reaction to the trauma experienced by a generation who had come of age in the Great Depression and spent their young adult years during a time of war. There is a nostalgia to the gender ideals that came to the fore in the aftermath of the Second World War—reflected in the neo-Victorian aesthetic of women's fashion—but there is also something distinctly modern. The disappearance of the male body, as well as the longing for conformity and the sense of self-abnegation felt in men's dress of the period, related to a new dogma of gender, influenced by the popularization and bowdlerization of Freudian psychology (Friedman and Downey, 1998). In this way, an emphasis on social harmony through gender conformity manifested itself both in an obsessive fear of male homosexuality, and, as Betty Friedan (1963) so brilliantly describes, through a cult of domesticity that confined women to childcare and the home. Thus, the *feminine mystique* that situated women as the sole locus of sexual desire also acted to suppress a masculine corporeality that suggested two dangerous possibilities: female sexual agency and the potential for same-sex attraction.

This new anxiety around and awareness of homosexuality in the 1950s is also discussed by John Ibson (2002) in his analysis of photographs of American men. Ibson convincingly demonstrates that unabashed physical affection between men—often pictured embracing, holding hands, or sitting on one another's laps, with no sexual subtext—was common in photographs of the late nineteenth century and into the 1910s and 1920s. But he finds that these forms of physical affection give way to much more formal and less intimate poses in the 1930s and even more pronouncedly in the post–Second World War context.

The early 1950s are a period of extraordinary and historically anomalous repression of physicality, physical intimacy, and male pleasure in the body. As Theweleit, Ibson, Cuenca, and Armengol describe, this "invisibilizing" of the male body was one that was decades in the making and that manifested itself both at the level of representation and in the way that men related to their own and others' bodies. Nevertheless, to invoke a law of Newtonian physics, *every action must have an equal and opposite reaction.* So too in the the emergent youth cultures of the 1950s, through which teenagers sought to rebel against the mores of their buttoned-up parents precisely by reinvesting the male body with sexuality and physicality. As Cohn describes:

> In terms of English teenagers, Teddy Boys were the start of everything: rock' n roll and coffee bars, clothes and bikes and language, jukeboxes and coffee with froth on it—the whole concept of a private teen life style separate from the adult world [...] Drapes apart, they wore tight drainpipe jeans, tapered to the ankle, yellow socks; creepers, large crêpe-soled shoes like boats [and] brass rings on several fingers. (1971: 28–29)

Indeed, from rock and roll stars like Little Richard, Chuck Berry, and Elvis Presley to filmic *wild ones* Marlon Brando and James Dean, as well as in popular fashion and dance, the youthful male body (one often marked as subaltern in terms of race and class) was reinvested with an erotic allure and a rebellious libidinal drive that was in direct conflict with the hegemonic petit bourgeois respectability of the period.

The liberated body

After the sexless menswear of the immediate postwar period, engineered to hide and repudiate the body, youth culture in the late 1950s and 1960s began, tentatively at first, to reinstate and reveal the male physique, nipping in seams and peeling away layers of grey flannel. What most differentiated youthful fashionable dress of the early 1960s was fit, as an increasingly shrunken silhouette, with close-cut trousers, short "bum freezer" jackets, and narrow pointed shoes, gained popularity. The Carnaby Street shops of John Stephen and his competitors complemented this new neat line by introducing unusual cloths: velvet, corduroy, and velour—soft against the skin, unlike the scratchy wools of old, asserting a newly phenomenal and corporeal masculinity. The importance of fit is felt in the comments of the young group of mods who styled themselves *the faces* (as in the previous chapter, their words are taken from an interview in *Town* magazine).

> "All the faces go to Bilgorri. And John Stevens [sic]. He's very good on trousers. Hardly any place in London makes good trousers. They're all baggy here." He tugs at the seat of his own trousers. Barely an eighth of an inch comes away. (Sugar 1962 cited in Barnsley, 1962: 51)

Like *the faces*, Nic Cohn, describing John Stephen's mini-empire of menswear shops in the early 1960s, also highlights the new figure-accentuating quality of his trousers as particularly worthy of note: "Above all, there were hipster trousers, cut so tight and so low that the backs came halfway up your arse and the fronts framed your genitals like a spotlight" (1972: 69).

This, then, was a new and radical approach to cut, and one that could hardly have been more different from that of the multiple tailors, Burtons, John Collier, Hepworths, and Tailors Associated, who had dominated the menswear market in the UK. And it is perhaps significant that the mod look, which was to prove so influential in Britain and America, was originally adapted and exaggerated from Italian tailors like Brioni—the Italians, with their corporeal, fleshy visual culture, never having developed quite the dread of sex and the body of the British. In the UK context, the pioneers of the styles that were to develop into the mod and subsequently the peacock aesthetic—Vince, Cecil Gee, John Stephen, and later Michael Fish (as well as the early mods themselves) were often those who sat somewhat outside the class and gender conventions of the time, either because they were Jewish or gay or sometimes both, and who thus had the least to gain from upholding the values of a reserved, class-conscious self-abnegating menswear.

By the mid-1960s a new ideal body was in vogue—thinner and more boyish. A 1966 advert for the "famous *guitare* swimwear" available "only at Simpson" illustrates the shifting aesthetic: a hand-rendered depiction of a summery group pictures the slim, tanned and enviably long legs of the ideal 1960s man (Figure 2.2). Cohn explicitly connects the new physique of the period to shifting notions of gender:

> Nothing seem fixed any more—all the roles were blurring, and there was an evolving concept of what makes men attractive. It seemed much less important, suddenly, to have biceps like grapefruit and hairs on your chest; if you were good in bed that was all that counted. (1972: 62)

Here, as elsewhere in the fashions of the 1960s and 1970s, there are strong resonances with the later innovations of Hedi Slimane and Raf Simons, both of whom drew on the modish, youthful silhouette of this period to articulate a similarly liminal and ambiguous masculinity in the late 1990s and early 2000s.

As well as being clad in increasingly close-fitting garments, the male body in the 1960s and 1970s also become steadily more exposed, as shorts and swimwear had became ever more abbreviated. Foreign holidays to France, and especially to Spain and Greece, had become much more affordable and popular for middle- and working-class Northern European consumers during the 1960s, while Americans were also flying or driving to sunny shores in ever greater numbers. A Mediterraneanization of men's beach and summer clothing—a feeling for the exotic, the daring, and the corporeal—accompanied these shifts in holidaying. In a Pacific, rather than a Mediterranean mood, *Town* magazine advertises Sabre "Waikiki" swimwear for summers of 1963 and 1964, with stylized illustrations of

Figure 3.1 Mayogaine Paris Advertisement (1971). *L'Uomo Vogue*, (11), p. 152.

deeply bronzed chiseled men in brief swimming trunks that "fit like second nature in Helanca bri-nylon" (Sabre Helanca Advertisement, 1964: 31).

By the early 1970s, these sorts of representations had both proliferated and shifted, becoming both somehow freer and more eroticized. An advertisement for Mayogaine Paris swimwear from *L'Uomo Vogue* of 1971 shows a tousled-haired young man pictured at the beach—the blue sea, sky, and a bank of verdant foliage captured impressionistically behind him. Photographed from below, so that his head, torso, and pelvis fill most of the frame, the model wears patterned swimming shorts cut low on the hip and extending an inch or so past the groin so as to expose the full leg (although the tight composition shows only a sliver of his upper thigh). His shirt, in the same swirling, stylized floral print, is open so that the eye is drawn to the smooth, tanned skin of the torso and up to the model's face, his high cheekbones, full lips, and heavy brow shaded beneath a slightly battered straw hat. Like the "Waikiki" swimwear of the 1960s, the Hawaiian hibiscus-like motifs of the model's trunks and shirt evoke a glamorous, exotic locale, but the proximity and angle of the photograph, as well as the swimmer's lithe physique, hint at a new intimacy (Figure 3.1).

In July 1972, British *Vogue* featured a double-page spread of men's beachwear amongst the women's fashions (a hint at what to buy the man in your life). There is a candid joyfulness to the photographs of the dancer/choreographer Micha Bergese who jumps and swings through the air in gaily patterned trunks, an open shirt, and form-fitting knit: Bergese's taut dancer's physique is framed geometrically, a series of diagonal lines that along with his fluttering long hair underline the dynamism of the shoot (Lategan, 1972: 74–75). *GQ* magazine of summer 1973 captures a similar feeling of bodily freedom (though with a more conventional photographic style). The front cover features a beachgoing couple—apparently on a detour to a photographic studio—the male model is in brief, tight trunks with an abstract print, his partner in a sun hat and bikini: inside, a photo story entitled "Trunk Show" captures models in a series of brief, boldly patterned swimming trunks and elsewhere in gauzy cotton voile shirts or barefoot in shrunken shorts.

All of these representations point to a newly unabashed attitude to the male body that had emerged out of youth cultural discourses, particularly those of the hippies, over the course of the 1960s, in which the values of honesty, naturalness, and pleasure took precedence over those of reserve, respectability, and self-control. These links to hippy ethics and aesthetics can be felt in the 1971 Mayogaine Paris advert, particularly in the model's silver jewelry, loose curls and peasant straw hat. But shifts in the framing of the male form, in representation and through dress, can't be ascribed to youth and subculture alone: there are also clear continuities between the avant-garde, Modernist body culture of the interwar period and that of the 1960s and early 1970s.

In a gesture to modernity, efficiency, and freedom—and in response to new synthetic fibers—athletic clothing in the 1920s and 1930s had become increasingly brief and close-fitting. After the hiatus of the Second World War, and 1950s reconstruction, this modernizing process continued into the 1960s and 1970s as footballers' and tennis players' strips became simpler and more streamlined (tendencies that increasingly extended into menswear proper). Only in the 1990s, in a new period of anxiety over masculinity and male sexuality, would this process go decisively into reverse as sporting garments become curiously ill-fitting and oversized.

Away from sporting and casual dress, the more elegant, dressed-up fashions of the peacock revolution during the late 1960s and early 1970s took on an increasingly corporeal quality as they borrowed from the slinky, sheer, tactile fabrications of womenswear. By the end of the 1960s, the loosening of social and sexual mores associated with the "permissive society" was strongly felt in the innovative modes showcased in the new men's magazine *L'Uomo Vogue*. For Spring/Summer 1969, a photograph of designer Roberto Capucci—captured by Helmut Newton—appears. The designer lounges against the cream leather interior of a luxury car, wearing a transparent shirt in black marquisette of his own design, a lizard-skin jacket draped over his shoulders, and steel choker at his neck (Newton, 1969: 77). It is one of a number of images in *L'Uomo Vogue*

Figure 3.2 Catalano, E. (1969). La Moda a Roma si recita a Soggetto. *L'Uomo Vogue*, (4), pp. 116–117.

of this period featuring translucent fabrics—chiffon, cut-velvet, broderie anglaise, and voile—that point to a new sensuality, sexuality, and daring in menswear (1969: 98, 135). This trend for sheer cloth is discussed in *L'Uomo Vogue* Spring/Summer 1969 alongside a fashion shoot by artist/photographer Elisabetta Catalano featuring the young actor Hiram Keller (shirtless and wearing a devoré waistcoat by Forneris). The article states, "shirts—when worn—are precious, embroidered, perforated, transparent [... there is] a new freedom in mixing fabrics and materials" (Figure 3.2). Keller, the star of the hippy "rock musical" *Hair*—which had featured a famous nude scene—and lead in Federico Fellini's decadent and sexually explicit *Satyricon*—was, in this sense, a representative of a shockingly disinhibited turn in sixties culture. Lounging bare-chested on the studio floor in a pair of silk shantung trousers and open waistcoat, Keller plays his part well, legs akimbo, pouting and eyeing the viewer/photographer with a frankly carnal gaze.

L'Uomo Vogue of the late 1960s and early 1970s featured clothes that banished postwar austerity, declaring it a distant bad dream, and that—in place of respectability—celebrated sexiness, informality, novelty, and the tactility of sleek satins, soft chiffons and smooth leathers. The newfound disinhibition, which underpinned these images, was, of course, a highly contested one, as numerous trials for obscenity over the course of the 1960s make clear[5] (Collins, 2007). Nevertheless, this corporeal candor steadily permeated the mainstream—particularly youth culture—through pop music, film, magazines, and, indeed, through shifts in popular fashion.

A hippy-influenced feeling of bodily freedom continues into the mid-1970s: *L'Uomo Vogue* of April 1976 including a multi-page photo story entitled "Afro-Look" featuring black Parisian dancers, in Kenyan- and Nigerian-inspired clothing by British knitwear designer John Ashpool (1976: 133–141). A photographic double-page spread captures a dancer in the act of leaping horizontally through the air, one leg kicking with pointed toe, his arms in the midst of a *port de bras*. The dancer, suspended in mid-jump, wears a chevron and stripe-patterned knitted top, copper bangles, and tight briefs that leave his shapely legs and taut buttocks exposed. And, in this way, the dynamism of the image, along with its folkloric styling, conveys strength, grace, and liberty, while simultaneously evoking a balletic atavism and an exoticism that calls to mind Nijinsky's *The Rite of Spring*. The accompanying copy declares:

> Another advancement from the frontiers of fashion: after moving through time (with retro), fashion now roams over land and after hitting China and Arabia, Greenland and India continues on to Black Africa. (1976: 134)

Thus the allure of "authentic," romantic, non-Western foreignness in fashions of this period reveals continuities between the early twentieth century

Modernist body and that of the 1960s and 1970s;[6] Afrocentric fashion operating as liberation through exoticization.

In this way, the late 1960s and 1970s were periods in which the male body was increasingly displayed and eroticized as clothing was cut closer to the body, and as the taboo against nudity lessened. Changes in the framing of the male body through fashion during the 1960s have been given less attention than other aspects of contemporary counterculture, "permissiveness," and sexual liberation (an absence of discourse that points both to lacunae in the history of fashion and to the under-theorization of the male body more generally). Nevertheless, the narratives of sexual liberation, political radicalism, and of an expanding youth-oriented consumer culture that underpin this history of representation have been explored thoroughly and engagingly in an existing literature and are well-understood (Hall and Jefferson, 1993; Collins, 2007; Mort, 2010). What is more noteworthy from a contemporary perspective is how much more unpolished, un-retouched, and diverse the fashionable bodies of the late 1960s and 1970s are in comparison to those of subsequent decades. The model physiques featured in the images I have reviewed are generally moderately slim and more or less athletic, but they are neither the gaunt, adolescent bodies that designers like Hedi Slimane have favored in recent years, nor the bulging, steroidally inflated musculature of 1980s and 1990s mainstream men's fashion.

The sixties and seventies fashion model is, of course, an aspirational and idealized figure, but he is recognizably a flesh and blood human being: smiling, perhaps with laughter lines around his eyes or with dustings of hair on his forearms and chest; perhaps in his late teens, he might equally be in his twenties of thirties—by the 1970s he might even be non-white. In this sense, whether lounging or leaping, there is a guilelessness, an unabashed corporality to representations of the male body in this period; one that was lost in the more polished representations to follow.

Holding out for a hero

As we move into the 1980s, contradictions between increasingly sharply polarized versions of masculinity and representations of the male body emerge. In addition to the subversive, subcultural, sexualized glamor of the Blitz Kids, The Human League, Depeche Mode, Spandau Ballet, and Prince, the decade also saw a resurgence of much more orthodox images of the male physique in fashion and popular culture. The "streetwise Hercules" sought by singer Bonnie Tyler (Steinman et al., 1984), muscle-bound and oiled-up, was to become a recognizable archetype of the period.

Corporeality retains a central place in eighties representations of masculinity, from the hard bodies of action stars Sylvester Stallone, Bruce Willis, and Arnold

Schwarzenegger to the Neoclassical nudes celebrated in the photography of Bruce Weber and Herb Ritts. As cultural critic Susan Jeffords suggests, this resurgence of strong, powerful, dominant models of masculinity in the 1980s—particularly as expressed at the level of the body—seemed to connect to a broader set of anxieties and preoccupations and to a new mood of cultural conservatism. As Jeffords describes in her account of the patriotic action movies of the period:

> the hardened bodies that emblematized Reaganism assisted citizens/viewers in perceiving not simply those bodies but themselves as masterful, as in control of their environments, as dominating those around them [...] Such bodies assist in the confirmation of this mastery by themselves refusing to be "messy" or "confusing" by having hard edges, determinate lines of action and clear boundaries (Jeffords, 1994: 26–27)

As Jeffords suggests, this reliance upon a highly conservative notion of maleness suggests a retrenchment in cultures of gender, and in attitudes to the body. In a US context, in particular, the culture wars of the 1980s saw gender politics become a highly fraught and polarizing issue. And across many developed, Western economies the certainties of the progressive postwar consensus were increasingly challenged as traditionally male manufacturing and extractive industries went into decline, as state functions were cut back in favor of private provision, and as reactionary voices fought back against the gains of feminism. In the words of Susan Jeffords:

> In the dialectic of reasoning that constituted the Reagan movement, bodies were deployed in two fundamental categories: the errant body containing sexually transmitted disease, immorality, illegal chemicals, "laziness," and endangered foetuses, which we can call the "soft body"; and the normative body that enveloped strength, labor, determination, loyalty, and courage—the "hard body." (Jeffords, 1994: 24)

In men's magazines, particularly *L'Uomo Vogue* and *GQ*,[7] a fairly sudden change in depictions of the body is perceptible between the end of the 1970s and the beginning of the 1980s. In magazine shoots of the 1970s, the body is revealed through closely fitting garments, bare chests, open shirts, and brief shorts. In these 1970s representations the models are more youthful and more lithe than the average "man on the street," but they don't appear as a separate, morphologically distinct species. By the beginning of the 1980s, however, various shifts in depictions of the fashionable male have become apparent. Articles explicitly focused on fitness, grooming, and exercise start to appear, as do adverts for gym equipment, moisturizer and cosmetics: crucially, and most noticeably, the model body shifts to become much more muscular, hairless, and critically more homogenous.

Two stories from *L'Uomo Vogue* of June 1982 typify these trends. An article entitled "Fitness—Barefoot Gymnastics on the sand" features a large double-page photograph in which two models, bare-chested and in shorts, grip each other's wrists as they engage in a seesawing, abdominal exercise on a beach (McKinley, 1982). The sun setting behind the figures casts a violet light over lapping waves; the sky is pink and orange. In the foreground, the figure on the right grimaces, as if in pain, his face flushed with effort as he holds his counterpart upward. Both figures shine with sweat and their bulging biceps and muscled backs glisten in the half-light. It's a strange and incongruous image, the picturesque backdrop seeming entirely out of keeping with the strenuousness of the exercise in the foreground. The article counsels:

> the interlude of holidays and leisure should not become synonymous with neglect, it may indeed be a good time to resume contact with a body too often overlooked [...] Doing gymnastics at the beach has several advantages: the sea air invigorates your lungs, the sand enhances your muscles, while unlimited space stretching out to the horizon frees your mind. (McKinley,1982 :191)

A second feature in the same 1982 edition entitled "Navy Story" presents a similar incongruity: a paragraph of text, framed by black and white photographs of a muscular, white vested model shadowboxing in the mirror, urges readers to:

> Come face-to-face with the mirror to confront your everyday problems: from razor-burn to finding the right shampoo, from *eau de toilette* to deodorant fragrance. The best solution is always to go for quality by choosing a complete line of cosmetics designed to meet the thousand aesthetic needs of a man. *Jules* the *Nouvelle ligne pour homme* receives its seal of approval from Dior [...] (McKinley,1982 :190)

A year later in the July 1983 edition of *GQ* an advert for an exercise machine features a black and white photograph of a moodily lit model: his pose—arms raised ready to bring down the bar of the machine—emphasizes the V shape created by his developed deltoids and tapering waist. The angled spotlighting lends the model's hairless torso a sculptural quality, exaggerating his defined abdominal muscles and biceps. Perhaps aptly, the tagline "Body by Soloflex" implies that it is the model's body (rather than the machine) that is for sale (Soloflex Advertisement, 1983: 4). By the late 1980s, the muscular body, if anything, has become even more dominant: in a photo shoot from *GQ* of January 1988 a male model turns away from the camera. His back, at a three-quarter angle, forms a sinuous line from his powerful broad shoulders to his waist (Figure 3.3). His right

Figure 3.3 Anon (1988). *Gentlemen's Quarterly* (January), p. 172.

arm—another curved diagonal line—is lifted and bent to frame his face which, though cast into shadow, betrays an even profile, pouting lips, and square jaw. The camera lingers on the model's deltoid and bicep—two elliptical volumes picked out in the strong directional light. His clenched fist resting against the back of his head grasps a gleaming, cylindrical weight. The sports apparel and equipment, ostensibly the focus of the image, are entirely secondary to the model's body, framed so expertly by the photographer, golden and rippling, its Neoclassical attitude recalling the sculptures of Rome's *Foro Italico*.

On page after page of 1980s *GQ, L'Uomo Vogue, Arena*, and *Mondo Uomo*, a recognizable type emerges: muscular models shirtless or in underwear, look back at the camera, their sculpted, hairless bodies as well as their small-featured, firm-jawed faces betraying a striking uniformity. In this way, dominant media representations of masculinity, during the 1980s and throughout the 1990s, increasingly privileged a muscular eroticism inspired by Neoclassicism and Second World War propaganda of various hues. The highly muscular, gym-honed body displayed in menswear shoots nodded to Greco-Roman statuary, socialist-realism and images of early twentieth century industrial workers. Herb Ritts' *Fred with Tires* of 1984 perfectly encapsulates this taste for the proletarian hero as sex symbol, the model shot in a manner that combined a frank eroticization of the male form with the suggestion of a powerful, highly physical and active masculinity (Ritts, 1984). Photographer Bruce Weber's iconic images for Calvin Klein, including his 1982 campaign featuring pole-vaulter Tom Hintnaus, had anticipated the tone of the decade: by 1987, his Obsession For Men campaign, seemingly channeling Leni Riefenstahl, reflected a recognizable archetype of fashionable masculinity (Weber, 1983: 16).

This return to an early twentieth century aesthetic of masculinity and male embodiment associated with the 1930s and 1940s is intriguing when one considers the ideological content of those thrusting images of statuesque, muscular, and "racially pure" bodies that characterized fascist—and much socialist realist—propaganda. As Klaus Theweleit (1989 [1978]) describes, this conception of the impermeable, invulnerable, heavily disciplined, steely masculine physique was absolutely central to fascist iconography, both *embodying* nationalist and patriarchal power, and obscuring the very real vulnerability of bodies in mechanized warfare.

> This, I believe, is the ideal man of conservative utopia: a man with machine-like periphery whose interior has lost its meaning ... The mechanised body as conservative utopia derives from men's compulsion to subjugate and repulse what is specifically human within them ... The soldier male responds to the successful damming in and chaoticizing of his desiring-production ... by fantasising himself as a figure of steel: a man of the new race. (Theweleit, 1989 [1978]: 162)

As well as the aesthetic connections between these modes of masculine representation, there are also thematic and symbolic links. While the fascist body acts as a repudiation of the "decadent," mixed, louche, and feminized Weimar Republic, the newly conservative representations of masculinity in the 1980s, especially in film, act to reject both 1960s/1970s "permissiveness" and the anti-normative, subversive, representations of masculinity that coexisted in contemporary sub- and youth cultures. The late 1980s marked a point of peak homohysteria that coincided with the devastation of AIDS (often referred to as a "gay plague" in the rightwing media) and in this context the slim male body fashionable in the 1960s and 1970s comes to be replaced with a much more powerful, muscular physique connoting health and resilience. The equation of thinness with the wasting symptoms of AIDS—and the fear and stigma that accompanied the epidemic—certainly contributed to the fashion for muscularity so predominant in the 1980s images I have described: indeed, a gay respondent to Pope, Philips and Olivardia's 2000 study into male body image makes this aesthetic analogy explicitly, stating, "thinness is ugly because it speaks of sickness and death. Muscles equal health" (anon cited in Pope et al., 2000: 218).[8] But a shifting fitness market, the expansion and mainstreaming of gym culture, and growing focus on the male body in advertising and the media all played their part, too.

Nevertheless, to apply either Klaus Theweleit's reading of early twentieth century representations or Susan Jeffords' analysis of the *hard bodies* of Reaganite film too uncritically to fashion photography of this period would be simplistic. Despite the consistency of the bodies found between the pages of 1980s *GQ, L'Uomo Vogue, Arena*, and *Mondo Uomo*, significant tensions *do* emerge in the corporeal representations of men in the 1980s—ones hinted at in the images reviewed above. On the one hand, there is a greater emphasis on the body, its maintenance and care, as an expanding range of moisturizing, hair styling, sporting, and other products are marketed at men. On the other hand, there is an evident desire to situate these images and products within a rhetoric of "traditional" masculinity, reflected not only in the hard bodies of the models, but also in sepia-tinted references to the military and navy, nostalgic styling, and *mise-en-scène* recalling 1940s cinema, along with gestures to Classical and Neoclassical art.

And while the framing of these images may sometimes be nostalgic—harking back to a period of more clearly defined gender roles—in an atmosphere of acute anxiety around masculinity and sexuality they nevertheless offered a mode of embodiment, physical pleasure, pride, and enjoyment which clearly resonated with many men. In this sense, the tendency of 1980s magazines and advertisements to pay a renewed attention to the male physique—both at the level of representation and of self-care, exercise, and cosmetic regimes—can be understood as resituating men in their bodies, giving men the permission to look after and take pleasure in their physicality. Despite drawing on the visual codes of hegemonic masculinity, these images and discourses simultaneously destabilize the instrumentalized, Modernist ideal of the unfeeling male alienated from his body. In contemporary academic and media discussion, this phenomenal masculinity was linked to the New Man—an ambiguous figure associated both with an increased engagement with consumption and appearance, and simultaneously with a new style of more liberated and less patriarchal masculinity (Beynon, 2002). Scholars of 1980s men's fashion such as Frank Mort (1987; 1996) and Teal Triggs (1992) convincingly argue that foregrounding the male body in this period can be read as a subversive act, one that implicitly placed men's bodies on a par with women's and that disrupted the economy of looking and "to-be-looked-at-ness."

The hard, affectless, invulnerable bodies of 1980s action films could certainly be argued to represent "the ideal man of conservative utopia." But the homospectatorial gaze invited by these scantily clad muscular figures—the fact that men where increasingly invited to survey other men's bodies, as well as the barely suppressed homoeroticism of both fashion and filmic representations of the male physique—tends to both queer and complicate such readings. The hard, sculpted body depicted in eighties *GQ, Arena* and *L'Uomo Vogue* may have represented a narrow and prescriptive ideal, but it also offered men a site of positive identification, of pleasure, and a license to look at one another and look after themselves without fearing accusations of effeminacy or narcissism.

Outside these mass-market representations in big-budget advertising, Hollywood film, and established men's magazines like *GQ*, titles such as *The Face, Blitz*, and *i-D* sprang from and catered to a very different set of youth and subcultures. In these new style bibles, a whole range of masculinities, androgynies (and indeed "male femininities") were visible at the level of dress, styling, and the body. For example, in *The Face* of January 1984 in a feature entitled "Out come the freaks," Blitz Kid and singer Marilyn gazes seductively from page 3: his immaculately made up face, bleached teased out hair, hand-on-hip pose, and low-cut, sleeveless dress—apparently hastily fashioned from an old sheet—connote both a self-consciously performative femininity and the suggestion of sexual availability (Johnson, 1984: 3). There is a sense in which these more *outré* representations of the male body existed in deliberate opposition to the mainstream, conservative archetypes I have discussed. But it is also true that male bodies coded androgynous or feminine and those coded masculine (or sometimes a combination of all three) were able to coexist in magazines like *The Face*, which, by adopting a playful, camp, *bricolage* aesthetic, ironized and decentered common sense readings of the gendered body.

While Jeffords, Theweleit, and others rightly point out the connections between the hard body and normative masculinity, the long-standing association between gay, male subcultures and bodybuilding—from physique magazines of the 1950s to the clones of the 1970s—complicates this narrative. In *Hard Looks,* Sean Nixon (1996: 180–185) describes the way in which "hard" and "soft" signifiers were employed in shoots styled by Ray Petri, suggesting that

Figure 3.4 Ritts, H. and Roberts, M. (1984). Grease Monkeys. *The Face* (54), p.70.

"the choice of model and some of the elements of clothing ... have a strong intertextuality with certain traditions of representation of masculinity aimed at and taken up by gay men" (1996: 185).

In this way, the boundaries between "normative" and "transgressive" representations of the male body during the 1980s were more permeable than might be imagined. An October 1984 shoot for *The Face* by Herb Ritts and Michael Roberts entitled *Grease Monkeys* features a shirtless, muscular male model smeared with black grease, who, across three black and white spreads, stretches and flexes his torso while sporting gothic jewelry and various leather accessories by Stephen Sprouse. Like Ritts' *Fred with Tyres,* the photographs celebrate a butch, built physique marked working-class through references to manual labor. But unlike this more commercial work, *The Face* shoot draws attention to a homoeroticism that would elsewhere be tacit through exaggerated styling and torn fragments of text superimposed onto the photographs declaring "Prime beef flexed in hell on wheelz" and "a pretty boy in Sprouse" (Figure 3.4) (Ritts and Roberts, 1984: 69–73). Lest this queer coding appear too subtle, an accompanying paragraph states that "From the garages of the New Jersey badlands to the uptown hustlers of Times Square, this fall the real boys on the block are looking dirty" (*The Face*, 1984: 69).

In this sense, from Marilyn to Herb Ritts there is a self-consciously postmodern quality to the presentation of the gendered body in the 1980s, one that queers and complicates these eroticized images of men, and that draws attention to the male body as a locus of desire. However, the polyvocal quality of these camp strategies means that they don't consistently challenge patriarchal norms.[9]

The fact that virtually identical images of the male body could variously connote heteronormativity and same-sex desire, mass-market populism and subcultural cool, is indeed paradoxical. But this paradox points to a larger set of tensions and ambivalences in 1980s representations of masculinity in which the model of the New Man—attuned to feminism, engaged in childcare, conscious of his appearance—battled it out against macho-reactionaries of Hollywood action movies. In a sepia-toned Athena poster of 1986 entitled *L'Enfant,* shirtless hunk Adam Perry cradles a naked baby: "out of the strong came forth sweetness." The image is simultaneously a gesture to the centrality of the muscular male body in 1980s aesthetics and an aspiration to a more caring, gentle way of being a man.

As Tim Edwards recounts in his 1997 text *Men in the Mirror*, the New Man occupied an ambiguous position: located in media discourses both in relation to second-wave feminism and to an increasingly acquisitive model of capitalism: overtly commercialized and sexualized, while simultaneously reliant upon a curiously conventional image of masculinity. Notwithstanding the association of the New Man with contestation and change, as Edwards suggests, the proliferation of New Man imagery in the 1980s was strangely repetitive:

> Yet despite this apparent plethora, the content of these representations remains quite extraordinarily fixed. The men in question are always young, usually white, particularly muscular, critically strong jawed, clean shaven (often all over), healthy, sporty, successful, virile and ultimately sexy. (Edwards 1997: 41)

In this sense, 1980s representations of the male body betray some substantial departures from fashion imagery of the 1970s. Firstly, as the 1980s progressed there was quite simply an increasing profusion of imagery and marketing aimed at men as advertisers focused on a lucrative potential market. As in the 1970s, fashion imagery aimed at men is often sexualized and focused on the body, but both the body itself and the way it is framed have changed. Gone is the *naïveté*, diversity, joy, and youthful abandon that characterized 1970s advertising.[10] In their place is an approach to both fashion and the body founded on a set of much more orthodox masculine archetypes, but nevertheless proving a potent site for identification, desire, and a newly embodied form of masculine representation.

In contrast to the 1970s, muscular, "traditional," and nostalgic images of the male body—whether subject to ironizing camp or not—are increasingly resurgent as the 1980s progress. Effeminacy, so crucial to the youth culture and music of the early to mid-1980s, was sidelined towards the end of the decade, no doubt influenced by homophobia in America and the UK which reached its zenith, according to attitudinal data, in the late 1980s (Anderson, 2009: 98; Ormston and Curtis, 2015).

In this way, corporeal fashions of this period reflect anxieties pervading the performance of masculinity within a still strongly heterosexist society experiencing rapid social change. The eroticization of the male body—which took place to an increasing extent in the late 1980s and 1990s—employed various strategies, most notably hyper-masculinity and nostalgia, as a way of displacing the unease that went along with the objectification of the male physique. In this way, advertisers, designers, and image-makers had their cake and ate it: giving themselves the permission to commodify men's bodies, while employing the symbols of male power to neutralize the subversiveness of the act.

The 1990s and its legacy

While Bruce Weber's iconic early eighties photographs for Calvin Klein were notable for their athletic, muscular models, by the early 1990s, the physiques depicted in the label's advertising had undergone an evolution. A 1993 underwear campaign featuring musician Mark Wahlberg and Kate Moss illustrates this change – Wahlberg's highly developed musculature thrown into sharp relief by Moss's waif-like form. Not only had the fashion for muscled male bodies become more extreme, it had also diverged radically from feminine modes (as characterized by 17-year-old Moss' childish frailty) (Ritts, 1992). This divergence in the bodily fashions of men and women represents a shift from the 1970s in which models of both sexes were generally slim, and even from the early 1980s in which more athletic female bodies were popular.

Harrison Pope, Katherine Phillips, and Roberto Olivardia in their 2000 text *The Adonis Complex* describe how the availability of anabolic steroids in the United States and elsewhere—during the 1980s and especially in the 1990s—allowed men to achieve a much greater degree of muscularity than had previously been possible. This bulking up of the body using enormous doses of synthetic testosterone, along with a punishing exercise regime and diet, represents—in a strikingly literal manner—the technologies of the self and techniques of the body to which theorists such as Foucault (1988) and Mauss (1973 [1934]) refer. Technologies of the self, to use Foucault's language, not only relate to the possibilities for corporeal transformation that medicine, diet, and exercise regimens afford, but also to the values, discursive regimes, and systems of surveillance that pertain in a given society.

The new forms of embodiment offered by steroid use may have been taken up by relatively few men at first, but as Pope, Phillips, and Olivardia demonstrate, their effect on aesthetic ideals was enormous: from bodybuilders and film actors to children's action toys, the ideal male body had swollen to previously unimagined proportions.

As I have suggested, self-consciously nostalgic representations of the proletarian male body plays a part in the resurgence of muscularity during the 1980s, in particular, but so too does the increasing *spectacularization* of the male physique: the postmodern emphasis on the male body as image and symbol that emerges out of the commercial culture of the 1980s. Writers including Mike Featherstone (2007), Jean Baudrillard ([1981] 1994; 1998), Anthony Giddens (1991), and Frederic Jameson (1991) have explored the ways in which the economies of industrialized countries, during the late twentieth century, shifted from an emphasis on production—physically making goods—to an emphasis on consumption. These changes, they argued, belonged to a new form of economic and social organization of late or postmodernity in which the circulation of signs and symbols became increasingly central to economic life. For all the nostalgia of sepia-tinted photography, there was something highly distinctive about the late 1980s and early 1990s body which had become substantially delinked from a Modernist masculinity defined by labor, functioning instead as a free-floating symbol of desirability and success.

A 1991 campaign image for Calvin Klein Obsession Cologne by Bruce Weber reprises the sculptural aesthetic for which he was now well known. A naked male model in a sunlit garden bears an emaciated, collapsed female figure on his shoulders (Weber, 1991). Turning away from the viewer he nuzzles his face into the woman's scant flesh as he holds her aloft. Sunlight plays upon the model's veined, muscular shoulder and arcuate thighs, while his buttocks are partially veiled in shade. It is an image of showing and hiding, both explicit and coy, one that sexualizes the male body while transforming it into an anonymous sculptural form, and that—in its inclusion of a slumped female model—partially transposes the implied male sexual passivity onto the female figure.

A few years later, an advert for Versace Underwear from Spring 1994 featured a brooding model photographed in black and white (Versace Intimo Advertisement, 1994: 14). Leaning against the bamboo screen of a tropical beach-hut, gazing pensively into the middle distance, he rests one hand on his chin in an expression of concentration as filtered sunlight strikes the side of his face and falls onto his torso to highlight his gym-honed physique. The camera lingers on the model's washboard stomach and on the clenched biceps and quadriceps of his right arm: his right hand, holding his hip, leads the eye down to a pair of branded, white jersey boxer shorts—bright against the model's tanned skin—and pushed up at the leg to highlight the bulge of his penis and scrotum. Like 1980s images of male models, the photograph encodes aspiration, both through the Neoclassical body that it takes as its object, and through its associations with luxury goods and exotic locales. A less conventionally photographed campaign of the same year, for Calvin Klein's perfume Escape, conveys a similar set of ideas (Weber, 1994: 16). A grainy close-up features a young man and young woman just about to kiss. The shirtless male model's developed upper arm and pectoral fill most of the image; the female model is positioned below, gazing up at him longingly. Sex, adoration, and power seem to be on sale alongside the perfume.

These are, as Roland Barthes might say, totally magical bodies—undulating smooth surfaces, sculpted contours—tactile, desirable, eroticized, but also somehow safely distant, fantastical, and unreal. This isn't to deny the reality of the models who posed for these images, of course, but there is something otherworldly not only in their statuesque physiques, but also in the dreamy, hazy way that these bodies are presented—the insistence on the smooth surface (soft yet hard, sculpted yet fleshy) that distances us from the real corporeality of these bodies, so that they function much more as symbols than as human beings. The sepia or black and white photography common to these images underlines this dreamlike atmosphere by suggesting an indistinct, mythic past.

It is also striking that these kinds of representations are much more common in advertisements than in editorial fashion stories and, moreover, that they are often used to promote perfume, watches, underwear—magical elixirs and talismans of desirability (rather than clothing itself).

But just as striking as these scantily clad, spectacular, pneumatic physiques are the disappearing bodies of men in fashion and in public life during the 1990s. While magical, fantasy bodies may appear between the glossy pages of magazines to promote the latest heady fragrance—Obsession, Opium, Allure— the clothing featured in magazines like *GQ, Arena, Arena Homme+*, and *The Face* during this period is in no way body-conscious. Oversized menswear that hides and obscures the body, a trend that had started in the 1980s, continued apace during the 1990s, extending from exaggerated suiting and blouson jackets to encompass all aspects of the male wardrobe. Suddenly, sportsmen's shorts extend down to the knee; the hems of T-shirts drop by several inches; suit jackets drape from the shoulders barely touching the torso and falling to mid-thigh; while snug 501s are replaced with loose, drop-crotched jeans. In this sense, men's fashion and clothing in the 1990s form part of a process of estrangement of men from their bodies as the contours of the male form are systematically shrouded, hidden, and obscured.

Sociologist Jonathon Watson—working in the context of health and social policy—has explored the problematic, distanced way in which men are encouraged to view their bodies in Western culture, describing the participants in his qualitative study as experiencing their bodies "in a fragmented contentious manner" (2000: 119). This is the flipside of Elizabeth Grosz's observation that women are assumed to be "somehow more biological, more corporeal, and more natural than men" (1994: 14). In times of anxiety surrounding masculinity, the male body—vulnerable, permeable, a site of pleasure, pain, hunger, longing, and a potential locus for violence and destruction—is either hidden from view, as in the 1950s, or transformed into an anonymous sculptural ideal.

An advertisement for Marithé et François Girbaud of 1991 typifies this disembodied tendency in menswear: a stocky, broad-shouldered, hooded figure, with his back to the camera, prowls through a narrow New York Street framed by high-rise buildings, parked cars, and tarmacadam (Marithé et François Girbaud Advertisement, 1991). The black and white image has a grainy, impressionistic quality, reinforced by a cloud of steam that partially engulfs the figure and renders the details of the cityscape indistinct. He wears a faded, distressed denim jacket, splattered with raindrops, an untucked denim shirt, and jeans in the same faded, stonewashed denim—oversized, bagging, and crumpling at the seat. This is an urban warrior, totally engulfed, swathed, and protected by his figure-hiding, identity-concealing clothing.[11]

Even in summer vacationing fashion, 1990s menswear remained all-encompassing. Against a black backdrop, a *GQ* photo story of 1991 features a model in an oversized, double-breasted sports coat by Pal Zileri, a rumpled, untucked silk shirt, and ballooning cotton chinos. In stark contrast, his female companion wears a short, sleeveless shift dress in pale pink ("The resonance of solids in subtle shades," 1991: 146–147). The treatment and framing of the fashionable body in 1990s fashion had radically bifurcated according to sex ("On days when denim seems a little too heavy," 1991: 242; Barcelona: Antonio Miró, 1991: 337).

Collezioni Uomo of Autumn/Winter 1992 captures the swathing, protective quality of men's fashion of this period as a model for designer Stefano Chiassai proceeds down the catwalk wrapped in layer upon layer of expensive Italian wool: a drop-shouldered flannel jacket ruched and crumpling around the model's arms as his hands are thrust into pockets, wide trousers collapsing into folds at the hem, a grey mélange moss-stitch cardigan layered over another cardigan, and a glimpse of a patterned shirt fastened at the neck (Firenze: Stefano Chiassai, 1991: 31). There is something Eastern, almost kimono-like, in this layering that so completely masks the contours of the body to create an abstract silhouette.[12]

Away from the luxury of Italian mills and a couple of years later, *Arena Homme+* presented sporty, waterproof outerwear in a dynamic photo shoot that nods to the football casual subculture. Notwithstanding the amorphous silhouette of the models' garments, a sense of corporeal masculinity is expressed through their unshaven shiny faces and lank hair as well as in the feeling of movement captured in the models' leaping poses. But the stiff, padded, impermeable performance-wear encompasses and obscures the models' torsos entirely: their bodies are shielded from the elements, from the rough and tumble of the football terraces, and from the desiring gaze (Figure 2.7).

The uncertainty and ambivalence around the representation of the male body, hinted at in these images, extends beyond the fashion pages of nineties magazines. In an article from *GQ* of February 1994, journalist Hilary Sterne is intrigued by the new phenomenon of the often partially clad, hunky, celebrity male model (1994: 126–128). Sterne arranges an evening with 25-year-old Steve Sandalis or "Topaz Man," a physique model and coverstar of pulpy romance novels whom she spends the rest of the article sending-up as a not-too-bright "himbo." It's an intriguing piece of writing that reveals a discomfort with the apparent role reversal implicit in the figure of the male model packaged to appeal to the supposed tastes of heterosexual women (the article's subtitle "Gender Gaffes" further underlines this sense of anxiety). The accompanying photos of the ersatz date are also significant since, despite Sandalis' fame being predicated on his body, it is Sterne and not he who is seductively attired in figure-hugging clothing. And in this way, the conventional gendered economy of looking is recuperated and reaffirmed.

A month earlier, Steve Friedman, in his review of New York's fashionable spa treatments, captures a related note of corporeal anxiety that the writer himself refers to as a "deep and twisted ambivalence" (1994: 50–52). An aspirational image of a muscular, tanned model, wearing a face pack and tended to by multiple female beauty therapists, illustrates the feature, but the writing betrays a more complex set of competing discourses than this image might imply. There is a curious hedging at work here: the writer, keen to reaffirm a heterosexual masculinity (that might perhaps be under threat), refers to sexual fantasies involving his masseuse while simultaneously telling us that "I hate and pity myself for my sordid desires." And the performativity of gender is alluded to in his description of enduring a painful massage: "This is stupid, but manly" (1994: 50–52). Surprisingly, the notion that visiting a spa might be in any way enjoyable or relaxing seems entirely absent from the article: there is little sense of the body as a site of pleasure; rather it is a repository for embarrassment, pain, and humiliation.

This sense of an ambiguous and uneasy relationship to embodied experience (and associated reticence to speak about the body amongst men) is described by sociologists of the body Rosalind Gill, Karen Henwood, and Carl McLean, who in their 2005 paper *Body Projects and the Regulation of Normative Masculinity* go so far as to characterize the respondents they interviewed as lacking the "verbal and psychological vocabularies" to make sense either of their own embodied experiences or the external pressures that "police" the male body (2005: 51–53).

Men's estrangement from their corporeal selves must be understood in the context of an orthodox masculinity in which the need to care for and to look after the body is in conflict with an idealized, socially mandated invulnerability. By the 1990s, the laboring, productive, proletarian male body, rendered heroic in the representations of the early twentieth century, was increasingly disappearing; at the same time, the sense of physical freedom which had enlivened menswear of the 1970s had dissipated, while the stigmatization of the 1980s New Man rendered the consumer body—the new desirable self resulting from gym membership and the application of expensive unguents—a problematic figure now associated with effeminacy and vanity. In this sense, the options available to men as subjects were in many ways becoming narrower during the early 1990s, while, as John Beynon suggests, representations of the male body became more conservative than in the preceding two decades (2002: 109). As a result, 1990s menswear carries with it a defensiveness that relates to the need to be "authentic" while any claim to authenticity seems increasingly in doubt.

As Gill, Henwood, and McLean suggest in their qualitative study of young men's attitudes to the body, "males may increasingly be defining themselves through their bodies in the wake of social and economic changes that have eroded or displaced work as a source of identity" (2005: 39). And, in this sense, the production of a symbolic masculinity, as embodied in an increasingly exaggerated muscularity, has acted to displace anxieties around the disappearance of other forms of masculine prestige.

As we shall see, this is far from the whole story, and by the middle and late 1990s, more subversive, waif-like representations of the male body began to remerge in earnest (a process linked both to a liberalization of social attitudes and to greater economic confidence). Nevertheless, the sexy "consumer body," sculpted and energetically maintained in the gym, that first emerges as a recognizable archetype in the early 1980s[13] remains a powerful symbol of male desirability throughout the 1990s. This body reappears in a somewhat altered form in the figure of the "spornosexual" in the 2010s, as described by journalist Mark Simpson (2014).

Like the metrosexual and New Man before him, the spornosexual emerges at the confluence of new types of representation and new forms of gendered practice. Simpson's portmanteau term alludes to the aspirational, artfully honed male bodies popular in sport and pornography and widely emulated by young men. In this sense, the spornosexual is a figure created out of media discourse but who corresponds to real changes in the lived experiences of men in the 2010s. The spornosexual body—despite its obvious connections to 1980s and 1990s representations—is a distinctively twenty-first century mode of self presentation that, as journalist Clive Martin has suggested (2014), is particularly associated with clubbing, foreign holidays, and social media. Martin illustrates an article critiquing this emerging demographic with "ethnographic" images of young, very muscular, tanned, tattooed, and carefully coifed young men out clubbing in a variety of body-conscious outfits, or partially dressed and engaged in "laddish" antics. This new style of self-presentation—derived from the idealized heavily crafted bodies of sportsmen, reality television personalities, and pornographic actors—is connected to the growing acceptability not only of working out, but also of waxing, tattooing, artificial tanning, teeth bleaching, and other forms of bodily remediation.

The spornosexual physique, then, is explicitly sexualized, commodified, and constructed: its rhetoric is one of attractiveness, success, and fun rather than of authenticity and, in this sense, the rise of this body style marks a shift from the values of not showing off and authenticity expressed by participants in Gill, Henwood, and McLean's study of nine years earlier.

Martin,[14] in his article "How Sad Young Douchebags Took Over Modern Britain," along with critics of the "neoliberal body" (Harjunen, 2017) problematize these explicitly constructed consumer bodies using a set of frames that recuperate Adorno and Horkheimer's critiques of mass culture: these, they suggest, are inauthentic, unreal bodies, a manifestation of false consciousness that ultimately serves the capitalist class. It is easy to condemn a corporeal aesthetic that may seem vulgar and brash, but to do so is to dismiss the pleasure, pride, and sense of identity that resides in the spornosexual body. There persists, beneath Martin's critique in particular, a puritanical fear of corporeal pleasure and of sexuality that expresses itself in a confused plea for a return to the values of orthodox masculinity.

Rather than reifying some nebulous notion of the "authentic body," we could recognize the ways in which spornosexual styles of corporeality allow men to connect with and enjoy their bodies in positive ways. It is, after all, perfectly legitimate to take pride and pleasure in a strong, physically powerful physique. On the contrary, what is problematic about the continued fetishization of muscularity (at least in some segments of popular culture) is that this body style remains bound up with normative notions of gender, and that considerable pressure on men and boys to be muscular *as proof of their masculinity* persists.

Until relatively recently, little work investigating dissatisfaction with the body among males had been carried out, and it was generally assumed that men were much more satisfied with their corporeal lot than were women (Grogan, 2008).

However, the cultural pressures on men are different to those placed on women. While women are often encouraged to take up less space—to slim, diet, and to become smaller—conversely, orthodox forms of masculinity encourage men to take up more space: to be tall, outgoing, and muscular. When researchers in the 1980s redesigned their methodologies to focus not only on issues of weight but also on muscularity, a previously hidden form of body-dissatisfaction was revealed (Drewnowski and Yee, 1987; Lynch and Zellner, 1999; Pope et al., 2000; Gill et al., 2005). This corpus of research demonstrated that feelings of physical inadequacy were widespread, and perhaps growing amongst males: that many men, boys, and adolescents felt that they were never big or muscular enough, that their bodies were scrawny, impotent, and undesirable.

The fourth sex: Androgyny and objectification

By the mid-1990s, the model of desirable masculinity defined by muscularity was increasingly challenged by youth and alternative culture: in music, by bands like Suede, Pulp, and Placebo, with their androgynous, wan, skinny frontmen; in magazines like *i-D, Dazed & Confused, The Face*, and *Sleazenation* with their "heroin chic" models; and in fashion design from the late 1990s onward by figures such as Raf Simons, Hedi Slimane, Ennio Capasa, and Helmut Lang. By the turn of the millennium, this slim and more ambiguous male archetype had moved decisively into the spotlight (not least on the catwalk of the newly founded Dior Homme). But he is already visible, at the periphery of youth and subculture, from the early 1990s onward.

Across the course of the decade, notwithstanding the dominance of highly muscular images of masculinity in mainstream popular culture, the archetype of a troubled, ethereally beautiful, man/boy (re)gained a currency in transgressive, youth culture; in indie music, in style magazines, and in alternative film.

In music, the mode of embodiment and self-presentation adopted by figures like Richey Edwards of The Manic Street Preachers (Harpin, 1992: 55), Kurt Cobain of Nirvana, and Brett Anderson of Suede very deliberately differentiated itself from the images of desirable masculinity that dominated mainstream fashion and film of the period. So too did the alternative fashion photography of Corinne Day, Willy Vanderperre, David Sims, and Collier Schorr, with its focus on adolescence, nudity, sexuality, and grungy social realism. In two fashion shoots for *The Face*, the first from 1990 by David Sims and the second from 1992 by Corrine Day, the photographers communicate a sense of guileless and unpolished vulnerability in their intimate portraits of longhaired teenage boys (Figures 3.5 and 3.6). A new kind of body-consciousness is felt, one quite different from the more mainstream

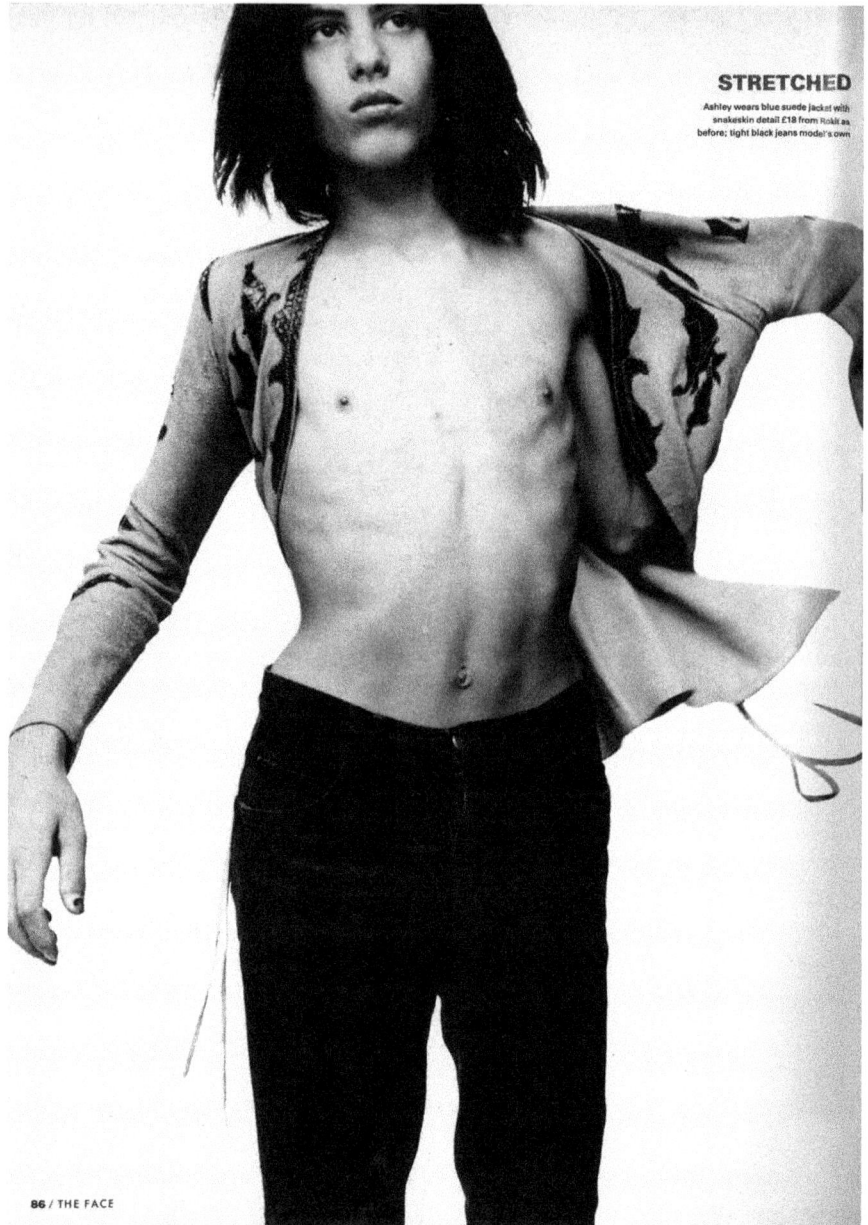

Figure 3.5 Sims, D. and Howe, A. (1990) "Snip it, rip it, colour it or patch it: in Denim the customiser is always right." *The Face*, p. 86.

BODY LANGUAGE

Spider's web customised T-shirt and Levi's jeans from Rokit as before

Figure 3.6 Day, C. and Ward, M. (1992) "Wah Wah." *The Face*, p. 85.

representations reviewed earlier in the chapter. Nevertheless, these images—with their svelte youthful models, exposed torsos, and tight black jeans—hint at an aesthetic that would go on to be highly influential in the decades to come. The slim and frequently androgynous form of embodiment favored in these hip, but somewhat peripheral, cultural forms gestured to the rejection of an orthodox, patriarchal masculinity in favor of something more questioning, vulnerable, and chaotic.

To frame it in poststructuralist, psychoanalytic terms, these skinny, effeminate figures, whether appearing in *The Face, i-D*, or in *NME*, represented the antithesis of the "phallic order" (Lacan)—as symbolized by the upright, rigid, disciplined, hard, muscular bodies that came to prominence in the 1980s and 1990s—in favor of a more chaotic, affect-laden, corporeality that relates to Julia Kristeva's *chora*[15] and to her notion of the abject.[16] Indeed, one could scarcely imagine a more abject figure than that of Richey Edwards self-lacerating and bleeding, but also beautiful, Christ-like, badly made up, glamorous.

In the world of fashion design in the late 1990s, it was the work of Raf Simons,[17] with his street-cast teenage models scouted from Antwerp's alternative hang-outs that most typified this new model of embodied masculinity. Like Day and Vanderperre (Vanderperre et al., 2003)—the latter of whom collaborated extensively with Simons—the liminality, awkwardness, and fragility of the skinny, "quirky" nonprofessional models he cast was integral to a message which thematized the alienated teenage years Simons himself had experienced in the Belgian countryside (Simons cited in Limnander, 2006). In Simons' Black Palms collection for Spring/Summer 1998, the first models to proceed along the concrete runway were shirtless, the titular black palms traced onto their backs, drawing attention to their protruding shoulder blades, vertebrae, and the hollow arcs of their lower backs. Later, web-like open knitwear exposed the models' bare torsos, and trousers were slung low to expose narrow waists—the fragile physicality of the models communicating a palpable sense of vulnerability (Figure 3.7). Despite the radical nature of these representations of the body, in the years up to his appointment at Jil Sander in 2006, Simons remained a somewhat subcultural figure, little known beyond a small, fashion-literate crowd. And in the late 1990s, in particular, the willowy, angular physique of Simons' models sat far outside the mainstream aesthetic which was predominantly square of jaw, white of tooth, athletic, and bronzed.

In contrast, the sense of excitement captured in contemporary journalistic accounts of the skinny silhouette and models introduced by Hedi Slimane reflects the very real novelty of seeing these kinds of alternative representations presented by a big fashion house in the full glare of the media spotlight (Menkes, 1998; Clark, 1999: 10; Porter, 2001: 62). Slimane's intervention in men's fashion at Yves Saint Laurent and most importantly at Dior Homme represents the point at which the skinny male model moves from the periphery to the center of men's fashion

BODY LANGUAGE 103

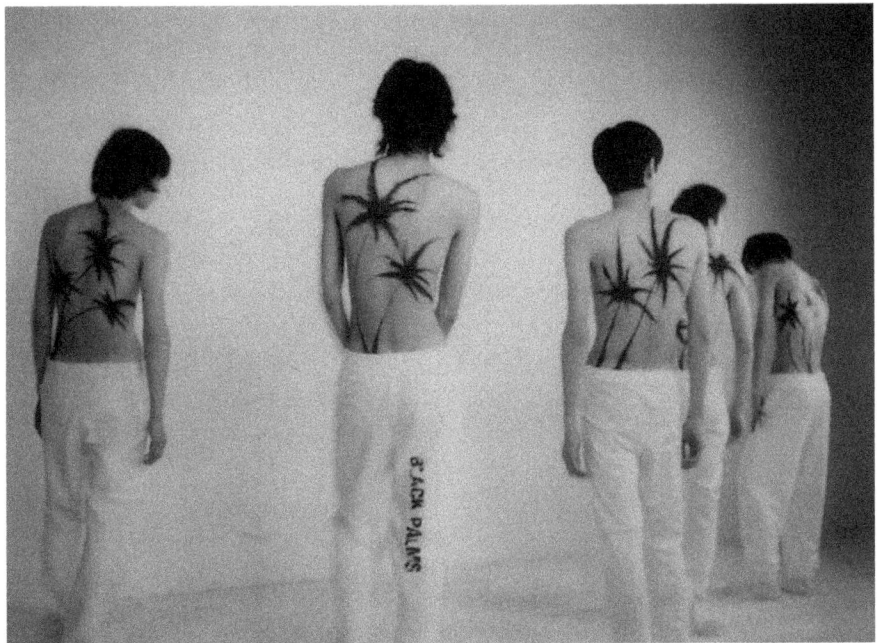

Figure 3.7 Takahashi, Y. (1997). *Raf Simons Spring/Summer 1998 — Black Palms*. [Polaroid] Paris: Bastille.

representation, a fact reflected in Murray Healy's 2001 interview with Slimane for *Arena Homme+*, entitled "Adam's ribs":

> the male model has transformed into a much sleeker animal. Gone are the grinning, pumped-up, all-American-types that dominated the Eighties […] In their place we have the less burly, more surly European skinny-boy. (2001: 163)

As the feature continues, Slimane himself explains the significance of this new model physique:

> It is not about a powerful body or big muscles which become completely like a caricature, but about a natural and lean body: martial arts instead of working out […] I never see big guys [when casting a show] only naturally toned boys, with a certain ease of movement […] do real exercise, such as swimming or martial arts. Stay and be as natural as possible. Lean doesn't mean vulnerability, but strength. (2001: 163)

Clearly, Slimane understood the slender body as representing a more authentic and less overtly constructed masculine identity. He saw his choice of model as a deliberate intervention in the language of gender, as reflected in an interview for The Guardian with Charlie Porter (2001) tellingly entitled *Body Politic,* in which Slimane explains, "Muscles don't mean masculinity to me [...] and long hair does not define your sexuality." These assertions capture the liberating possibilities of a model of gender that seemed to allow for a less built, less narrowly defined form of male embodiment and identity. But the notion that a slender silhouette represents authenticity is itself clearly a highly problematic one, failing to account for the bodily regimes required to retain an appearance of perpetual adolescence and—whatever Slimane's own intentions—at risk of fetishizing youth and vulnerability.

Nevertheless, in the early 2000s, magazines, stylists and photographers seemed increasingly inclined to concur with Slimane, favoring a more slender, "natural" boyish figure. As journalist Charlie Porter commented:

> Slimane is heralding a more sensitive interpretation of male self image at odds with the pumped-up gym stereotype that has dominated menswear for the past two decades. (Porter, 2001: 62)

By the early 2000s, the lean, supple physical type championed by Slimane had begun to gain currency: suddenly, the heavily muscled, tanned models of the 1980s and 1990s look decidedly old-fashioned, like heavy, mahogany Victorian furniture destined to be replaced with tubular steel.

> Relations of power-knowledge are not static forms of distribution; they are "matrices of transformations." (Foucault, 1978: 99)

Closely connected to Slimane's new representations of the male body (whether on the runway or between the pages of a magazine) was the way that he spoke about corporeality—emphasizing the *realness, naturalness*, and *authenticity* of the models he cast who had "a certain ease in the movement," and whose "body has to have evolved effortlessly" (Slimane, 2001 cited in Healy, 2001: 163). By characterizing the slender male body as natural and real, he positions other kinds of more explicitly constructed "built" model bodies as inauthentic. And in this way, Slimane was engaged in what Michel Foucault (1978: 101) might describe as "reverse discourse": legitimizing a previously stigmatized form of physicality and masculinity by drawing on an existing set of values (authenticity and naturalness) reconfigured in relation to a new form of embodiment.

And it was not only the form of the male body that shifted but also the way that body was framed by clothing. Soft, draping, fluid fabrics caress the skin of menswear models from the late 1990s onward on the catwalks of Capasa, Slimane, Simons, Helmut Lang, and Tom Ford at Gucci, suggesting a more sensing, sensual, embodied form of masculinity than the hard workwear fabrics

Figure 3.8 Dior Homme by Hedi Slimane (2007). *Collezioni Uomo*, (60), p.259.

and boxy tailoring that preceded them. In Slimane's Spring/Summer 2007 collection (Figure 3.8), a sexy, body-conscious mood is felt in the use of fine-gauge, draping translucent jersey, cutouts and in the collection's fitted silhouette, which emphasizes and exposes the models' narrow thighs and slight frames.

In this way, placing the skinny male body at the center of their new vision of menswear was integral to Slimane's and Simons' rejection of a phallocentric, heteronormative masculinity. And this renunciation of hegemonic masculinity in the world of men's fashion connected to a much broader cultural shift in the early years of the new millennium. Sociologist Eric Anderson—conducting ethnographic fieldwork amongst young British and American men between 1999 and 2004—found striking and unexpected changes in masculine identities taking place during this period, as young men increasingly embraced identities that were more affectionate, more diverse, less delimited by sexism and homophobia, and in which they were able to engage in behaviors historically categorized as feminine. He states, "Whereas gender expressions coded as feminine were edged to extinction in the 1980s, today they flourish" (2009: 97). The "androgynous" bodies celebrated by Slimane and Simons strongly related to what Anderson characterizes as *inclusive masculinity*: while coexisting with more orthodox representations of gender, they offer the possibility of new and sometimes "transgressive" modes of subjectivity.[18] Changes in the way that people think about gender and about bodily "relations of power-knowledge," in Foucault's term, relate to the kinds of strategies of representation and "discourse" which cultural actors (like designers, stylists, editors, and fashion photographers) employ. But as Foucault suggests, these discourses exhibit "tactical polyvalence" (1978: 100): a variety of different and sometimes contradictory approaches. While Slimane's initial intervention in the language of gender relied on a set of essentialist discourses around the natural, pure and authentic, other designers and cultural commentators drew on a more ambivalent, ambiguous set of ideas, albeit with a similar end result.

Reflecting this set of inherent tensions, in 2003 (just two years after Slimane's debut collection for the newly founded Dior Homme), two books were published which placed notions of youth, adolescence, and gender at their center—a coincidence seeming to point to a moment of cultural preoccupation with representations of liminal, sexualized masculinities. The feminist thinker and literary critic Germaine Greer's art historical text *The Boy* explored representations of male beauty in Classical and Renaissance art through the prism of boyhood. Meanwhile, Raf Simons collaborated with curator Francesco Bonami to produce a volume entitled *The Fourth Sex: Adolescent Extremes,* which accompanied an exhibition of the same name. Simons and Bonami's catalog used images drawn from fashion and documentary photography and from contemporary fine art—again with a focus on fragile teenage masculinities.

In *The Boy,* Greer asserts that "the male human is beautiful when his cheeks are still smooth, his body hairless, his head full-maned, his eyes clear, his manner shy and his belly flat" (2003: 7). And she goes on to discuss the boy as an archetype of male beauty that signifies, amongst other things, "male vulnerability," "the passive love object" and "the female gaze." Greer writes intriguingly when she describes how the figure of the boy sits outside, and threatens to disrupt, patriarchal relations: "every male who survives boyhood must agree to annihilate the boy in him and confine himself to the narrower scope available to him in patriarchal society" (2003: 28), and she is insightful in her analysis of female visual pleasure and its relations to power, stating:

> the boy is the missing term in discussions of the possibility of a female gaze … the boy, being debarred from phallic power, is endowed simply with a responsive penis rather than a dominating phallus and can be sexualised with impunity. (2003: 228)

But while Greer may be right to describe how a celebration of boyishness as a quality could serve a wider project of deconstructing and reforming gender relations outside patriarchy, her tendency to collapse together images and descriptions of childhood with those of early adulthood, is, for me, problematic. Greer, it seems, *is* able to perceive something amiss in the brutalized "icons of male vulnerability" beloved of Classical, Renaissance, and Neoclassical artists— figures pierced by arrows, flung from chariots, bound in ropes and chains or, like Phaeton, "killed by Zeus with a thunderbolt […] his divinely perfect young body plummet[ing] earthwards on ceilings and walls all over Europe" (2003: 195). And she brilliantly exposes the normative view of early twentieth century-art historians who were perturbed by any suggestion of male beauty characterized by gentleness or estranged from power. Nevertheless, in her project to reinstate male beauty, vulnerability and passivity, along with female visual pleasure into an art historical narrative that has sought to suppress them, Greer fails to give sufficient space to a discussion of the more troubling, objectifying and exploitative aspects of these representations of boys.

With a similar set of preoccupations to Greer, Simons and Bonami's exhibition and catalog aimed to capture the disruptiveness, creativity, and transgressive aspects of adolescence (2003: 12). Just as Greer characterizes boyhood as sitting outside patriarchy, and thus outside the expected rules of gender, Simons and Bonami see the adolescent as belonging to a "fourth sex" in which "freedom and lightness combine" and identity "explodes" (2003: 12). And while they assembled works that feature both male and female figures, images of quirky, awkward, sometimes bashful, sometimes eroticized male figures predominated. A painting by Elizabeth Peyton (2003: 281), almost certainly from a photograph, captures a young Leonardo DiCaprio, his face and upper torso filling the composition as he reclines diagonally across the picture frame: DiCaprio gazes up at the artist, his eyes blue, clear, and reflective, his lips vivid red, his open shirt exposing nipples and pale chest. Peyton's technique of simplified tonal contrasts (in this case violet washes that define the cheekbone, neck, collarbone, and pectoral muscles) emphasizes the prettiness of her subject while also his recalling fashion illustration of the mid-twentieth century. In this way the artist explicitly situates DiCaprio as an object of the desiring, romanticizing gaze.

Elsewhere, the fashion photographer Collier Schorr, who became well known in the early and mid-1990s for her photographs of young men and adolescent boys, describes a set of motivations for producing her distinctive photographs that also connect to the preoccupations of Simons, Bonami, and Greer. In an interview for *Dazed & Confused* she suggests that her focus upon androgynous, adolescent masculinities in the 1990s was designed to avoid the dynamics of objectification that she associated with photographing women.

> The pressure not to represent women in the 80s was so strong where I was coming from. I felt like there was a real problem with how women had been packaged and sold back to women [...] So any anxiety, desire or aggression I felt I directed towards boys. (Schorr, 2014 in Gavin, 2014)

These new forms of representation were understood, by fashion practitioners and commentators alike, to signal a new set of desires and social aspirations for men, aspirations that, as I have suggested, connect with Eric Anderson's notion of *inclusive masculinity* (2009)—a form of masculinity no longer predicated on the disavowal of femininity, effeminacy or homosexuality, and one in which a much greater plurality of behaviors can be integrated into a masculine identity. So there is certainly something positive and progressive here. But there is also something disturbing, since this celebration of youthful indeterminacy and vulnerability—representing a set of subjectivities that have often been denied to men—so easily transforms into a fetishistic gaze.

In the years following Slimane's and Simons' early shows of the late 1990s and Slimane's campaigns for Dior Homme in the early 2000s, images of the sorts of slim, young, and "quirky" models that these designers had championed became increasingly widespread on the catwalk, in magazines and in advertising. And by the end of the decade, these representations had themselves become dominant in the context of high fashion.

In the Spring/Summer 2015 edition of *Man About Town*, a photograph features a close-up of a young model who lies uncomfortably on a bare concrete floor, his head propped awkwardly against the unpainted grey plaster wall that forms a diagonal line across the composition (Sejersen and Volkova, 2015: 143). The model's face is impassive, resigned, and waxy with pale makeup; he wears a very tight, pale-pink "nude" long-sleeved top embroidered in orange and silver sequins in a semi-abstract cubist design. The fine, almost sheer, clinging polyester jersey exposes the model's very thin body beneath—angular shoulders and long, fragile arms.

This image is one of many in the issue of *Man About Town* to feature youths in prone, awkward, or suggestive positions. And in the past decade there seems to have emerged a genre of fashion photographs in which male models—almost invariably, thin, white, and very young—are depicted as if collapsed, passed out, often in states of partial undress, slumped, gazing bashfully or mournfully into the camera (Harris and Irvine 2013; Rubchinsky and Spence, 2013: 188–205). While it might be argued that these images make space for new kinds of masculine subjectivities, they also invite a voyeuristic gaze and imply a troublingly asymmetric power relationship (between the viewer and subject and between the photographer and the model) in which the vulnerability of the models seems an intrinsic element in the economy of desire.

In addition to these "boy lost in forest," "boy collapsed" scenarios that celebrate a liminal, wan, adolescent masculinity, magazines such as *10 Men, Another Man,* and *Man About Town* also regularly feature head and torso shots of multiple, shirtless "fresh faces," as well as images of models getting changed behind the scenes at catwalk shows (sometimes headless or cropped to show just a pair of legs or torso). In this way model bodies become interchangeable, commodified, and fragmented.

Martha Nussbaum (1995: 257), drawing upon the work of feminist theorists Andrea Dworkin and Catherin MacKinnon and on the philosophy of Emmanuel Kant, defines objectification as "treating as an object what is not really an object, what is, in fact, a human being," and she delineates seven distinct attitudes that may lead to objectification: instrumentality, denial of autonomy, inertness, fungibility, violability, ownership, and denial of subjectivity. Though, as Nussbaum describes, some of these qualities may be present in an image or representation without it being morally reprehensible. What makes the photographs I have described problematic—in my judgment—is not that they present beautiful young men as desirable—though some models do, at least, appear too young for this to be appropriate—nor that they suggest erotic subtexts, but rather that this desirability and eroticism seems to be predicated on the inertness, fungibility, and (if not violability per se) the implied vulnerability of the models. In attempting to make possible qualities and identities that have been forbidden to men, fashion producers too often find themselves trapped within the problematics of female objectification merely displaced onto a male figure. And while androgyny can indeed be a source of liberation in men's fashion, the way in which androgyny is imagined at the level of the male body as adolescence and extreme thinness can be rather worrying. Androgyny and the transgression of normative masculinity, it seems, find a space in our culture only when embodied by a slender, beautiful young man, or, as Greer suggests, a *boy*.

The celebration of fragility and androgyny that characterizes these sorts of representations enabled an escape from normative masculinity, but what happens to those beautiful doomed youths who, unlike Jim Morrison or Johnny Thunders, fail to consign themselves to oblivion before they begin to fade? Adolescence as a metaphor for the liminal and slenderness as a symbol of emotional fragility is all very well, but what culturally sanctioned images of alternative masculinity exist for those who are no longer young, who grow plumper, or lose their hair? The tendency towards idealization in these images of transgressive, alternative masculinities leads to a sense of alienation for men who can no longer maintain their elfin, puckish looks, who must either consign themselves to the effacement of orthodox masculinity, or be seen as rather sad faded figures.

Nevertheless, the validation of the slim and androgynous physique implicit in the work of Slimane and Simons and in magazines like *Man About Town* represents an important challenge to the orthodox representations of masculine embodiment that regained dominance in the late 1980s and 1990s.

Theorists of fashion familiar with the East Asian context, notably Yumiko Iida (2005) and Masafumi Monden (2015), suggest that this very slim adolescent corporeal ideal became mainstream in Japan rather earlier than in the West and one might speculate on whether Japanese representations exerted an influence on the European context. There are also significant intertexualities between this form of fashionable embodiment and the figure of the "twink"—the hairless, slim, young gay man—who, as Filiault and Drummond have described, gained currency as a recognizable type within gay culture in the early 2000s (2007: 179–181).[19] Intriguingly, despite the visibility of these alternative physical ideals in gay culture, subculture, fashion, and the mainstream media during the 2000s and 2010s, very little academic discourse surrounds them.

4
MILLENNIAL MEN

Having investigated shifts in representations of the male body at the turn of the millennium, let's turn now to an exploration of menswear proper during this period of flux and dynamism.

Men's fashion in the early and mid-1990s experienced very little formal or aesthetic innovation. Although youth culture and subculture continued to generate distinctive modes of dress, the contemporary style press (with a few notable exceptions) lacked the dynamism, confidence, and sense of purpose of the early 1980s, while mainstream menswear, insulated from stylistic innovation, timidly played it safe. In men's magazines like *L'Uomo Vogue, GQ,* and even the newly founded *Arena Homme+*[1], the eighties formula of big suits and brawny bodies remained dominant well into the middle of the new decade: these representations, as sociologist Tim Edwards has described, seemed to signify "a return to traditionally masculine values of money, work, and success" (Edwards, 1997: 42–43). In edgier magazines like *i-D* and *The Face,* grungy anti-fashion was combined with influences from skateculture and American hip-hop to result in an oversized, casual, logo-oriented, but deliberately understated menswear in which there was little room for experimentation at the level of form. As I have argued, the conformity and blandness of menswear in the early 1990s signaled a moment of retrenchment and anxiety as the social and economic underpinnings of twentieth century masculinity became increasingly precarious.

In this sense, the images that emanated from the menswear industry and mainstream fashion media during early 1990s continued to reify a highly normative, orthodox model of masculinity in much the same way as in the late 1980s. Despite the continuing dominance of these hegemonic representations, however, the emergence of new, countervailing discourses surrounding gender and identity also accompanied the beginning of the new decade.

The 1990s saw the mainstreaming of a set of identity politics that had developed in the 1980s, as well as a series of important cultural and political changes: the popularization of third-wave feminism, emphasizing choice and the freedom to play with femininity and sexuality; the emergence of a gritty, working-class mood in pop culture reflected in the rise of grunge and in edgy fashion photography by the likes of Corinne Day and David Sims; the gradual displacement of Thatcherism and Reaganism by rebranded aspirational social democratic politics (taking a much more relaxed attitude to consumerism than the old left); and the amplification of gay politics, increasing gay visibility, and the emergence of anti-homophobia as a symbol of progressiveness.

Few looking at menswear in the early or mid-1990s would have imagined that it was a discipline poised for creative experimentation and radical change, and yet these emergent discourses point to some of the shifts that would go on to transform men's fashion at the turn of the new millennium. The first hints of an alternative approach to the masculine ideal is felt in the work of photographers like Day and Sims[2] and stylists such as Melanie Ward, who rejected the glossy, glamorous, gym-honed look of *GQ* and *L'Uomo Vogue* and instead embraced a more raw, grunge-influenced subcultural aesthetic (Figures 3.5 and 3.6).

Mark Simpson, in his influential article "Here Come the Mirror Men" (1994), writes about a new demographic of male consumers he dubs "metrosexuals," who, in common with adherents of third-wave feminism (and perhaps influenced by its rhetoric), adopt a much more ludic, playful consumerist approach to masculinity (Simpson, 1994b: 22). At a point at which popular discussions surrounding representations of masculinity were largely focused on the figure of the "New Lad," Simpson's observations and predictions were to prove prophetic.[3] The spirit of anxiety and straitened economics of the early 1990s had resulted in retrenchment and stasis in menswear. But moving into the middle and late 1990s, as the economy improves, as per capita consumption increases, and—crucially—as the dominant cultural mood becomes more liberal (indicated by the election of Clinton in 1993, Blair and Jospin in 1997, and Schröder in 1998), significant shifts in menswear at the level of design and representation begin to surface.

In this way, though it was far from self-evident at the time, by the middle and late 1990s, some of the elements that were to define the coming revolution in menswear were already falling into place. As Amy Spindler, writing in *The New York Times* in 1997, was to argue:

> Fashion has proved time and again that even superficial goals have layers of meaning. So, it was a powerful shift when Gucci's designer, Tom Ford, changed the superficialities of men's fashion [...] Instead of gearing designer suits to make men look successful, powerful and established (the Armani goal), he has made them younger, thinner and sexier. (Spindler, 1997: 14)

The highly influential aesthetic Tom Ford had developed at Gucci during the late 1990s is visible in two images that appear in *Arena Homme+* of Spring/Summer 1997 (*Arena Homme+,* 1997: 89; Testino, 1997). In a shoot featuring Ford's latest collection, five male models and a female dresser pose informally against a glossy black background as they casually sip champagne. A Gucci advertisement from the same issue takes the form of an intimate portrait of model Edward Fogg sporting gold tinged aviators, and a black jersey shirt open almost to the waist, his skin glistening in moody half-light. The lean body-conscious silhouette and sensual mood highlighted in these two photographs is communicated through supple leathers, soft translucent jerseys, lightweight wools, and silks which — along with the exposed chests of the models, glints of gold and wide frame glasses — strongly evoke a glamorous seventies milieu: Studio 54, Halston, Mick and Bianca Jagger. Although the specifics of these references to New York glitz remained signatures of Ford's collections for Gucci, the silhouette and nostalgia for the 1970s were felt in several other designers' collections of Autumn/Winter 1997–1998 and Spring/Summer 1998.

Amy Spindler in her *New York Times* article draws attention not only to Ford but also to two young and at the time virtually unknown designers: Hedi Slimane, who had recently been appointed to rejuvenate Yves Saint Laurent's lackluster menswear offering (and who would go on to establish a new men's label at Maison Christian Dior), and Raf Simons, who had just debuted his first Paris collection (1997: 14). For Spindler, these young designers' work seemed particularly fresh, striking, and prescient, and she was not alone in suggesting that they were just what menswear needed. Six months later, in a feature rather tellingly entitled "Touches of Spice in a Tepid Stew," Constant White (again in *The New York Times*) reported:

> Mr. Simons possesses as strong a vision as any recent fashion talent, freely combining elements of punk with the style of the traditional gentleman. Mr. Simons used his lipstick-wearing models to display his virtuosity in sculpting black pants, whether sharp stovepipes or wide-leg trousers [...] At Yves Saint Laurent, too, there was a pleasantly unexpected spirit at work in the designs of Hedi Slimane, who like Mr. Simons is exploring a kind of subversive gentleman's dressing. Pierre Bergé, the irascible chairman of the company, pushed Mr. Slimane onto the runway after the show to take a bow. There was much for which Mr. Bergé could be proud: the chocolate twin set, the black leather trench jacket [...] and the long tuxedo with a black midriff top. (White, 1998)

While Giorgio Armani in Milan and Calvin Klein in New York, amongst others, played it safe with the square boxy tailoring and heavily branded sportswear, which had been the early 1990s chief sartorial gifts to the world,[4] Ford, Slimane and Simons, along with Costume National's Ennio Capasa, pioneered a radical silhouette allied to a new physical ideal, one which Suzy Menkes of the *International Herald Tribune* evocatively described as: "Like a pen stroke on graph paper [...] a thin, straight line" (Menkes, 1998). It was a gesture widely understood by fashion commentators to hold significance beyond the aesthetics of menswear, signaling new modes of masculinity for the coming millennium (Clark, 1999b: 10; Porter, 2001: 62).

Not only did the silhouette and choice of models change under the influence of Capasa, Ford, Slimane, and Simons, but fabrication, detail, and construction were suddenly also considered ripe for innovation. In the case of Capasa and Ford, their revelation was in moving away from the 1980s and 1990s silhouette (in the hands of Armani, oversized yet draping, but amongst his lesser competitors, a carapace of stiff fabric encasing rather than describing the body). They did this by referring extensively to the 1970s in their choice of textile and approach to cut. But, they combined this feeling for fit and drape with a sense of chromatic and stylistic restraint, and, in the case of Capasa in particular, of minimalism. It was an approach that brought a new sensuality to menswear and which captured the zeitgeist to alter the course of contemporary fashion. Ford's and Capasa's allusions to seventies menswear were significant because they acted to reclaim the corporeality, inventiveness, and sense of freedom associated with men's fashions of that period. And the drapey, sheer, lustrous cloths and soft leathers they employed—though reinterpreted in pared-back forms—recall some of the late 1960s and early 1970s images I reviewed in Chapters 2 and 3.

> My aim, my ambition has always been to create a style, an aesthetic viewpoint if you will […] I would say that the most important things [in my work] are an aesthetic blend inspired by eras: the rock and roll of the 1970s with a minimalist slant: minimalism, which I believe played a part in creating the 1990s, combined with a passion for Italian tailoring. For me fashion is not only a dream but a form of intense pleasure which seduces others and seduces oneself. (Capasa, 2011)

The younger and less established designers Slimane and Simons also adopted a closely cleaving silhouette and both incorporated a sensual use of supple leathers and soft fabrics, sometimes drawn from womenswear, into their respective design methodologies. However, unlike Capasa and Ford who, for all their prescience and skill, relied essentially on core sartorial forms—the jacket, the trouser, the shirt, the cashmere pullover—Slimane and particularly Simons increasingly adopted an approach characterized by formal innovation. At the same time, both designers integrated subcultural references into their practices, drawing not only on the glamor of the early 1970s, but also on the gritty, edgy look of the latter half of the decade as expressed in proto-punk, punk, and the arty demimonde of New York City.

For Slimane, inspiration was drawn from CBGBs musicians Johnny Thunders and the Heartbreakers, Richard Hell and the Voidoids, The New York Dolls and from photographer Robert Maplethorpe. Simons, meanwhile, immersed himself in the European post-punk moment with references to Joy Division, Kraftwerk, and contemporary bands like the Manic Street Preachers.

Raf Simons had demonstrated a fascination with marginal masculinities from his first Antwerp collection of 1995 (which took the form of a low-key video presentation) and throughout his work of the late 1990s and early 2000s. His collections for Autumn/Winter 1996, entitled *We Only Come Out at Night,* and Spring/Summer 1997 *How to Talk to Your Teen,* incorporated motifs of subverted school uniforms and recurrent allusions to rave, punk and New Wave. The Raf Simons look of this time was characterized by close-fitting, uniform-inflected tailoring (often sported with Crombie-like coats), along with edgy youth culture references: slashed garments, leather, and sheer slouchy knits (Sinclaire and Mondino, 1997; Simons and Daniels, 1998). The aesthetic was complemented by Simons' characteristic use of non-professional, street-cast models scouted from Antwerp's teenage hangouts.

Having debuted in Paris with his Autumn/Winter 1997 collection, in which subcultural references remained key, Simons gradually developed a visual language over his subsequent collections that combined these allusions to youthful alienation with an abstracted formalist approach. For his Autumn/Winter 1999–2000 collection, *Disorder Incubation Isolation*—nodding to Joy Division[5] songs in its title—Simons used the overcoat and the trench as points of reference. Abstracting away from these classical forms, he pleated, layered, and sculpted fabric to exaggerate the trapezoid shape of the coats. Simultaneously, he eliminated the extraneous seams, fastenings, and details to draw attention still further to the sculptural qualities of the draped cloth. Other garments were yet more extreme: in a cloak for the same collection, pleats fall from the left hand side of a stand-collar to create an off-center diagonal opening; the garment recalls the eighteenth century, but—in its asymmetry, fluidity, and lack of visible fastenings—feels entirely modern (Vanderperre, 2014). Elsewhere, Simons' Crombies, shirts, and jackets retained his characteristic neat fit, but the line was stretched and elongated, lending his boyishly slender models—still a novelty in the late 1990s—a wraith like ethereal quality.

Slimane's collections for Yves Saint Laurent in the late 1990s garnered increasing attention, but it was his 2001 launch of new label Dior Homme that acted as his decisive critical intervention in menswear, pointing towards the formal and aesthetic approaches that would go on to characterize the practice of men's fashion in the coming decade. The claims made for Slimane at the time evoked messianic imagery: "It was on the last day of the presentations, however, that Paris was saved, by Hedi Slimane" (Clark, 1999b). With the eyes of the world upon him, Slimane proposed a vision of menswear that seemed, at that moment, entirely new, fresh, and exhilarating. In the words of Charlie Porter in *The Guardian:*

> Nothing exciting is meant to happen in men's fashion. Yet in Paris right now, the talk is all of Hedi Slimane, the designer whose work at the newly

established Dior Homme is provoking a radical rethink in the stagnating ateliers of menswear. (Porter, 2001: 62)

In Slimane's inaugural collection for Dior, as well as his final collection for Yves Saint Laurent, some of the core semantic and formal elements that went on to define his practice in the 2000s are already evident. Firstly, there is an emphasis on tailoring, as evidenced in Richard Avedon's iconic campaign photograph of Eric Van Nostrand for Autumn/Winter 2001/2002, in which the jacket has simultaneously regained its structured form—darted through the waist and padded and rolled at the shoulder—while losing the excess of canvas that characterizes traditional tailoring (Avedon, 2001). This prioritization of elements of formal and evening wear, though the pieces were rarely worn as conventional suits, reflects a dandyish aspect in many of Slimane's collections: a reaction to the dominance of sportswear and the oversized silhouette of the 1990s that, ironically, rendered the hyper-traditionalist elegance of men's evening wear a subversive pose. In case this subversiveness be too weakly felt, Slimane introduced an abstracting approach, shearing away at garments to reveal their pure forms. For Yves Saint Laurent Autumn/Winter 2000/2001, shirts were finished without buttons or, more dramatically, reinterpreted as a bolt of cloth suspended from the neck, animated as the model progressed along the catwalk (Slimane, 2000). In these two outfits, a knowledge and respect for the core sartorial forms of menswear is combined with a willingness to challenge and radically subvert them. Moreover, the bared skin and more especially the sensuousness of the drape introduces an eroticism that would have been much less strongly felt had the model simply been shirtless. This sense of ambiguous eroticism was also evident in the monochrome palette, deep necklines, and sheer fabrics creating a graphic juxtaposition between the white of the models' chests and the black of their garments (Slimane, 2000). A *Diamond Dogs* aesthetic is reflected in nods to Bowie and Roxy Music throughout the collection including gold lamé trousers, tipped fedoras, sharp tailoring and glittering paillettes (Figure 4.1, Figure 4.2). But the exuberance of these gestures was always balanced against the coolness and minimalism of the styling. In *Solitaire* for Dior Homme, the cleanness of the stripped back tailoring is complemented by subtle elements of decoration. The fabric corsage on the lapel of a black dinner jacket was made using haute couture womenswear techniques for which Dior are well known; these potentially conflicting elements of precision and decoration balanced with a measured restraint. The impression we are left with, reflected in the fashion journalism of the time, is of both the audacity of the work and simultaneously its strong and determined sense of purpose.

By the mid-2000s, Hedi Slimane's stylistic approach—the slim, elongated line; the closely fitted tailoring; the womenswear fabrications; the feeling for an underground seventies glamor in a Roxy music, New York Dolls, David Bowie vein—had influenced many purveyors of high-end menswear. Having moved

YVES SAINT LAURENT RIVE GAUCHE HOMME BLACK VEST.
BLACK SATIN JEANS AND BLACK LEATHER BOOTS AND RING

Figure 4.1 "Simmons, T. and Munro, T. (2001). A+ Collections: Yves Saint Laurent Rive Gauche. *Arena Homme+*, (14), p. 144.

beyond the innovations of Ford and Capasa to adopt a much more radical aesthetic, Slimane's mixture of grungy glamor, precise cut, and attenuated silhouette was seen in the output of labels as diverse as Fendi, Burberry Prorsum,

YVES SAINT LAURENT RIVE GAUCHE HOMME. BLACK WOOL SWEATER, BLACK WOOL TROUSERS, BLACK WOOL FEDORA, BLACK LEATHER BOOTS AND RING

Figure 4.2 Simmons, T. and Munro, T. (2001). A+ Collections: Yves Saint Laurent Rive Gauche. *Arena Homme+*, (14), p. 145.

Prada, Spastor, Alessandro dell'Aqua, and even Italian casual wear brand Iceberg (which had previously been strongly associated with oversized denim and gimmicky knit). The feeling for softly draping silks combined with fitted jeans, leather, and motorcycle finishes—so characteristic of Slimane's collections in the early to mid-2000s—is evident in Silvia Venturini-Fendi's menswear catwalk presentation for Fendi Autumn 2004 and Spring 2005 (Venturini-Fendi, 2003; 2004), which have a distinctly seventies "de luxe" feel in their use of sheer, lustrous, and shot fabrics combined with glossy leathers: this mood is also present in Miuccia Prada's very close-fitting silhouette for Miu Miu Uomo of the same season.

Perhaps, however, one of the most significant effects of Slimane's aesthetic occurred beyond the world of high-end fashion. During the late 2000s, even after his departure from Dior Homme in 2007, the fitted tailoring he had pioneered exercised an increasing impact on the high street—in mass market shops including Topman and Zara—and in the wardrobes of style-conscious men of relatively modest means (Topman, 2009; Westgarth and Ellis, 2009; Mackie and Lloyd, 2010). Not only had the defining look of the period—skinny jeans worn with a tailored jacket—been popularized and largely originated by Slimane for Dior Homme, so too had the punkish influences, fine-gauge jerseys and knits, and low necklines. Slimane communicated his aesthetic through advertising campaigns, often photographed by himself and featured in the newly expanded market of men's fashion magazines including *10 Men,* launched 2004; *Another Man,* launched 2005; *Fantastic Man,* launched 2005; and *Numéro Homme*, launched 2007 (Slimane, 2005; 2006a; 2006b). Equally importantly, his collaborations with various rock groups including The Libertines and Franz Ferdinand (whom he dressed and who sometimes played at his catwalk presentations) reached beyond a highly fashion-literate crowd to permeate more generally into the cultural consciousness of the period, so that the Hedi Slimane look became familiar even to those who had never heard his name. Slimane's pervasive influence on men's fashion of this period can perhaps be explained with reference to industrial designer Raymond Loewy's maxim that design should present for the consumer "the most advanced yet acceptable" style (Pawley, 1992): Slimane's early collections were new enough to capture the industry's attention, but were legible and comprehensible enough for a relatively wide range of consumers.

After leaving Dior in 2007, Slimane's influence continued to be felt in the designs of Lucas Ossendrijver at Lanvin and Kris Van Assche, the new designer at Dior Homme, both of whom had previously worked under him. The design philosophy reflected in Dior's menswear offering had been completely transformed from the outset of Slimane's tenure at Dior Homme (the label which he had effectively created),[6] but it was his transformative effect on the bottom line that ensured that major brands "sat up and took notice" of the potential of menswear. Profits continued to grow at Dior Homme even as Slimane prepared to leave the label he had brought into the world, with Christian Dior chairman Bernard Arnault commenting that "Dior Homme experienced sustained growth across its entire product line (city, sportswear, and accessories)" (Arnault, 2007: 17). As both Miles

Socha in a 2007 report for *Men's Week* and William Drew in his profile of Lucas Ossendrijver (for *Wish* magazine) suggest, menswear and its potential revenues had been largely ignored by the major French fashion houses until the mid-2000s:

> [Lanvin] men's wear has also been explosive, thanks largely to a new fashion line introduced two years ago, overseen by Elbaz and designed by Dior Homme alum Lucas Ossendrijver. [Lanvin president Paul] Deneve said Spring 2008 men's orders jumped 80% as the brand re-entered such fashion and luxury-conscious markets as the U.S. and Italy. (Deneve, 2007 cited in Socha, 2007: 1)

> Despite Lanvin's individuality [in menswear design] it can also be seen as leading the revival of traditional French fashion houses. Venerable institutions, such as Givenchy, Yves Saint Laurent, Balenciaga, and Balmain, long reliant on womenswear and accessories to the detriment of their men's business, are all rediscovering their masculinity. These companies are benefiting from a raft of radical designers rather than play-it-safe patsies. (Drew, 2009: 46)

In retrospect, it seems extraordinary that these labels took so long to awaken to the possibilities of menswear. But, as I have suggested, the sense that men's fashion could or should be a creative discipline to rival womenswear contradicted received opinion around the nature of men's dress and masculinity that had reasserted itself with a vengeance in the late 1980s and 1990s. As Hedi Slimane himself stated in an interview with Charlie Porter for *The Guardian* newspaper: "At the end of the day, the men running the companies wanted the clothes to look like the kind of clothes they would wear, and they didn't really see a world beyond that" (Slimane, 2001 cited in Porter, 2001: 62).

Subculture, music, and fashion

The work of Simons and Slimane drew upon and connected both to contemporary subculture, and to those of the 1970s and 1980s, weaving together a diverse set of allusions to form a hybrid style. Bands like the Manic Street Preachers, Suede, and Pulp—marginal, indie-identified and opposed to the mainstream—had begun to gain popularity during the mid-1990s, and there were certainly hints at the glam-inflected Ziggy Stardust-manqué aesthetic of Jarvis Cocker, Richey Edwards, and Brett Anderson in Simons' and Slimane's early designs. Both the music and the visual aesthetic of these groups, expressed in their clothing, makeup, hair, and videos, evoked a series of overlapping subcultural milieux: the grunginess of punk; fitted secondhand suits that nodded both to the mods and to new wave; and a good dose of new-romantic androgyny—silky unbuttoned shirts and chin length tousled hair. The rake-thin silhouette of the band's frontmen was also part of the appeal.

Nor were these musicians alone in championing this retro aesthetic. Slimane's and Simons' designs (along with photographers and stylists like Sims, Day, and Ward) should be understood as in dialog with a 1990s indie/alternative subculture. By the middle of the decade, in a UK context, an identifiable scene of vintage-clad teenagers who congregated around Camden Market and frequented clubs like the Camden Palace, the Scala in Kings Cross and Trash (The End)—off Tottenham Court Road—had emerged. Integral to the sensibility of the scene was the rejection of the commercial values of mainstream fashion and music expressing itself in an adoption of miscellaneous seventies references. In this sense, indie subculture kept the subversive flame of seventies and early eighties radical youth culture alight—acting as a space for alternative, non-normative representations and expressions of gender that were pushed to the margins during the late 1980s and early 1990s. Far from an act of appropriation, it was quite natural that designers like Slimane and Simons, with their explicit interests in exploring and celebrating marginal, subordinated masculinities, would engage with this scene and aesthetic. Echoing this seventies "vibe" in a New York CBGBs mode, The Strokes emerged in 2000, their Ramones-like look and guitar-oriented sound becoming immensely influential. As Alex Needham, culture editor of *The Guardian*, formerly of *The Face* and *NME*, described to me:

> The Strokes were immediately embraced by the fashion world. When you think what The Strokes were wearing at the time—jeans with suit jackets—that pretty much lasted the whole decade, and Converse as well. It was an updated version of a New York punk-band look which goes right back to the Velvet Underground, and that was what the music was like too. (Needham, 2013 [interviewed in] McCauley Bowstead, 2013)

Of course, Slimane did more than draw on a diverse set of allusions. From the early 2000s, newly installed at Dior Homme, with a large advertising budget and increasing media profile, he did much to popularize and bring into the mainstream a look that had hitherto remained on the periphery of popular culture. For me personally, with my slim and androgynous appearance, these shifts in fashion were especially welcome: I was never going to ripple with muscles, nor achieve a deep tan. The corporeal ideals of the late 1980s and 1990s were being replaced with something that, in my case, was much more achievable, and, just as importantly, with a style and ethos—liminal, ambiguous, glamorous, and playful—to which I could relate. People's reactions to me changed quite noticeably—my look had come into fashion.

As I have suggested, club nights like Trash and subsequently Nag Nag Nag acted as incubators and disseminators for this look. In photos from Trash taken in 2002, or thereabouts, many of the elements of Slimane's and Simons' aesthetic are visible—the narrow silhouette, the rock and roll references, hints at Gary

Figure 4.3 McCauley Bowstead, J. (2002) *Clubber at Trash*. London: The End.

Newman-ish strangeness (Figure 4.3). Though notably, the sense of refinement and of a pared-back elegance that characterized the early collections of Slimane, Simons, and Capasa are less discernable—an indication of the ways in which these designers elevated and transformed the raw material of their references. Looking back at my photographs with the benefit of hindsight, what is also very noticeable is the emergence of what would go on to be called—rather dismissively—hipster culture (though this term wasn't in common parlance at the time).

Queering men's fashion

Developments in the economics of menswear and in contemporary popular culture go some way to explaining the momentum that creative men's fashion has enjoyed since the early 2000s. Connectedly, these shifts in fashion practice and representation also functioned as a response to profound and rapid changes in attitudes to gender and sexuality in the mid-to-late 1990s and early 2000s.

France in the 1980s under Socialist President François Mitterrand had already enacted progressive laws granting recognition for same-sex cohabiting couples (with some of the entitlements of marriage), as well as providing legal protection against discrimination for gay and transgender people. However, in Great Britain and the United States, under right wing administrations, homosexuality, along with single-parent families, had re-emerged in the 1980s as potent issues in a set of "culture wars" that pitted "traditional family values" against "permissive" social liberalism. As theorists of masculinity including Máirtín Mac an Ghaill and David Plummer suggest, homophobia is important not only in the way that it oppresses gay people, but much more widely in the way that it structures and shapes attitudes to gender (and to masculinity in particular): "In men's spheres, the yardstick for what is acceptable is hegemonic masculinity and what is unacceptable is marked by homophobia and enforced by homophobia" (Plummer, 1999: 289). Which is to say that homophobia functions to discipline, regulate, structure, and shape the behavior of heterosexuals as much as to stigmatize a homosexual minority.

By the early 2000s, however, attitudes had changed considerably. Not only were homophobic statutes increasingly removed from law[7] but public opinion across much of Europe and metropolitan America had also shifted (Pew Research Centre, 2013). With less fear associated with the contravention of acceptable "heterosexist" modes of dress and comportment, for both gay and straight consumers, men's fashion in the 2000s was free to explore a much wider set of aesthetics and signifiers. This context also allowed new forms of male subjectivity and fashion practices to emerge. Mark Simpson, coining the term "metrosexual," suggested that the ways in which heterosexual masculinity was performed, embodied, and experienced were changing. And the emergence of various classifications to describe men in the decades following Simpson's intervention—from "hipsters," "metrosexuals" and "new lads" to "bros" and "spornosexuals"—provides evidence of a pluralization of masculinities that points to an increasing license for men to experiment with identity and appearance. As qualitative research has indicated (Hall, 2015), these forms of identity certainly are meaningful (at least to certain men at certain times in their lives), although the boundaries between these notionally distinct identities remain leaky and their definitions unstable and contingent.

Notwithstanding this mutability and instability, such terms provide a discursive framework—a way of talking and thinking about heterosexual masculinity, in particular—that challenges orthodox assumptions surrounding gender. The naming of metrosexuality as a phenomenon in the mid-1990s can be understood in relation to the "queering of heterosexuality" advocated by feminist scholars such as Lynne Segal. Segal (writing in the same year as Simpson) argued that:

> All feminists could, and strategically should, participate in attempting to subvert the meanings of "heterosexuality," rather than simply trying to abolish or silence its practice. [...] The challenge is to acknowledge that there are many "heterosexualities." (Segal, 1994: 259–260)

Queering can be understood, in this sense, as subverting and overturning the common sense understandings of gender that have tended to lock men and women within rigid binary codes of behavior and, relatedly, as a way of fracturing hegemonic identities into more plural and diffuse subjectivities.

Slimane's customers and admirers were, no doubt, too sophisticated to identify with so crude a label as metrosexual, nor would they necessarily have been steeped in Lynne Segal's synthesis of queer theory and feminist research. Nevertheless, as I have argued, the intervention in the language of gender which designers like Slimane, Lang, Capasa, and Simons made in the late 1990s and early 2000s should be understood as growing out of a set of concerns that relate closely to those of both Simpson and Segal: namely, a desire to disrupt, challenge, and destabilize essentialist and heteronormative models of gender.

Millennial men

While Slimane had garnered much attention—and proved highly influential—during the mid-2000s, Raf Simons—appointed to the (then ailing) label of German designer Jil Sander[8] in 2005—continued to work more quietly, attracting favorable reviews but fewer claims of paradigm shifts. Designing his own eponymous collection, while working on the Jil Sander men's and women's lines, Simons slowly developed an approach in which he played with elements of construction and experimented with new garment types. It was a direction that had been hinted at in his collections of the mid-1990s but which had matured to propose a new menswear wardrobe that innovated at the level of *form* as well as at the level of *style*.

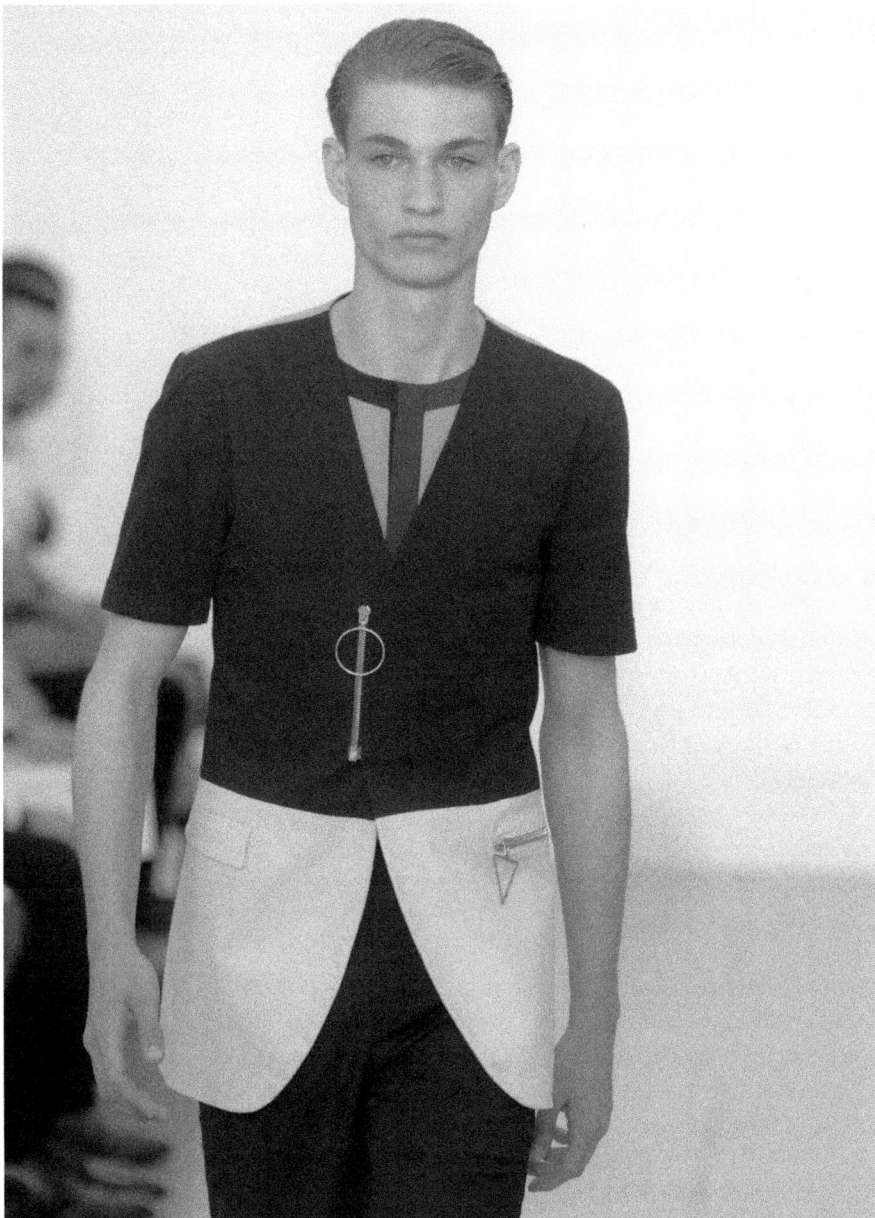

Figure 4.4 Madeira, M. (2008) Jil Sander Spring/Summer 2009 by Raf Simons. Available at: http://www.vogue.com/fashion-shows/spring-2009-menswear/jil-sander/slideshow/collection#2 (Accessed: 19 November 2012).

Simons' work of the mid- to late 2000s frequently demonstrated a concern for geometry and simplicity, as indicated in both his Spring/Summer 2005 collection for his own label and, strikingly, in his Spring/Summer 2009 menswear for Jil Sander. A purity of line was expressed in the uncluttered simplicity created by concealing fastenings and pockets, displacing seams to the back of garments, and avoiding darts and style lines: an approach that indicated affinities with twentieth century Modernism. On the Spring 2009 catwalk, these Modernist references had become explicit as tailored jackets, shorn of their collars and revers, are paneled in bands of contrasting hues,[9] shirt fastenings are concealed beneath plackets, and zipper pulls articulate pure primary forms (Figure 4.4). This bright, vivid, Modernist collection, evoking Bauhaus and Constructivist utopianism, contrasts against the more melancholic mood of Simons' earlier work.[10] And in its optimism, abstract qualities, and experimentation with construction, Simons' designs also connect to the formalism that I found in *L'Uomo Vogue* of the late 1960s and *Tailor & Cutter* of the early 1970s (as described in Chapter 2).

Tom Ford in the late 1990s and Slimane in the early and mid-2000s had frequently referred to the glamor of various seventies creative and subcultural scenes and through these references had found fresh approaches to silhouette, drape, and fabric choice. By contrast, Simons by the middle to late 2000s was engaged in an exploration of new types of garments and methods of construction that innovated predominately at the level of form. In this sense, Simons' project in the mid-2000s recalls some of the seventies approaches I have discussed in previous chapters—an attempt to redefine, restructure, and reimagine men's garments in the contemporary world. By the mid-2000s Ennio Capasa of Costume National—who, along with Ford, had reworked the silhouette of the 1970s for the 1990s—was also engaged in a formal investigation of menswear garments with references to armor and protective clothing stitched into his tailored collections (see Figure 4.5). By drawing attention to menswear in innovatively styled garments that captured the spirit of the time, Slimane had catalyzed structural change in the industry along with stylistic change in the discipline. Nevertheless, as the first decade of the millennium progressed into the second, it was Simons, rather than Slimane, that heralded the direction for a newly rejuvenated and confident design practice, one that increasingly looked to reinvent a men's wardrobe beyond its core sartorial forms.

On the one hand, the developments in menswear initiated by this small band of designers, photographers, and stylists in the late 1990s seem to have appeared out of nowhere. Slimane's collections for Yves Saint Laurent and Dior Homme at the turn of the millennium embodied an aesthetic that was startlingly different from other contemporary labels, rejecting the corporate power look for a more ambiguous, sensual style, one which—perhaps surprisingly—was to enjoy considerable commercial success. In the first decade of the new century,

Figure 4.5 Costume National Spring/Summer 2005 (2005) *Collezioni Uomo*.

a small group of iconoclasts had been able to make big luxury houses and high street retailers alike sit up and take notice of men's fashion, substantially transforming the discipline through bold experimentation that challenged the industry's conservatism. Both Slimane and Simons were notable for producing books and exhibitions and for collaborating with journalists, writers, musicians, and artists in an attempt to disseminate their vision beyond the world of fashion.

On the other hand, the aesthetics and ideas that these designers explored—as I hope I have demonstrated—had a much longer lineage. With their dramatic silhouettes; deconstructed, figure-revealing garments; and decorative flourishes, Slimane, Simons, Capasa, and Helmut Lang quoted from a miscellany of queered, subcultural styles—from the peacock revolution to post-punk. But their work also related, much more broadly, to a shifting ethos of gender at the turn of the millennium, one that connected to contemporary feminism—notably the queered heterosexuality described by Lynne Segal (Segal, 1994)—as well as to a longer history of progressive, reforming masculinities, from the "men's liberation" of the 1970s to the inclusive masculinity researched and theorized by Eric Anderson (Anderson, 2009). Slimane and Simons in particular had an explicit interest in gender and a desire to challenge the hegemony of normative, orthodox masculinity. As Slimane stated in 2001, "There is a psychology to the masculine: we're told don't touch it; it's ritual, sacred, taboo. It's difficult but I'm making headway, I'm trying to find a new approach" (Slimane, 2001 cited in Cabasset, 2001). These pioneering designers at of the turn of the millennium were drawing upon tendencies that had lain dormant in mainstream culture and the collective psyche: their achievement was to reactivate these discourses, to disseminate them to a wider audience, and to make them relevant for a new generation of menswear consumers.

5
THE SHOCK OF THE NEW

Perhaps every discipline experiences a historical period in which it shines with a particular brightness and in which, if only for a moment, it seems to articulate something special and particular its contemporary (world). In painting, you we might argue that this époque of importance fell between 1870 and 1900 as artists, in a dialog with emerging technologies, found ways to describe modern life, the experience of nature: (light, water, fresh air) and the city in flux in new and exciting ways. In womenswear, the era between 1910 and the late 1940s produced radical innovation after radical innovation as hems fell and rose by feet, corsets were rejected and rediscovered, and techniques including the bias cut were pioneered. In this present decade, menswear as a design discipline has experienced a seemingly unprecedented vitality, questioning the sartorial forms inherited from the twentieth century, and finding new approaches to an aesthetic of masculinity.

> Where has menswear's growth sprung from? Menswear has officially arrived. As today heralds new beginnings for a market which has long sat on the very furthest edge of fashion's landscape and in the murky shadows of its women's counterpart, menswear has been given an independent voice of its own. As the first ever menswear-only fashion week showcase, The London Collections: Men, kicks off, 90 British menswear designers are being given the chance to challenge the established men's collections shown across Milan and Paris. (Fashion United, 2012)

As the *Fashion United* quote above suggests, at the beginning of the second decade of the new millennium, menswear had never been in a stronger position either as a creative discipline or as an industry. The previous decade had seen the major French couture houses from Lanvin and Givenchy to Balmain relaunch their faded menswear offerings—and a stream of innovative menswear designers establish their own labels (Juun. J in 2006, JW Anderson and James Long in 2008, Astrid Andersen in 2010). By 2012, a new men's fashion week had emerged in London (New York was soon to follow) and global menswear sales in the luxury sector, were growing apace.

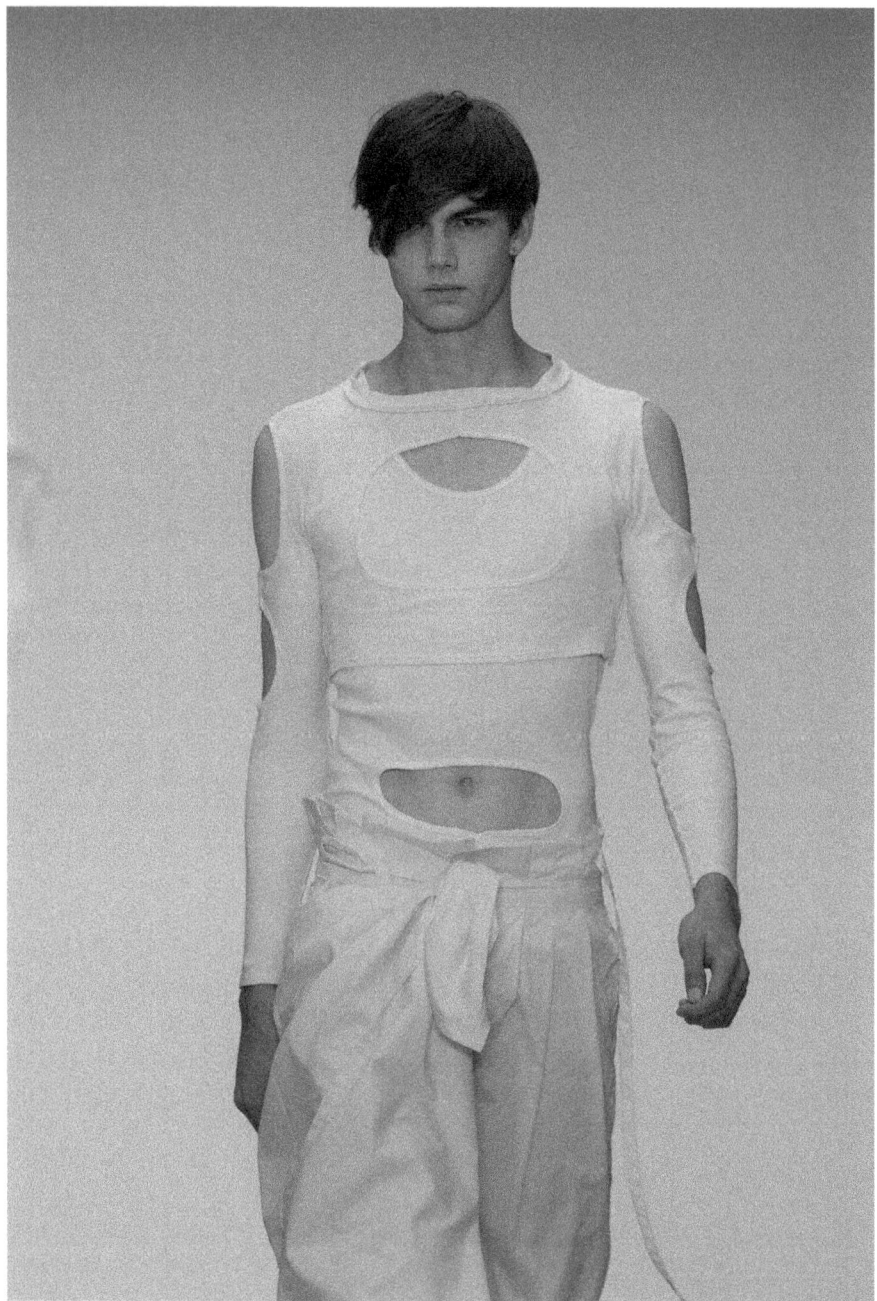

Figure 5.1 Fewings, T. (2015). *Craig Green Spring/Summer 2015*. [Menswear Collection] London. Craig Green's deconstructed and experimental collection references earlier work by designer Helmut Lang.

Menswear is growing twice as fast as womenswear in the luxury sector, analysts have revealed [...] Consultancy Bain & Co revealed that the luxury menswear market, which makes up 40 percent of the global market, is worth £150 billion—and is currently growing by 14% per year, whilst womenswear is only growing by 8%. (Milligan, 2011)

Menswear is bucking the dismal retail trend with overall sales in the category rising 3% over the past six months [...] Research found that branded menswear sales grew at a higher rate than own label over the period, with total spend on branded menswear up 4% from £1.61bn to £1.67bn. Sales of own labels increased 2% from £2.82bn to £2.89bn. (Gallagher, 2012)

Even in large Western fashion markets, such as the US, the UK and Germany, the sales of menswear has been growing at a faster pace than womenswear for the past few years. Euromonitor has named this trend "Menaissance" and attributes the sales boom to men becoming more and more aware of their personal appearance, adjusting their grooming habits accordingly. [...] Since 1998, global sales of menswear has soared over 70 percent and there seems to little signs of it slowing down anytime soon, as the men's fashion market is predicted to reach 450 billion dollars this year. (Fashion United, 2014)

The state of the art: Menswear since 2010

Les Soldats pas de guerre mais les Soldats de la paix, c'est ça l'histoire. "Soldiers not of war but of peace, that is the story." (Elbaz, 2011)

The innovation of figures like Capasa, Slimane, and Simons had brought a newfound freedom to menswear: as the first decade of the new century slid into the next, a new generation of designers would go on to utilize this freedom to articulate responses to economic and cultural shifts in the wider world. The economic downturn of the late 2000s—originating in the collapse of failed financial institutions—reawakened a yearning for *authenticity*. It was as if the chimerical, volatile, insubstantial nature of the leveraged financial instruments that had caused the crash required a return to solidity, tangibility, and craft manifested in a handmade, homespun aesthetic. But whereas in the late 1980s and 1990s a return to "authentic masculinity" had tended to inhibit novelty and originality in men's fashion, in the first years of the 2010s this new direction was incorporated more thoughtfully into the collections of creative menswear designers. The collections of practitioners including Lucas Ossendrijver, Juun. J, Neil Barrett, and Damir Doma increasingly emphasized a certain toughness that diverged from the fine-gauge and shot fabrics (with their attendant aura of luxury and glamor) typical of the preceding decade. But it was a toughness inflected by a sense of questioning, an ambiguity, one that combined fragile and ethereal beauty with unexpected elements of archetypal masculine attire. This approach was later echoed in a number of Spring/Summer 2017 collections by labels such as J. W. Anderson and Vetements, with their playful takes on the boiler-suit, sportswear, and workwear. Speaking in 2011, Lucas Ossendrijver summarized his Spring/Summer collection as follows:

> It's about oppositions, it's the contradictions between the soft and the hard. We took the first look from security guards one sees in the airport but we have translated the look using mousseline, pastel colours, and using a technique whereby utility garments are coated in a fine layer of leather which is then pressed on: a technique which allows a certain lightness along with the sense that something lies beneath the surface which, in this way, acts as a metaphor for the collection. (Ossendrijver, 2011)

The Lanvin Spring/Summer 2012 collection by Ossendrijver (under the overall creative direction of Alber Elbaz) was introduced in a runway presentation that, even mediated by a computer screen in another city and another country, as I experienced it, nevertheless energized and delighted. It was a collection that impressed not so much through its originality, but through its exquisite conception, prescience, and sense of poise. Soft tunics in what appeared to be nappa were in fact made from cotton twill laminated in a film of leather, the seams and panels beneath discernible as an embossed pattern (Figure 5.2). These were cut with soft rounded shoulders, or left sleeveless, their unusual construction giving an impression of both lightness and durability. Crêpe trousers and unstructured blouson jackets communicated softness and opulence through their generous fit and drape, though this was counterbalanced by exposed zipper-tapes, taped seams, and brass press-studs (applied judiciously to ensure an uncluttered quality). In Figure 5.3, the sleeves were "grown on" to the pattern to avoid seaming, which instilled a sense of airy volume as the springy cloth fell in billowing folds.

Plays of volume fit and texture were deft, the cloth coated, washed, and embossed with technical finishes, matt leathers and glossy wet-look treatments, contrasted against dégradé fine-gauge jersey. Lanvin creative director Alber Elbaz described the military theme thus: "These are soldiers not of war but of peace, that's the story" (Elbaz, 2011). And so the hardness of the military finishings was countered by the soft drape of the fabrics, the long utility tunic looking particularly beautiful dancing around the model's body as he hurtled down the catwalk (Fashion TV, 2011). This textural softness was coupled by a chromatic softness as the washed black of the opening outfits faded to dove-grey, blue-grey, a saffron-like warm yellow, a neutralized phthalo blue, and carmine pink.

"Soldiers of Peace," a combination of "soft" and "hard," something "lying beneath the surface." Such concepts spoke to the state of contemporary men's

Figure 5.2 Lagneau, N. (2011). *Lanvin Spring/Summer 2012 by Lucas Ossendrijver* [image]. Available at: http://www.vogue.co.uk/shows/spring-summer-2012-menswear/lanvin/collection/ [Accessed 23 Mar. 2014].

Figure 5.3 Lagneau, N. (2011). *Lanvin Spring/Summer 2012 by Lucas Ossendrijver* [image]. Available at: http://www.vogue.co.uk/shows/spring-summer-2012-menswear/lanvin/collection/ [Accessed 23 Mar. 2014].

Figure 5.4 Virgile, V. (2011). *Lanvin Spring/Summer 2012 by Lucas Ossendrijver* [image]. Available at: http://www.vogue.co.uk/shows/spring-summer-2012-menswear/lanvin/collection/ [Accessed 23 Mar. 2014].

fashion and contemporary masculinity: a rejection of the overt theatricality of preceding years, not as an embrace of a traditionally conceived masculinity, but rather as a search for something else. This play of oppositions exerts a kind of *Verfremdungseffekt* (Brecht, 2005 [1936])—an alienating or distancing effect not so much between the model protagonists and their audience, as between the garments and their usual significations.

A similar distancing effect or sense of the uncanny, is visible on the runway of Korean designer Juun. J. For Spring/Summer 2014, he presented a collection that combined formal innovation with iconic garments that had been transformed to become unfamiliar, ambiguous, and otherworldly (Figure 5.5). In this way, Juun. J's Spring 2014 collection demonstrated an engagement with archetypal menswear forms, but strangely exaggerated to become distorted echoes of their original prototypes.

In Figure 5.7, an American football jersey has been abstracted and enlarged to *hanbok*-like proportions, the shoulders dropped to form one continuous curve with the sleeve, while style lines and raised lettering take on an exaggerated, sculptural quality reinforced by the marbled digital print of the stiff-spongy technical jersey. The designer has combined this reimagined football jersey with the briefest of tailored shorts, worn high on the hip—not quite at the natural waist –accessorizing the ensemble with heavy bracelets that also recalled marble, as well as white rubber boots. Elsewhere in his collection (as in the outfit featured on the cover of this book) high-waisted tailored shorts were combined with shirts that resembled the *hanbok* even more closely, the brevity of the shorts emphasizing the length of the models' bare legs—both provocative and alien—while double-breasted tailored jackets, again teamed with shorts and tucked in at the waist, featured shoulders padded to wild proportions (Figure 5.8). It is not resorting to hyperbole to describe this as an audacious collection: in its unexpected proportions and strangely exaggerated use of iconic menswear garments it resembles Raf Simons, but whereas Simons' work often suggest a narrative Juun. J's collection seems to resist one. Tellingly, the designer entitled the collection UNUNIFORM, issuing a press release claiming his aim was to "disintegrate the barrier of the familiar by breathing new life into an already told story" (Juun. J, Samsung Everland, 2013).

While Juun. J seeks to play with and parody archetype, his collection remains legible, if only just, because of its inclusion of recognizable but exaggerated garments. In this sense UNUNIFORM is a collection which speaks of its time, not only of the frustrations and limitations of those conventional masculine modes of representation which it both resists and incorporates, but also in anticipation of new aesthetic possibilities.

In the work of designers like Juun. J and Ossendrijver,[1] contemporary men's fashion has increasingly explored *form*—the compositional, three-dimensional, structural, and constructional qualities of garments—as a way of escaping the restrictive archetypes of twentieth-century menswear and masculinity.

THE SHOCK OF THE NEW

Figure 5.5 Virgile, V. (2013). *Juun. J Spring/Summer 2014 Catwalk Show* [image]. Available at: http://www.juunj.com/collections/2014_ss/index.jsp [Accessed 20 Mar. 2014].

Figure 5.6 Virgile, V. (2013). *Juun. J Spring/Summer 2014 Catwalk Show* [image]. Available at: http://www.juunj.com/collections/2014_ss/index.jsp [Accessed 20 Mar. 2014].

Figure 5.7 Virgile, V. (2013). *Juun. J Spring/Summer 2014 Catwalk Show* [image]. Available at: http://www.juunj.com/collections/2014_ss/index.jsp [Accessed 20 Mar. 2014].

Figure 5.8 Virgile, V. (2013). *Juun. J Spring/Summer 2014 Catwalk Show* [image]. Available at: http://www.juunj.com/collections/2014_ss/index.jsp [Accessed 20 Mar. 2014].

THE SHOCK OF THE NEW

In these formal reimaginings of menswear it is easy to see parallels with the innovations that took place in women's fashion in the early twentieth century. Just as designers like Madeleine Vionnet and Coco Chanel[2] brought a new simplicity to dress, as well as a new relationship to the body so too have Juun. J, Ossendrijver, Raf Simons, and, more recently, practitioners such as Ximon Lee and Sean Suen. Womenswear in the nineteenth century had stiffly encased women—literally and metaphorically—in a restrictive femininity, but Chanel and Vionnet, using new lighter fabrics and inventive approaches to cut and drape, created a feeling of suppleness, liberty, and sensuality. Chanel's borrowings from menswear, sportswear, and tailoring and Vionnet's bias cutting—the intricate seams of her dresses describing and softly caressing the contours of the body beneath—ushered in an aesthetic revolution in which femininity was reimagined and reinvented for a more liberated age.

Perhaps the most direct analogue for the work of Chanel, Vionnet, and the innovators of the early twentieth century can be found in Raf Simons' Spring/Summer 2013 menswear collection, in which vivid color and precise construction convey an equivalent sense of modernity, clarity, and optimism. Also present is a feeling for softness and drape—what the French call *flou*: most evidently in the supple jersey tunics, decorated by LA artist Brian Calvin (see Figure 5.9), their simple tubular construction and fluent movement recalling the dresses of the 1920s—a silhouette Simons was to reprise, for Spring 2014.

Along with the tunics—printed with enormous, multicolored, abstract faces and teamed with shorts just peaking from below the hem—Simons offered an elegant, pared-back approach to tailoring. Jackets in black, grey, iridescent ultramarine and emerald green—some with exaggerated peaked lapels and some, Modernist and Cardin-like, without revers—were paired with abbreviated shorts in matching cloth, slashed at the front so that the models' upper thighs flashed as they proceeded determinedly along the catwalk (Blanks, 2012). Like Chanel before him, Simons collapses together sporty and dressed up elements: sleek bomber jackets and nylon coats in lilac, hot-pink, and madder-red were paired with highly polished, whole-cut formal shoes. And amid all this clarity and precision, floral patterned coats and shirts (the former like curiously refined housecoats) appeared along with collarless jackets and woven T-shirts in geometric prints (see Figure 5.10). The vivid color, athleticism, the dynamism of the draping tunics, the economy of the tailoring, and the long bare legs of the models all spoke to an energy and sense of liberation that recalled Chanel and Vionnet's designs of almost a century before. As Simons, speaking in 2013, suggested, these collections were about form and experimentation, not feeling "the obligation to be dressed in a uniform" and crucially "about the freedom that a man has to express himself" (Simons cited in Levy, 2013: 160). In this sense Simons not only proposes a new aesthetic, but also celebrates a new way of being a man no longer bound by a strict, normative masculinity.

Figure 5.9 Vlamos, Y. (2012) *Raf Simons Spring/Summer 2013*. Paris.

Figure 5.10 Vlamos, Y. (2012) *Raf Simons Spring/Summer 2013*. Paris.

An interest in new forms of masculinity and evidence of their expression can also be seen in a body of recent scholarly research (published roughly contemporaneously with the collections of Ossendrijver, Juun. J and Simons that I have reviewed). Sociologists such as Eric Anderson (2009), Ann-Dorte Christensen and Sune Qvotrup Jensen (Christensen and Jensen, 2014) as well as Richard de Visser (2009) have drawn attention to shifting practices of masculinity in contemporary European (British, Danish, Scandinavian) and American societies, suggesting that more inclusive, egalitarian masculinities were emerging and that orthodox forms of masculinity are losing their hegemony. Anderson, reporting on his extensive qualitative investigations, found that groups of young men were increasingly practicing masculinities in ways that are "less concerned with [policing] the expression of femininity among other men", that "displayed irreverence" for essentialist thinking, and even "questioned the usefulness of categorising things as gendered in the first place" (2009: 128).

In various ways all four of these academics have highlighted significant changes in the organizing structures of contemporary masculinity, especially in comparison to the early 1980s—the point at which Raewyn Connell formulated her highly influential theory of *hegemonic masculinity* in collaboration with a number of other writers (Connell et al., 1982; Carrigan et al., 1985).

Anderson's and Christensen and Jensen's more recent scholarship draws on Connell's insights into masculinity as part of a dynamic set of structures and practices but develops her theories in line with research conducted over the past decade.[3] Connell situates hegemonic masculinity within a hierarchical gender structure in which patriarchy is maintained through the oppression of women, the subordination of stigmatized masculinities, and the rejection and devaluation of feminine characteristics. She implicates the informal cultural "policing" of gender—including the idealization of a heroic, dominant, violent masculinity—in the maintenance of hegemonic masculinity and patriarchy. And, in an echo of Foucault's "discursive formations," she highlights the fact that masculinities are multiple, contested, and open to change (2005). In her 1987 text *Gender and Power* Connell argues that the creation of subordinated masculinities, made up of stigmatized groups like homosexuals who fail to meet the hegemonic ideal, is fundamental to the continuation and justification of patriarchy. She states that though the exaggerated, aggressive masculinity of film stars like John Wayne or Sylvester Stallone may hardly be typical, it nevertheless signifies a culturally sanctioned and idealized archetype against which other men are judged. In Connell's words, the "overall subordination of women requires the creation of a gender based hierarchy among men" (1987: 110). And thus masculinities can be classified within Connell's schema as being hegemonic, complicit, or subordinated.

Anderson, Christensen, and Jensen, however, have questioned the extent to which this tripartite form of masculinity persists. Strikingly, their qualitative studies not only have located multiple sites of resistance to hegemonic masculinity[4] but more significantly revealed, that by the late 2000s, orthodox, patriarchal masculinity had become so destabilized (at least in certain contexts) that it was being replaced by an inclusive, non-patriarchal form of masculinity, especially amongst young men. Anderson states:

> Men performing inclusive masculinities participate in tasks traditionally defined as feminine and support women who perform tasks traditionally defined as masculine. (2009: 101)

Christensen and Jensen find that: "the gender equality regimes of Scandinavian welfare states are succeeding in making masculinities dominant that do not in an unambiguous way contribute to the reproduction of patriarchy. Such 'new masculinities' may be said to dominate other masculinities" (2014: 70).

Meanwhile a recent YouGov poll of 1,692 adults (Dahlgreen, 2016) found conspicuous differences in the ways in which younger and older men valued "masculinity" and the extent to which they identified themselves as "masculine" (the terms were left to the respondents to define). YouGov found that only 2 percent of men in the 18–24 age bracket in the UK perceived themselves as "fully masculine" in comparison to 56 percent of over 65s. The poll found that masculinity was perceived negatively by 42 percent of young men aged 18–24 with only 39 percent of the demographic viewing it as a positive trait! Indeed, young women had a more positive view of masculinity than young men.

All of this research, particularly Anderson's extensive ethnographic fieldwork, points to real and significant changes in the structure of gender today, suggesting that men no longer internalize the values of orthodox masculinity as uniformly or as unquestioningly as hitherto. Inclusive, hybrid, anti-sexist, and metrosexual masculinities act as discursive formations through which men, especially young men, can construct or uncover subjectivities that feel more real, authentic, and meaningful to them. And both the YouGov poll and Richard de Visser's work provide evidence of a profound disenchantment with orthodox masculinity—as one of his respondents declared, "I'm not a very manly man, really. Like … it doesn't really grab me. It just seems a bit ludicrous to me, frankly" (anon cited in de Visser, 2009).

In this context, men's fashion has offered a set of discursive practices—ways of dressing, ways of framing the body and identity—that allow men to express alternative and inclusive masculinities and to resist and reject the narrow confines of orthodox masculinity. This new sense of permission is felt in Matthew Hall's account of *Metrosexual Masculinities* (2015) in which "metrosexuality" is found to give space for men to develop subjectivities that run counter to normative masculinity as well as in Margaret C. Ervin's earlier research (2011) in which she argues that metrosexual practices challenge the presumed "naturalness" of orthodox masculinity.

Yumiko Iida, writing of the emergence of highly style-conscious young men in contemporary Japan, states:

> The employment of feminine aesthetics and strategies by young men [...] provides them with a means to refute silently imposed ideological assignments and cultural expectations to reproduce the conventional masculine order in the cultural hegemony of Japanese society. In shifting my perspective this way, I view what is described by some as the "feminization of masculinity" as counter-hegemonic practices that challenge conventional masculine values and ideals upheld by the phallocentric hegemonic discourse. (2005: 57)

In this way, fashion practices are closely connected to an expanding repertoire of masculinities. As Iida and Hall attest, men use fashion to express alternative and inclusive forms of gender identity, while fashion as worn, as designed and as promoted frequently acts to refute, challenge, or deconstruct orthodox masculinity. As I have described, practitioners such as Ossendrijver and Juun. J—building on the work of Simons, Slimane, Capasa, and Lang—have taken apart, interrogated, and played with masculine archetypes in ways that unsettled and denaturalized them. Meanwhile, designers such as Alassandro Michele, J. W. Anderson, Grace Wales Bonner, Katie Eary, Charles Jeffrey, and Meadham Kirchhoff have introduced a provocatively queered and feminized menswear aesthetic that explicitly challenges the values of aggression, dominance, and invulnerability that characterize what Connell termed hegemonic masculinity. Grace Wales Bonner, whose work responds to the hyper-masculinized stereotyping of black men in popular culture, states:

> I've seen enough images of black men looking really aggressive, very hypersexualised or "street." That's not how I think about men at all. That's not the men in my life. (Wales Bonner cited in Madsen, 2015)

Androgyny in contemporary menswear

As I have described, the turn of the millennium sees a prodigious opening up of menswear as a site of creative expression for both fashion practitioners and consumers: key to this process was designers' flirtation with aesthetics coded as androgynous, feminine, or queer (McLellan and Rizzo, 2015). These tendencies are seen in the pared-back, dandyish designs of Slimane, Capasa, Simons, and Lang, with their close-cleaving silhouettes and flashes of skin in the early 2000s, and later in the increasingly colorful and flamboyant collections of labels such as Fendi, Dior Homme, Burberry Prorsum, Spastor, and Dries Van Noten during the mid-2000s. Some of the feeling for dandyish glamor seems to have dissipated in our current decade; nevertheless, as I have described, menswear practitioners have continued to explore, transgress, and deconstruct masculinity. Indeed, in recent years, androgyny on the catwalk has become ever more pronounced.

The strict binaries that underpin orthodox systems of gender define normative masculinity as much by what it is *not* as by what it is, and therefore tend to position anything not classed as masculine as de facto feminine. As Michael Kimmel says, "Masculine identity is born in the renunciation of the feminine, not in the direct affirmation of the masculine" (2005: 32). To this extent, the embrace of some level of androgyny has been fundamental to achieving innovation and dynamism in men's fashion, since new styles that sit outside classical twentieth-century menswear are frequently read as androgynous even if they emphasize the male body and even if they owe little to womenswear. Nevertheless, the deliberate, sometimes provocative, adoption of styles explicitly coded as feminine in contemporary men's fashion also owes its fascination to the note of danger that they communicate, since men who dress effeminately remain vulnerable to violence, and connectedly, because the policing of masculinity has rested upon the taboo of femininity. While womenswear borrowings from men's dress have become commonplace, the reverse proposition still carries with it a frisson of daring, transgression, and eroticism. As Siri Hustvedt suggests, "eroticism thrives on borders [...] the excitement of crossing into forbidden territory—the place you need special permission to trespass into" (2006: 46).

The liminal, hybrid nature of Grace Wales Bonner's work is founded not only on a playful transgression of gender boundaries, but also on a cross-fertilization of European and African aesthetics and more generally an exploration of black style. In the four collections from her debut Spring/Summer 2015 *Afrique* to her Autumn/Winter 2016 *Spirituals,* Wales Bonner has developed a distinctive set of codes referencing West Africa through cowrie shells, skull caps, opulent fabrics, and a high-waisted 1970s silhouette that recalls the photographs of Malick Sidibé and Samuel Fosso. A lush, bejeweled, neo-exoticist androgyny expresses itself in Wales Bonner's Chanel-style jackets —in their original iteration, men's tailoring reworked to become womenswear, here reappropriated and reintegrated into menswear: hybridized, embroidered with cowries and rendered in crushed velvet (Chandler and Wales Bonner, 2015). Wales Bonner's show notes refer to the Harlem Renaissance poet Langston Hughes and to the portraits of Carl Van Vechten as sources of inspiration (Wales Bonner, 2016). In her work, the flux, hybridity, ambiguity, and creative fertility of 1920s New York finds its echo in post-independence Africa—Mali, Cameroon, Côte d'Ivoire, and Ghana in the 1960s and 1970s (and more generally in a moment of Afrocentric political consciousness during the late 1960s and 1970s).

In Wales Bonner's Autumn/Winter 2015 collection *Ebonics,* crystal chokers gleamed against bare skin, while a white waistcoat and cummerbund worn without a shirt drew attention to the model's sinuous body—his bare arms sparkling with bijouterie and streaked in iridescent blue (Wales Bonner, 2015). Models both willowy and muscular, dark and lighter skinned, with conked or natural hair raised their fists, their hands dipped in glitter, in the a black-power salute. This subversion and rejection of normative masculinity on the part of Wales Bonner is felt all the more strongly since black masculinity has so often been caught within an ultra-macho, ultra-phallicized set of racist representations that deny full personhood to black men[5] (hooks, 2004b: 45–47, 63–79; Fanon, [1952] 1967: 196–202) or alternatively within the effacement of identity implied by assimilation.

Wales Bonner's Spring/Summer 2017 show *Ezekiel* built upon the dandyish, diasporic, androgynous aesthetic codes explored in her previous collections, but this time drew upon Ethiopian imperial garb to communicate a strong sense of refinement and elegance. Black evening dress—tailored jackets; high-collared shirts, some with white cravats; white capes with self-colored embroidery (Figure 5.11, Figure 5.12); and long pleated skirts followed an opening look consisting of an elongated tailored tunic in white (Figure 5.13). Later, a sumptuous white suit featured high-waisted trousers, short at the ankle like a toreador's, with an intricate pattern of palms embroidered the length of the leg; these were accompanied by a short, stand-collar jacket upon which fronds of intertwining trees, in satin cord, wound their way up the sleeves to bear fat garlands of pearls as their fruit (Figure 5.14). It was an ensemble that encapsulated the lushness, sensuality, and fecundity that is expressed in Wales Bonner's androgynous exoticism: her vision for a black masculinity liberated from racist and patriarchal norms.

As I have suggested, androgynous and feminine styles in men's dress have often carried with them an erotic charge and an association with queer sexuality. This eroticism, as Hustvedt suggests, lies in part in the transgression of gendered norms, but it also owes something to the sexualization and objectification of femininity as theorized by such figures as Laura Mulvey (1985) and Martha Nussbaum (1995). Mulvey's notion of the male gaze, as I have described, is predicated on the scopophilic pleasure the male subject finds in the female "object" of his gaze—with all the implications of power and control implied in this one-way transaction of looking. There are clearly limitations to Mulvey's concept, since it ignores oppositional ways of viewing a text (image, film) and assumes a heterosexual subject. Nevertheless, there remains a profound truth to her observation that looking and being looked at is a highly gendered activity deeply implicated in networks of power, knowledge, and pleasure. Thomas Waugh has suggested that the homoerotic gaze that developed in the nineteenth century often focused on the object of the "ephebe," the androgynous adolescent—a figure easily absorbed into existing systems of gendered looking and power—and thus, despite its taboo nature, homoerotic looking was not so structurally different from the heterosexual male gaze. It seems today, too, that male

Figure 5.11 Getty Images (2016) Grace Wales Bonner *Ezekiel* Spring/Summer 2017. London.

Figure 5.12 Getty Images (2016) Grace Wales Bonner *Ezekiel* Spring/Summer 2017. London.

THE SHOCK OF THE NEW

Figure 5.13 Getty Images (2016) Grace Wales Bonner *Ezekiel* Spring/Summer 2017. London.

Figure 5.14 Getty Images (2016b) Grace Wales Bonner *Ezekiel* Spring/Summer 2017. London.

androgyny or femininity attracts the gaze both because clothing perceived as feminine is often sexualizing—in the way it exposes or cleaves to the body and in the softness and drape of certain cloths—and also because femininity is coded as "to-be-looked-at-ness", in Mulvey's distinctive phrase. Androgynous menswear unsettles practices of gendered looking, rendering it unclear who is looking at whom and to what end, but it doesn't necessarily escape from the economy of power to which theorists of the gaze have drawn attention.

In this sense, as James Smalls (2013) and Grace Wales Bonner suggest, the eroticizing attention that seems to be invited by androgynous menswear can be liberating and progressive—it can disrupt existing systems of gender domination, and provide new sites of identification. But simultaneously, the objectifying nature of the gaze can, if we're not careful, also act as a form of subjugation humiliation, and denial of autonomy.

Anticipating Wales Bonner by several years—but perhaps without some of the intellectual drive that characterizes her work—(Jonathan) J. W. Anderson has consistently played with what he refers to as "sexual ambiguity" in his design. Debuting in 2008, Anderson's men's collections featured, variously, ornate jewelry, long quilted skirts, translucent open knitwear, sheer chiffon shorts, mica-like glistening surfaces, and transparent vests fashioned from multicolored leather lattices. The see-through elements that characterized his aesthetic, from 2008 to 2011, as well as his liberal borrowings from womenswear, spoke to a strange, sexualized effeminacy. But it was Anderson's Spring and Autumn 2013 menswear collections that cemented his reputation as *enfant terrible* and provocateur: organza and taffeta suits teamed with housewifely headscarves, shorts hemmed with oversize ruffles, basques and tube-tops, wellington boots with corrugated decorative edges, and white rubber gloves. There was something unnerving about an aesthetic that combined exaggerated feminine detailing with latex accessories, suggesting both domesticity and fetishism. And while Anderson is certainly an intelligent and thoughtful designer who successfully tapped into the zeitgeist—eventually being appointed to direct the Spanish luxury label Loewe—there remain questions around his motivation in exploring effeminacy. Unlike such figures as Slimane, Simons, and Wales Bonner whose embrace of androgyny was clearly linked to a desire to reform and open up masculinity, Anderson's interviews sometimes seem to hint at a cynicism. And while both Wales Bonner and Slimane[6] design garments that carry with them a strong sense of empowerment—Wales Bonner with her references to black artists and intellectuals and Slimane in his admiration for the rock musicians who model his collections—Anderson's designs, particularly for his own label, can seem humiliating, a joke at the expense of his models, an expression of power and control.

Workers of the world unite

As we know, the Slimane aesthetic, with its ties to rebellion and rock and roll, was developed at Dior Homme and then from 2012 to 2016 at Saint Laurent Paris. It retains a certain currency today: in a June 2016 article for the free daily London newspaper *Metro,* the model and musician Dougie Poynter, sporting a silver and gold leather biker jacket by Saint Laurent, black mesh top, ripped skinny jeans, assorted pendants and rings, and a pair of chunky-heeled Saint Laurent Chelsea boots, opines, "Hedi Slimane is like the second coming to me right now" (Poynter 2016, in Harmsworth 2016: 22). But it's notable that while the sexiness and glamor communicated by translucent fabrics, silver and gold leather, and a skinny silhouette remain popular, at least amongst certain young men in the public eye[7]—having moved from fashion journals into the popular press and from indie musicians onto more mainstream celebrities—the look has lost some of its edgy sense of surprise. Slimane's vision—fine drapey fabrics, shrunken tailoring, rock and punk influences, and touches of androgyny—came to dominate 2000s men's fashion. But as menswear has continued to expand and diversify, the 2010s has witnessed both an evolution of some of these tendencies and, particularly at the level of silhouette, a break from them.

Fashion moves in trends and counter-trends and so amongst the increasing foppishness of the late 2000s—jewel colors, tight trousers, satin lapels, cowl necks, and patent leather shoes—an altogether quieter aesthetic was emerging. By 2010, fashionable brands such as Our Legacy, Albam, YMC, Bleu de Paname, and Engineered Garments were exploring a look with a strong emphasis on traditional fabrication, detailing which heavily referenced workwear, and hippyish, folk-inspired touches, particularly in knit. And while this style was associated with specific designers and labels, its origin lay in fashionable dress as worn on the street by creative people who mixed secondhand, customized, and reclaimed garments, as well as carefully sourced contemporary pieces, to achieve their own look.

This shift towards a folky-workwear aesthetic in menswear—all chambrays, twills, *bleu de travail*, patch pockets, double-needle, and run-and-fell seams—revealed an intriguing desire to engage with the process of manufacture and make. Magazines such as *Monocle,* founded in 2007, and *Inventory,* founded in 2009 (the latter, in particular, an important early adopter and innovator of this style), spent as much time explaining to their readers how garments and accessories had been crafted, as discussing their visual qualities. Their photographers lovingly captured images of workshops: calloused hands gripping tailor's sheers or hammering leather uppers onto lasts, industrial machines, orbital sanders, and concrete floors. This was a look that favored texture (and even coarseness) over smooth, lustrous, or drapey fabrics; there was a sense in which the consumer wanted to see evidence of how the fabric had been woven or knitted, how and by whom the garment had been manufactured. It is perhaps significant that this desire for something perennial, authentic, and solid emerged at the same time as uncertainty in the global economic system came to the fore in the shape of the 2008 credit crunch and its subsequent after effects.

A photograph from Autumn/Winter 2013 (Figure 5.15) typifies the *Inventory* look. It depicts a tall, bearded (rather un-modellish) model shot against the backdrop of a tarmacadam forecourt; he wears a grey boiled wool, three-button rever jacket by Engineered Garments with large patch pockets, a reinforced stitching detail at the shoulder and topstitched cuffs and lapels. The jacket is layered over a worker's cotton twill jacket, and an untucked white shirt with a

Figure 5.15 Kassam, F. (2013) "Fall/Winter Look Book," *Inventory*. Available at: http://thecvrator.com/inventory-magazine-2013-fallwinter-editorial.

curved opening at the hem; the model wears jeans with turned up cuffs and, no doubt, with the selvedge edge on the outside seam; as well as thick soled, welted and handstitched tan Derby shoes by Trickers. It's an outfit that speaks powerfully of the past while being unmistakably of the 2010s, and one that evokes quality, simplicity, and discernment.

For consumers, the advantages of a style that conjured up an image of an early twentieth century industrial or agricultural worker was that it allowed them to engage in fashion, to look a bit different, while adopting a subdued and, in many ways, traditionally masculine aesthetic. But the concern for construction, provenance, and authenticity implied by this look (and the brands that catered to it) also spoke to a much wider interest in craft and making that emerged in the late 2000s and early 2010s. In 2011 the Victoria and Albert Museum put on a show entitled the *Power of Making* with the express aim of placing craft, skill, and construction at the center of economic, educational, and creative discourses, to make the case, in the words of design historian Martina Margetts:

> that making is a revelation of the human impulse to explore and express forms of knowledge and a range of emotions; an impulse towards knowing and feeling [...] The reward of making is the opportunity to experience an individual sense of freedom and control in the world (2011: 39).

The exhibition provided a focal point for a wider movement of craftspeople, designers, and scholars (Adamson, 2007; Schwarz and Elffers, 2010; Frayling, 2011; Gauntlett, 2011; Harrod, 2015) who argued that reconnecting with making as a meaningful activity was essential to combat challenges of sustainability and to counter the profound sense of alienation wrought by globalized, post-Fordist systems of manufacture, consumption, and distribution.

And while the menswear look associated with this moment may be somewhat on the wane—now more frequently combined with sportswear and hypebeastly "athleisure" garments—its continued currency is no doubt closely linked to this broader cultural tendency, the concept of "peak stuff" and the notion that one should consume in a more deliberate, conscientious manner and in smaller quantities. This renewed foregrounding of construction (especially as expressed in workwear references) has also inflected upon the work of high end designers as diverse as Lucas Ossendrijver, J. W. Anderson, and, latterly, the label *du jour* Vetements, albeit in a less nostalgic and literal fashion.

The discourse around hipsters that arose in the late 2000s and early 2010s tended to stigmatize this approach to menswear by associating it with gentrification: an association, as I have argued, that not only confounds cause and effect, but which also betrays a set of rather sexist assumptions. And while it is easy to critique this consumption of craft as a co-option of something "authentic" by commercial forces—or to point to the unintended ironies of pseudo-proletarian getups—the sneering discussions of hipsters and "lumbersexuals" in the press and in popular discourse more generally have tended to obscure the positive, progressive aspects of this menswear aesthetic: truth to materials, an emphasis upon making, and the idea that work should be a meaningful activity.

Athleisure

In addition to androgyny and a renewed interest in craft and making, the 2010s have seen sportswear styles in various forms, along with elements of 1990s retro, increasingly finding their place within designer menswear. This shift towards sportswear represents a significant departure from the dressed-up dandyism of the 2000s (although the very slim trouser silhouette of the previous decade has persisted reinterpreted as leggings and jogging bottoms).

At the turn of the millennium the loud branded sportswear of the 1990s— its amorphous shapes and brash logos once associated with subculture and streetwear—had come to signify merely a gauche and somewhat vulgar commercialism. The look was swept aside by a tide of skinny tailoring, and rock and roll references. Indeed, a unifying theme of the aesthetic tendencies of the 2000s, from nostalgic dandyism to tight fitting garments and references to punk and glam, was their departure from anything that resembled mid-1990s casual wear. And while loud branding and garish color-ways were seen less and less on the catwalk and between the pages of fashion magazines, sports apparel companies were in a process of reform: repositioning themselves as culturally engaged lifestyle brands producing technologically sophisticated performance garments. Prada Sport, founded in the late 1990s, reimagined athletic clothing as chic, streamlined, and monochrome. And activewear companies began to work with high-profile designers, such as the joint venture between Yohji Yamamoto and adidas resulting in the launch of Y-3 in 2002. Since then collaborations between sports apparel brands and fashion designers have proliferated: Raf Simons with Adidas and Eastpack, Kim Jones with Umbro, Public School and Riccardo Tisci with Nike, Tim Coppens with Under Armour, Rick Owens with Adidas, and so on.

Perhaps as a result of these shifts, sportswear references have increasingly been reabsorbed into contemporary menswear, including designer collections, as a way of gesturing to modernity, progress, and to a more flexible, comfortable way of dressing (WGSN, 2016a). We can look to practitioners like Neil Barratt and Alexander Wang as innovators of a hybrid wardrobe in which high-tech garments, tailoring, and elements of casual dress are combined with an increasing freedom, as well as to designers such as Riccardo Tisci, whose Spring/Summer 2012 menswear collection—with its boxy silhouette, baseball caps, airtex, and buff models— reclaimed the late 1990s sport and streetwear look, but rendered it modern with the use of oversized botanic prints, skirts, and sequins. For 2014, Tisci went further, combining digital prints of collaged mechanical elements (notably cassette tapes and boom boxes) with Masai colorways, leggings layered under shorts and dramatically patterned tailored jackets: all this, together with his models' faces, painted with stylized aeroplanes, seemed to evoke a futuristic, tribal society, or perhaps a rogue skater gang: an exoticism of a type, but a benign one (Faudi, 2013).

As well as this renewed interest in sportswear on the catwalk, we can also look to a more organic resurgence of sneaker culture and streetwear as reflected in the founding of the hugely popular and influential website Hypebeast in 2005. The site lovingly details the ins and outs of newly released trainers and streetwear garments as well as commenting upon hip-hop and skater culture. And in this way, Hypebeast both firmly places sportswear in the context of desirable, high-end consumer goods and simultaneously situates the clothing within a rhetoric of subculture and authenticity (one that acknowledges the significance of hip-hop and other subcultures in the development, dissemination, and popularity of trainers sportswear). This dual function is particularly strongly felt in the user comments beneath the site's articles, in which the merits, demerits, and authenticity claims of garments are hotly debated. And this amplification of discourse around sportswear has contributed both to the advent of new sportswear oriented designer labels and the expansion of cult brands such as Stone Island and Supreme (Leach, 2016).

One could argue that there was nothing new about sportswear's absorption into mainstream fashion. The process can be traced back to the adoption of adidas basketball sneakers amongst hip-hop and proto-hip-hop subcultures in late 1970s and 1980s New York (Shabazz, 2002; Turner, 2014); to British "football casuals" in the 1980s with their fondness for expensive European sportswear like Sergio Tacchini; to the popularization of jeans, canvas basketball shoes and sporting apparel in 1950s and 1960s America, and even to the fashion for knitwear, jersey, and sporting dress in the 1920s and 1930s. What is new, however, is the degree of interconnectedness between what would once have been seen as distinct markets and groups of consumers, as well as the freedom with which sporting garments are combined with other types of clothing. This integration of sportswear garments and techniques into fashion proper, points to contemporary social and economic shifts in which the boundaries between work and leisure have become more porous and diffuse. Designers are keen to mine sporting and active apparel because it represents the field in which research around materials, fabrics, and manufacturing processes is at its apotheosis: sportswear brands have the infrastructure and resources to manufacture fibers, spin yarns, and knit cloths that hold new and unexpected possibilities, and their advanced methods of garment construction—with eliminated, displaced, taped, and flat-locked seams—suggest new formal possibilities. Similarly, sports apparel companies are no longer exclusively manufacturing and product design entities and are now much more engaged with aesthetics and with the lifestyles and aspirations of their consumers.

Meanwhile, fashion in general has shifted away from the dandyism that dominated the 2000s and towards a more casual, layered aesthetic that embraces elements of sporting apparel—leggings worn under shorts, jersey sweatpants, hoods, zippers, trainers—though sometimes paired with more tailored pieces. Part of this shift is to do with nostalgia (and the demographic of young practitioners currently gaining success) as designers such as Gosha Rubchinskiy and Nasir Mazhar draw knowingly on precisely the brash branding and vulgarity that precipitated 1990s sportswear's fall from grace. Rubchinskiy's designs of geometrically patterned shell suits; high-waisted sweatpants; satiny shorts and vests; turquoise, lime green, and red colorways; and be-logoed sportswear—along with his use of skinny teenage models—speak of the turbulence of the Perestroika-era Soviet Union and of the period of confusion, desperation, and creativity that accompanied its collapse in the 1990s as Western fashions flooded in.

Mazhar's Spring/Summer 2014 collection was emblazoned with his logo appearing on the pink terry toweling of a tracksuit, on the waistbands of boxer shorts (worn several inches above the models' low slung trousers), and on baseball caps and socks (Mazhar, 2013). These autographed elements were combined with cropped shirts that revealed the models' midriffs, as well as glittering holographic materials, and straps and braces against the models' bare skin. Mazhar celebrates 1990s sportswear, but amps up and revels in its ostentation to produce something transcendently joyous in its repudiation of "good taste." And in his ethnically and morphologically diverse model casting, too, there was an inclusivity connected to Mazhar's interest in subculture and grime music—a gesture against the conventional strictures of the fashion industry (Healy, 2016).

With a more sinister ambiance than Mazhar, the avant-garde New York brand Hood by Air, designed by Shayne Oliver, riffs off sportswear in sometimes bizarre and unexpected ways: asymmetric deconstructed garments, trailing sleeves, awkward proportions, and borrowings from fetish clothing including PVC, leather, chaps, and cutouts. In a similar vein to Oliver's work, Vetements collections designed by Demna Gvasalia take the familiar—hoodies and logoed T-shirts—and defamiliarize them by scaling them up and combining them with patched and reconstructed garments. In this way, designers Rubchinskiy, Mazhar, Oliver, and Gvasalia have reinstated some of the edginess to contemporary sportswear that originally accompanied its adoption by subcultures. Hip-hop and football casual youth cultures appropriated garments intended to be worn by athletes as well as branded, high-end goods that signified dominant, mainstream values. But when these garments were worn on raced and classed bodies that sat outside the hegemonic "ideal" (and the brands' own expected demographics), styled and combined in novel ways, they shifted in meaning: remaining symbols of aspiration, but also taking on connotations of rebellion, resistance, and (amongst the casuals especially) violence.

Deconstructing tailoring

Perhaps a more overarching tendency than avant-garde designers' reinvestment of edginess and danger in sportswear has been a much more general breakdown between formerly distinct genres and types of clothing. *Vogue's* Luke Leitch, writing in 2016, describes the waning significance of the conventional "city suit" as fewer men are obliged by their workplaces to wear one. Leitch interviewed various designers who emphasize that, amongst the risks to the menswear sector that these shifts bring, there are major opportunities, too, as design houses are free to develop more imaginative responses to the male wardrobe. Stefano Canali of Canali suggests that the "uniform market" in which customers buy suits because they are obliged to do so is in decline, but other markets are opening up. This view is echoed by Stefano Gabbana of Dolce and Gabbana who states that "What we are selling very, very well is elegant, interesting, and individual tuxedos. And sportswear. But the normal suits? People don't want those." Elsewhere Brunello Cucinelli offers a "jogger style" drawstring trouser to match his tailored jackets, while Paul Smith's lightweight suits come with trousers in the same cloth but in a myriad range of non-matching colors, an approach that has also enjoyed success, with Smith stating that "our suit sales have actually gone up" (Canali, Gabbana, Cucinelli, and Smith, 2016 cited in Leitch, 2016).

For Spring/Summer 2017 Lanvin, Prada, Hermès, and others offered suiting worn with knitwear, T-shirts, trainers, and parkas or accessorized with backpacks and nylon straps. Sportif "lifestyle" brand Tommy Hilfiger proposed lightweight blazers and floral print trousers, jackets, and anoraks, as well as tailored trousers with vividly colored tuxedo stripes along the outside seam. And at the cheaper end of the market, Topman Design was in on the act too layering track tops under suits and styling them with trainers.

For the same season, E. Tautz, the "ready to wear fashion label with a Savile Row aesthetic" had moved decisively away from this former signature look of nostalgic tailoring (Etautz.com, 2017). The preppy, 1930s-ish double-breasted jackets, button-down collars and bow-ties, that had characterized early collections, were replaced with collarless shirts in bold abstract stripes; deep-pleated, high-waisted shorts coming to the mid-thigh; oversized woven T-shirts with diagonal seams, and T-bar sandals (Figure 5.16, Figure 5.17). Tailored jackets and trousers still formed part of the collection, but the way of styling and assembling these pieces had radically changed.

In response to these shifts, established Italian tailoring houses like Brioni, Canali, and Corneliani—sensing a move away from traditional suits—have proposed more casual, decorative, and sportswear inflected collections on the runway for the past several seasons: billowing windbreakers, matching trousers and T-shirts, sandals and trainers mixed in amongst more formal

Figure 5.16 Getty Images (2016). *E. Tautz Spring/Summer 2017*. London.

Figure 5.17 Getty Images (2016). *E. Tautz Spring/Summer 2017*. London.

garments creating a look reminiscent of Lucas Ossendrijver's collections for Lanvin a few years previously. But for Spring 2017, under the pressure of falling sales, Brioni's new (and short-lived) creative director Justin O'Shea attempted a different tack. The result was a strange, vulgarized version of Tom Ford's Gucci with added fur and alligator skin, but without the sartorial knowledge that had underpinned Ford's assured style. It was a collection so crass that even the "gangsters" O'Shea claimed he wanted to attract failed to be impressed (O'Shea, 2016 cited in Sajonas, 2016) and, after 400 job cuts were proposed in response to continued underperformance, O'Shea was ejected (Abraham, 2016; Turra, 2016).

Nevertheless, it would be quite wrong to think that the lounge suit was in its final death throes. For Spring/Summer 2017, the buoyant sales of Paul Smith and Dolce and Gabbana's colorful tailoring was reflected in a similarly upbeat trend report for the prediction agency WGSN, who suggested, "Traditional tailoring and modern sartorial dressing remain a growth area in menswear. Fresh styling ideas and mass appeal from familiar cuts are in equal supply" (WGSN, 2016b: 2). In the accompanying photographs, single-button suits in light greys, caramel hues, and vivid blue—along with shawl-collared tuxedos in black and off-white—are teamed with trainers to lend them an informal air. Suits appear in light pink, worn with open-necked patterned shirts or T-shirts, in crumpled linen, or double-breasted in cream, grey, and deep purple. And while some of the less colorful suits featured in the report are perfectly conventional, their styling lends them a freer, more contemporary feeling that demonstrates, as WGSN puts it, a "mov[e] away from the traditional rules around tailoring" (2016b: 11).

Fashion-conscious men are quite happy to buy suits, it seems, but they want them to be fun, flexible, and free from arcane etiquette of the "never wear brown in town" variety. To paraphrase designer Thom Browne, tailoring today must be something men actually want to wear, not something they feel they have to wear (Browne, 2016 cited in Leitch, 2016). In this way, the contemporary men's market is in a process of reintegrating tailoring, casual clothing, and sportswear, a process which, in offering a much greater variety of options to men, represents a shift away from some of the assumptions about menswear that predominated throughout much of the twentieth century. As well as representing innovation and novelty, there are also echoes of the past in this process. In the eighteenth and early nineteenth centuries—a period of social and sartorial flux which gave birth to men's tailoring as we know it[8]—fashionable men's dress borrowed extensively from military uniform and from equestrian clothing, while garments like trousers—which in 1800 would only have been suitable for casual pursuits—became gradually accepted as smart dress (Rothstein et al., 1984: 58–64; Breward, 2016: 40–44).

The new monasticism

After a period in which men's clothing moved closer and closer to the body, clutching and holding it in a tight embrace, at the beginning of this new decade, garments began to release their tight grip as a new spirit of airiness and capaciousness slowly began to emerge. A shift in silhouette is already visible in the work of Lucas Ossendrijver and Damir Domar from about 2010 onward, as fluid volumes of draping cloth begin to swathe the angular frames of their young models. But, from around 2012 a decisively new silhouette emerges in designer menswear; in stark contrast to Slimane's "thin, straight line" which dominated the 2000s, outfits instead adopt a billowing monastic form: architectural volumes built up from the shoulders and falling in stiff folds; padded, abstracted shapes that speak of Kabuki Theatre; American football; and esoteric religious rites. In the work of designers such as Craig Green, Juun. J, Nicomede Talavera, Rory Parnell Mooney, and Ximon Lee, there is a decisive move away from the familiar cut of men's tailoring (and even from recognizable sportswear garments) in favor of references to Greek Orthodox headdresses, martial arts uniforms, Korean *hanbok*, and South Asian *salwar kameez* representing a "Re-Orientation" away from the classic forms of Western menswear.

Green's Autumn/Winter 2012 MA graduate collection for Central Saint Martins exemplifies this new aesthetic tendency, featuring large geometric volumes, slung from the back, like a peddler's pack, to create a dramatic silhouette (Kuryshchuk, 2012). Both these geometric forms and the simple tunic-like garments with which they are paired feature digital prints initially developed by projecting light onto prototype garments (toiles). Like Green, Ximon Lee's billowing pleated, deconstructed forms are informed by process:

> building [an idea] from paper to a three dimensional object: I felt so obsessed [...] This collection I was exploring all different kinds of, you know, denim materials and how different colours can be extracted from the indigo (Antonioli.eu, 2015)

And like Juun. J, Lee adopts an approach that abstracts away from recognizable menswear forms like the shirt—massively exaggerating the collar, opening up the side seams, stiffening the fabric with interfacing, and using run and fell seams and patched pockets to create latticed textural effects.

The work of these young designers recollects the radicalism of the "Japanese invasion" of the late 1970s and early 1980s—Rei Kawakubo, Junya Watanabe, Issey Miyake, Yohji Yamamoto—as well as the Antwerp 6—both groups bringing a much-needed strangeness to Franco-Italian fashion hegemony,[9] but it is a mark of how far men's fashion as a discipline has come that today, some of the

Figure 5.18 Pruchnie, B. (2016) Craig Green Spring/Summer 2017. London.

most innovative designers are primarily menswear practitioners. Green, Juun. J, and Lee are heirs to those quintessential "designers' designers" Raf Simons, Helmut Lang, and Martin Margeila: practitioners whose work is characterized by an interest in form and process more than in product, and whose collections often require an understanding of garment construction—especially how this is being played with or subverted—in order to be read and understood. In Figure 5.1 Green's homage to Helmut Lang's 1990s oeuvre is made particularly explicit.

If Slimane's sexy, dandified vision for menswear was the quintessence of a new millennial optimism, Lee, Juun. J, and Green's aesthetic propositions seem to relate to a much more ambivalent and stranger set of millenarian visions—ones that—in the wake of financial crises, a disintegrating Middle East, repeated European and American foreign policy failures, and declining living standards—speak to the nihilism that is the flip side of fashion's customary glamor. And while the rock and roll dandy lives on as a recognizable archetype in fashion collections, he no longer feels so fresh and relevant. Rather, a type of creative destruction—deconstructing menswear only to put it back together again—has become the order of the day (Figure 5.18).

Creatively, in the manner of moving sculptures, these formal experiments on the body are refreshing and fascinating, but unlike the work of Slimane—which was relatively easily "re-interpreted" by high street labels in cheaper fabrics—the degree to which the work of Juun. J, Lee, and Green is likely to impact on mainstream menswear, as more widely worn, remains open to question. In a nod to this new silhouette, long robe-like coats made up in a lightweight cotton, and worn indoors, as well as tunic-like tops and T-shirts, are already a discernable trend amongst the fashion cognoscenti (and long oversized robe-like coats and cardigans are already available at a Zara near you) but we still await a popularizer of this new aesthetic who can translate it into a more generally applicable form.

Perhaps part of the reason for the emergence of this new abstracted silhouette (as in the late 1970s and 1980s in womenswear) is the increasing internationalization of fashion. Designers like Ximon Lee, Juun. J, and Sean Suen, sometimes implicitly and sometimes more explicitly, draw upon non-Western sartorial forms and approaches to cut and construction in creating their distinctive aesthetics. Even where similar garments are worn across different cultures and continents the precise meanings of these pieces of clothing, the ways in which they are worn, and their history within that particular culture, are highly specific and nuanced: the language of fashion is subject to subtle lexical shifts as it moves across borders. As an increasing number of practitioners hail from outside Europe and North America, the dominant "common sense" understandings of menswear, the meanings ascribed to specific garments and styles, as well as

THE SHOCK OF THE NEW

technical approaches used to make them, will no doubt continue to evolve, transform, and become subject to hybridizing, creolizing forces.

The designer Ali Abdulrahim of Mai Gidah—whose beautiful and intricately paneled designs I mention in my introduction—is indicative of this internationalization of fashion (Figure 5.19). His work bears traces of both Ghana and Belgium as he described during an interview I undertook with him:

Figure 5.19 Abdulrahim, A. and Sels, T. (2015). Mai Gidah Spring/Summer 2016. London.

I'm Ghanaian but I'm also Belgian and I live in London. So it's all intertwined in my work, and these cultural influences come out without me necessarily being aware of them. The abstract, architectural silhouette definitely relates to my training in Sint-Niklaas, but I think it also relates to the way that people dress in Ghana. For instance, my mother even on a hot, hot day would never wear fewer than three layers of cloth—and layering and mixing different fabrics is key to my work. In my tribe, in my family, the clothes that are worn are really structured. And the textures are those of stiff, waxy African fabrics, like the waxed head wraps *gele*.

But the last collection for Autumn/Winter 2016/2017 was initially inspired by the Flemish Primitives, and by Van Eyck specifically. A lot of the paintings are still there in Gent, which Thomas [Sels, Ali's collaborator] and I visited recently. I love the art of that era, and so the rich colours of the collection were drawn from Van Eyck's palette. (Abdulrahim, 2016 [interviewed in] McCauley Bowstead, 2016)

The shock of the new

The inventive and expressive nature of men's fashion over the past two decades echoes earlier periods of radicalism and change in menswear—notably the youth style of the 1960s and 1970s, as well as the avant-garde aesthetics associated with 1980s subculture: these previous moments of inventive and dynamic men's fashion represent the progenitors of today's exciting scene. And as in these earlier periods, changes in men's dress have occurred in tandem with social shifts that have both augured and reflected evolving attitudes to masculinity. It would be wrong, however, to imagine that this current flowering of creativity is simply a brief interlude after which men's clothing will inevitably return to a perennially unchanging form (if indeed such a form existed). The practice of masculinity has simply transformed too radically in the West over the course of the past several decades for the kinds of orthodox, normative standards implicit in "classic menswear"[10] to persist unquestioned.

Menswear exists in dialog with the beliefs, values, and aspirations of men and of society more generally, feeding into and contributing to discourses surrounding gender and identity. *L'Uomo Vogue*'s *"Nuovi Papa"* (New Dads) feature, published in 1971, in which young fathers were photographed along with their offspring and described their approach to childcare, represented an intriguing example of the intersection between fashion, lifestyle, and shifting attitudes to masculinity in a period prior to the invention of the New Man (but in which many of his essential features were beginning to take shape). At the time, fathers who took their daughters to nursery were clearly seen as a novelty (Toscani, 1971: 102–104), but they were pioneers of a new style of fatherhood.

In recent years, as the research of sociologists such as Cornelia Behnke and Michael Meuser (2012: 129–145) suggests, forms of involved fatherhood—including those in which the father is the primary carer—have become more common.[11] The research of Eric Anderson (2009) and others, reviewed earlier in this chapter, points to a very real dissatisfaction with orthodox models of masculinity amongst young men in particular, and a desire to escape its confines and limitations. The set of attitudinal shifts Anderson explores in *Inclusive Masculinities* may not be precisely analogous to those described in the growing body of literature surrounding involved fatherhood, but both point to masculinities in the twenty first century that are becoming more plural and diverse.

As writers Mechtild Oechsle, Ursula Müller, and Sabine Hess have stated, "the period in which changes in gender relations and images was restricted solely to the modernization of women's lives is now drawing to a close" (2012: 10). In public, family, health, and industrial policy the structural barriers and normative codes that have impeded gender equality by trapping men within "traditional" roles are at last beginning to be recognized and investigated. In commerce too—as the marketers quoted at the beginning of this chapter suggest—new kinds of products, services, and indeed identities are increasingly being sold to men. By moving beyond the orthodox models of masculinity of the early twentieth century, businesses and entrepreneurs have found themselves able to access a previously untapped, underexploited reserve of consumers. While in previous economic downturns, like that of the early 1990s, men's fashion was hit hard; the menswear market continued to grow and expand during and after the 2008 financial crash. According to the market research company Euromonitor, the value of menswear sales has increased by 70 percent worldwide since 1998 (Bailey, 2015).

It is important to remember that fashion is not only worn, but also styled, photographed, and disseminated via a myriad of digital and analogue a channels. Fashionably attired men gaze out from between the pages of glossy magazines, from websites, blogs, and from billboards on the street and in the subway. This proliferation of high-fashion imagery means that designer menswear is increasingly influential—a simultaneously élite and popular medium—available only to a few in its commodity form, but accessed by millions as images, videos, and knock-off garments. And as such, it exerts a powerful influence on the ways in which men conceive of their bodies, their identities, and the ways in which they experience aesthetic and sensual pleasure. While actually buying a Dior Homme or a Grace Wales Bonner jacket is something few of us can afford to do, inspirational and influential images of these designs are available in magazines for a few dollars or euros and whole collections can be viewed completely gratis online.

Moreover, the notion that design-led fashion automatically equates to expense has been challenged by stores like Topman in the UK (and America) and retailers such as Aland in South Korea, who combine inventive and directional design with affordable prices. Unlike the 1960s and 1970s when relatively affordable youth-oriented clothing led the way, designer menswear has been the major site of innovation in men's fashion over the past two decades. But, the high street has followed where Dior Homme and Yves Saint Laurent have led. This proliferation of men's fashion imagery, the accelerated rate at which trends move from the runway to mass market, along with the new possibilities facilitated by e-commerce, have all helped to popularize men's fashion.

CONCLUSION

As I write this conclusion in 2017, men's fashion remains a dynamic, energetic, and innovative field of practice. On the Paul Smith catwalk for Spring/Summer 2018, for instance, a fantastic sense of fun, color, and excitement could be seen: high-waisted trousers with multiple pleats appeared in vivid burnt orange, paired with fluid drape jackets in fuchsia and acid yellow. Bowling shirts, intarsia knit, trousers and shoes were patterned with oversized poppies, fish and fronds of seaweed, creating an 1980s-tinged fantasia.

At Rick Owens, a futuristic mood prevailed: models wore sleeveless tunics with ballooning woven panels, some in transparent mesh, teamed with shorts; space-age, slouchy, sneaker-boots; and utilitarian bags and pouches strapped to the legs and thighs to create a strange bulging silhouette.

These two collections, and many others of the same season, point to the continued vibrancy of menswear, which, over the past two decades, has explored and interrogated masculinity more engagingly and thoughtfully than any other field of creative practice.

With the transgressive example of subculture as their model, designers from the turn of the millennium to the present day have used menswear to advance a form of "reverse discourse": challenging the values of orthodox masculinity by reclaiming and reframing qualities such as fragility, sensitivity, and sensuality as positive and desirable. I have explored the ways in which this "reverse discourse" was central to the early work of Hedi Slimane, Raf Simons, and Helmut Lang, designers who—quite literally—sheared away and deconstructed conventional men's dress to reveal something new and enlivened.

Over the past two decades, as sociologists such as Eric Anderson (2009) and Christensen and Jensen (2014) have demonstrated, contemporary masculinity has been significantly reformed, opening up to become more inclusive and more plural as young men, in particular, have become increasingly disenchanted with orthodox gender values and instead embraced more inclusive, egalitarian forms of masculinity. This realignment is reflected across a range of attitudinal data collected using a variety of methodologies (Anderson, 2009; de Visser, 2009; Dahlgreen, 2016). The transformation of men's fashion, which has been the subject of this book, has acted both to catalyze these shifts (by creating new forms of subjectivity, experience, and new patterns of consumption for men) and simultaneously to reflect the movement of broader cultural tectonics.

The dynamism of menswear in recent years has owed much to an embrace of innovation and flux. The dogma that men's clothing must remain conservative, perennial, and unchanging has waned and, as a result, menswear has opened up to become a field in which men are able to express and explore identity, to fashion and refashion themselves. The sense that men's fashion had become a space of self-actualization and self-expression is felt in many of the garments and collections that I have reviewed over the course of this text, and it is also felt in the way that contemporary designers, from the turn of the millennium onward, spoke about and conceptualized their work. In 2001, Hedi Slimane suggested, "A men's collection can be creative, desirable, enlivened [...] Menswear can become fashion too. I don't think this should be forbidden for men." Twelve years later, Lucas Ossendrijver declared his aim was to "make clothes that are special, that are different, that are not a uniform [...] For me clothes are a means to express your personality." In the same year, Raf Simons articulated an almost identical set of concerns, stating that his collection was about avoiding "the obligation to be dressed in a uniform" and instead "about the freedom that a man has to express himself" (Slimane, 2001, cited by Cabasset, 2001: 70; Ossendrijver, 2013, cited in Barneys New York, 2013; Simons cited in Levy, 2013: 160).

These statements represent a flight from uniformity towards a new plurality in both menswear and in cultures of masculinity more broadly. Over the past decades, notwithstanding a vociferous reactionary backlash, notions of masculinity as essentially unchanging, conformist, single, and unified have been on the wane—theorists of gender increasingly use the term "masculinities" to reflect the plural nature of male identities.

Nevertheless, it would be complacent to suggest that the explosion in new forms of masculine subjectivity through dress and fashion represents unequivocal evidence of sexism's demise for good. Paradoxically, the increased visibility of aggressively reactionary forms of masculinity—most powerfully symbolized by the election of Donald Trump—has coincided with radically inclusive forms of gender identity of the sort described by Eric Anderson. And these two mutually opposing forms of gendered practice point to the fragility and internal contradictions of orthodox masculinity which, delinked from its economic basis, becomes either an exaggerated and self-conscious form of bravado, or is replaced by something else. The achievements of men's fashion since the turn of the millennium form an integral part of a process of contestation: new modes of representation and practice that have acted, and continue to act, to repudiate essentialist dogmas of gender. As Margaret Ervin puts it in her account of the of the 2000s:

Every response to the metrosexual is revealing of the panic that ensues when gender is defined as fluid rather than fixed, or as contingent rather than natural [...] Thus, when the metrosexual who both does and does not act straight is proven by marketing surveys to exist, badass defenders rush to reclaim masculinity as an essential category and to deny the possibility of this other masculinity. (Ervin, 2011: 71)

In this sense, the reverse tendency, to underplay the very real changes in men's identities that have taken place in recent decades, is if anything even more dangerous because it delegitimizes and effaces the inclusive forms of masculinity that *have* emerged, and implies that gender inequality is inevitable.[1]

The importance of fashion in activating, opening up, and making space for new subjectivities can be seen in the qualitative research of scholars Ben Barry and Barbara Phillips (2016: 17–34) who found that engaging with images of fashionably dressed male models enabled their participants to "express new masculine identities" (2016: 30). Cultural theorists such as Yumiko Iida (2005) and Margaret Ervin (quoted above) have also located men's fashion as a site in which orthodox forms of masculinity are refuted and challenged.

As with all periods of progressive cultural change, the shifts that have animated menswear in recent decades relate to previous moments of radicalism—not least the earlier menswear revolution of the 1960s and 1970s, with its experimentation at the level of form, silhouette, color, and fabrication. The vivid, playful, formally inventive menswear of the middle and late 1960s and early 1970s, in particular, grew out of a period of affluence and of rapidly changing social attitudes. As I have argued, there are clear continuities between the project to reform masculinity that emerged out of the "men's liberation" discourses of the 1970s, the New Man of the 1980s, and more contemporary shifts in the conception of male identity. It is perhaps not surprising, then, that contemporary fashion practitioners have turned continually to the 1970s as a source of inspiration. To this extent, the innovation on the catwalk of recent years can be seen as the fruition of a set of processes set in motion many decades previously, a process of reform that has been strenuously resisted by essentialists of various stripes, but which has nevertheless exerted a considerable impact on men's fashion and on cultures of masculinity more generally.

So what does the future of menswear hold? After a prolonged period of expansion and change, perhaps the rate of innovation will slow, but it seems unlikely—the genie having escaped the bottle—that men's fashion will return to the periphery it occupied during the 1990s or to the dogma of an unchanging sartorialism that once held sway. In contrast to other periods of economic uncertainty—for example the early 1990s—menswear in the aftermath of the 2008 credit crunch continued to expand at rapid rate as designers continued to propose creative and inventive collections. In addition to the changes in masculinity that I have discussed, the advent of digital, networked, instant communication on a global scale has created online communities of men's fashion aficionados and instigated a proliferation of discourse, all of which has tended to drive the dynamism of the sector.

Contemporary menswear has been characterized by increasing choice and diversity both at the high end of the market and on the high street, but there remains plenty of room for greater experimentation and for expansion: while the youth market represents a dynamic and creative space, older customers seeking distinctive menswear outside of traditional tailoring and conventional casual styles remain poorly served. There remains a problematic assumption within the industry that men of middle age and older must, automatically, wish to dress in conventional and understated clothing.

After a period in which men's fashion sought independence from the dominance of womenswear by founding separate labels, magazines, and fashion weeks, today we are witnessing an increasing porosity between the two sectors. Male and female models are now frequently seen on the catwalk together in the same show and there has been a resurgence in "unisex" or what is often referred to as "gender-neutral" fashion. Labels like Rad Hourani and Toogood present collections that can be worn by anyone (as long as they can afford the price tag) and, echoing earlier moments of androgyny in the 1970s and early 1980s, it has become increasingly common for male celebrities—Jaden Smith, Kanye West, G-Dragon, and Young Thug, amongst others—to wear womenswear garments including skirts and dresses. This gradual, tentative disintegration of the boundaries between menswear and womenswear is reflective of a broader set of debates surrounding gender, as radical anti-essentialist discourses shift away from projects to reform masculinity or femininity and towards a skepticism around the usefulness of binary gender categories altogether. Such anti-essentialist ideas—rejecting the notion that chromosomal sex reveals the "real," "authentic," essential truth about a person—were key to feminist and queer theory discourses of the 1990s (Butler, 1990; Grillo, 1995; Wilchins, 2002) and have gradually permeated into popular culture. And while most people continue to identify as either female or male, the possibility of gender identity outside of these strict binaries (or at least one less strictly demarcated by them) has moved from the margins of activism and academia to increasingly enter popular consciousness. The extent to which these new developments will continue to inflect upon fashion remains to be seen.

At the time of writing, the trend prediction agency WGSN is drawing attention to menswear in Southern Africa, highlighting the inventive and sophisticated work of designers like Rich Mnisi and Lukhanyo Mdingi with their distinctive approaches to color, fabrication, and silhouette (WGSN, 2017). Mazi Odu of *Business of Fashion*, writing a few months earlier in January 2017, also discusses the expansion of African menswear, focusing on practitioners based both in Southern and West Africa (Odu, 2017). The avant-garde aesthetics of labels like Orange Culture of Nigeria point to a vision of menswear that connects to broader global trends while simultaneously being distinctively African, as evidenced by designer Adebayo Oke-Lawal's sensibility for color, motif, and in his treatment of form. Having already benefited from a new wave of East Asian design, Southern and Western Africa (and specifically cities like Lagos and Cape Town) now represent exciting centers of creative activity in men's fashion. The increasing cosmopolitanism of menswear adds fresh impetus to the discipline by contributing new perspectives, aesthetics, and narratives.

Perhaps not every development in men's fashion of recent years should be welcomed as an unalloyed good: I have expressed some concerns about the lack of diversity of model bodies on the catwalk and around the sometimes-objectifying ways in which the male body is framed in fashion photography. But despite these concerns, the prodigious opening up of men's fashion which I have described in this book remains an exciting and immensely positive phenomenon, one that has enriched my life and the lives of many other men.

NOTES

Introduction

1   By "textual analysis" I mean the investigation of both visual texts (photographs, garments, drawings, magazine spreads) and written texts.

Chapter 1

1   Shifting attitudes to masculinity and men's role in childcare, domestic relationships, and at home, which emerged in response to second-wave feminism, can be traced at least as far back as the early 1970s. For example, in 1971, *L'Uomo Vogue* published an article entitled "The New Face of the New Dads" (1971: 102–105) describing a new form of parenthood in which fathers are much closer to their children and highly involved in their daily care. But the term "New Man," with its associations of caring, antisexism, and sensitivity, really gains currency and enters into popular discourse in the 1980s (Beynon, 2002: 100; New Man, 2017).

2   Toynbee states, "The New Man is not here, and it does not seem likely that we shall see him in our lifetime, nor in our children's," with the implication that masculinity is highly resistant, or perhaps impossible, to reform. However, research by the US-based Pew Research Centre (2013) found that the amount of time fathers spent on housework had more than doubled between 1965 and 2011 and that the amount of time fathers spent looking after children had nearly tripled. So while there are still large gaps in the amount of childcare and housework carried out by men and women, it would be inaccurate to say that men's roles have not changed. Qualitative research by Behnke and Meuser (2012) examined the ways in which new forms of masculine identity they term "involved fatherhood," more focused on the family and less on work, were emerging in response to legislation providing parental leave for fathers in Germany. Research by Wall and Arnold (2007) found that, far from exaggerating fathers' involvement, representations of fatherhood tended to relegate men to a secondary role in parenting. They argue that increased institutional, workplace, and cultural change will be required for men to be able to meet their aspirations to be more engaged parents.

3   Chapman's and Toynbee's distrust of reforming masculinities find their echo in the later masculinity studies of Demetrakis Demetriou. In his (2001) critique of Connell's theory of hegemonic masculinity, Demetriou argues that while new

"feminized and blackened" forms of masculinity have emerged in response to the politics of feminism, racial equality, and gay rights, this hybridization is "a strategy for the reproduction of patriarchy" (2001: 349). There is a strange circularity to this argument that masculinity has changed to stay the same, and Demetriou fails to describe how these newly reformed masculinities contribute to the domination of women. By seeming to assume that men have an inherent interest in the perpetuation of patriarchy and—despite copious evidence to the contrary—that it exerts no costs upon them, Demetriou's council of despair leaves little room for agency or for change. Rather than reflecting on the possibility that men might wish to be more involved as fathers, less defined by work, or simply able to express themselves more freely, his heavily structural account, like Chapman's, ascribes all shifts in masculinity to an attempt to cling to power.

4 Effemiphobia (sometimes called sissyphobia, effemimania, or femme-phobia) describes a pathological fear of effeminacy (male femininity). It is, I admit, a rather clunky neologism; nevertheless, the term serves the useful function of naming a key organizing principle of orthodox or (what Connell, Kimmel, and Messerschmidt term) hegemonic masculinity. Connell describes a hierarchy of masculinity (2005) in which certain male subjectivities are subordinated, and clearly effemiphobia is an important aspect of this process of subordination. But the term develops Connell's concept by accounting for the dual nature of the stigmatization of feminine behavior amongst men—a stigmatization that is rooted both in a misogynist devaluation of femininity in general and in gender normativity that demands men and women adopt "appropriate" behaviors. The dual etiology of effemiphobia perhaps accounts for its prevalence in both gay and straight and in both progressive and conservative spheres.

5 Although not all gay men are effeminate, all transgress the codes of orthodox masculinity simply by being gay.

6 Those involved in the dissemination and legitimation of culture—such as curators, disc jockeys, university lecturers, stylists, and journalists—can be described as cultural intermediaries (I am employing the term to include designers as well, since they are frequently engaged in the active dissemination of aesthetics and ideas as well as in the creation of discrete works). Pierre Bourdieu's theories of cultural capital, habitus, and cultural mediation help us to understand the ways in which particular kinds of cultural artifacts come to signify "artistic genius" or "good taste" through a process of cultural legitimation. They also help us to consider how certain forms of knowledge and taste are inculcated—often osmotically and implicitly—through our immersion in a particular milieu or "field."

7 MAN was founded jointly by Topman and Fashion East; designers are selected by a panel of industry experts and receive funding that enables them to stage a catwalk show and launch their labels. The success of MAN was central to the eventual establishment of London Collections: Men. Its foundation demonstrated a canny understanding, on the part of Topman, of the ecosystem in which it was situated as a brand. By investing in new designer talent, Topman was effectively investing in trends and ideas it would go on to disseminate itself (and in men's fashion more globally as a site of expression and commercial activity).

8 Claiming consumption as a legitimate site of agency and self-expression may disturb some cultural critics. In contrast, the notion of "the worker" as a meaningful identity and as a site of power is well established in economic and sociological

thought. To claim the consumer as a *potentially* disruptive, progressive figure is not to advance an uncritical celebration of all forms of consumer capitalism any more than a championing of the worker celebrates "wage-slavery." Rather, it is to account for empirical evidence that consumption frequently does exist as a space in which dominant meanings and structures of power are challenged, overturned, and reformed—a space of contested meanings (Fiske, 1987, 1989; Campbell, 2005).

Chapter 2

1. John Stephen's first shop opened on Beak Street in 1956; his first Carnaby Street shop opened in 1957. With their relatively low-price points, Stephen's boutiques catered mostly to young, subcultural, working, and lower-middle-class consumers. By the late 1950s and early 1960s, however, smarter, more expensive London tailors and shopkeepers, John Michael of the Kings Road and subsequently the rather exclusive Blades of Dover Street, got in on the act. They catered to a more well-heeled, dandyish consumer seeking a modern silhouette and unusual fabrications but with a concern for quality. By the end of the decade, Carnaby Street was to lose some of its luster, having come to be seen as a rather tacky tourist trap.

2. This equation between the suit and modernity is made in John Flügel's *The Psychology of Clothes* (1930) in which Flügel describes the advent of simpler and more uniform male dress as a function of a declining aristocracy and the rise of the bourgeoisie in the nineteenth century. John Harvey in his 1995 text *Men in Black* associates the rise of the funereal black tailoring of the Victorian age with the grime of industrialization and with the fetish for austere dress amongst the Low Church Protestants of the new mercantile classes (in the UK and North America). Christopher Breward also makes this connection between Nonconformist Wesleyan and Quaker Christianity and the increasing simplicity of menswear in the eighteenth and nineteenth centuries, while simultaneously drawing attention to the expansion of clerical jobs and the necessity to find "an appropriate costume for the new professions thrown up by empire, industry and commerce, one that communicated an appropriate sense of respectability and responsibility" (2016: 49). The other side of this coin, of course, is the simplicity and elegance of early nineteenth century dandyism, again predicated on perfect tailoring in simple and muted colors, but with a rather complex relationship to class, since it was a deliberately understated but identifiable uniform of the fashionable élite (not least of whom the low-born but aspirant Beau Brummell).

3. Though, the Wolfenden Report (Home Office, Scottish Home Department 1957), which recommended the decriminalization of homosexuality, had been published some five years earlier and attitudes were (slowly) changing.

4. Sadly, the black and white photography doesn't capture these brilliant hues.

5. Often those sitting at some remove from the dominant classes because they were gay, Jewish, working-class, or all three.

6. A term, it's significant to note, coined by the left-liberal economist John Kenneth Galbraith as the title of his manifesto for a society in which a thriving private sector is complemented by a well-funded, activist public sector.

7   Michael Fish of Mr. Fish is perhaps best known for his promotion of skirts, dresses, and tunics for men—including the dress (come coat) sported in nonchalant Pre-Raphaelite splendor by David Bowie's on the sleeve of his 1969 album *The Man Who Sold the World*. However, Fish's elegant roll-neck shirts, sometimes with a zip fastening at the back or side of the neck were—I would contend—rather more significant since they proposed a new kind of formal men's attire that was both "wearable" and that diverged significantly from the conventions of twentieth century sartorialism.

8   Brother of singer and composer Alberto Anelli, with whom he shares the page.

9   The title *La Nuova Pelle dei Nuovi Papa* translates literally as "The New Skin of the New Dads."

10 As Barbara Burman (1995) describes, the Men's Dress Reform Party's (MDRP) key aims were for "better, brighter" and healthier clothes. They sought to encourage the wearing of sporting and casual clothing, knitted garments, shorts, and open-neck shirts, already becoming popular for leisure during the 1920s, for more general usage (Burman, 1995: 278). Despite MDRP reputation as cranks (and unfortunate connections to eugenics), their central sartorial claims that menswear was uncomfortable and unhygienic—since before the advent of dry cleaning woolen suits couldn't be washed—were, in retrospect, entirely correct. In fact, if you take a look at what is being worn on your nearest high street today, you will find that many of the proposals of the movement—including softer fabrics, unstructured garments, and sportswear finishes—have indeed been adopted by mainstream menswear albeit rather more slowly than they might have expected.

11 Evidence for this feeling of corporeal freedom can be found in Stefan Zweig's *The World of Yesterday* (2009 [1942]: 89–114), as well as in the new sports, cycling, and nudist movements that emerged in the early twentieth century to challenge "Victorian hypocrisy" and to promote "natural living."

12 An elevated, educated way of looking that celebrates reserve and distance.

13 Such as Stephen Linard, Michiko Koshino, BodyMap, Jean Paul Gaultier, and Boy London.

14 Iain R. Webb, who became fashion editor of *Blitz* magazine, was also involved in the Blitz Kid/New Romantic/alternative clubbing scene that, as he put it, "like a blazing phoenix [...] emerged from the ashes of punk," spawning a new generation of designers, musicians, stylists, filmmakers, and artists (2015). Like Webb, Simon Foxton had studied fashion at St. Martins and was immersed in London's clubbing scene from which he drew much of his inspiration (Martin, 2009). Ray Petri, the most famous of the three and often attributed with having invented the term "stylist," was older but had also been heavily involved in counterculture. His styling methodology was influenced both by black Afro-Caribbean aesthetics and by the bricolage of punk (for example, by attaching text, headlines, and typography to his models).

15 Sheffield in the case of The Human League and Cabaret Voltaire, Leeds in the case of Soft Cell, and Basildon for Depeche Mode.

16 Diana Fuss (1992) coined the term "the homospectatorial look" in response to Laura Mulvey's earlier conceptualization of the male gaze. While for Mulvey the gaze operates to code "the erotic into the language of the dominant patriarchal order" (1985: 805)—that is to glamorize the objectification and subjugation of

women—Fuss argues that ostensibly objectifying images of women (particularly in the context of fashion) can activate more complex forms of identification and desire. For a woman viewer, the female model of a fashion photograph may represent an idealized form of heterosexual femininity, but she may also represent a lost connection to her mother and/or an object of erotic fascination. We can use Fuss' framework to think about the complex ways in which fashion imagery of male models might be viewed by men: the intended or "first order" meanings of the image—if you look like this you'll be attractive to women and sexually successful—may operate alongside more ambivalent responses of fraternity, desire or love, or indeed, of hatred and envy.

17 Of course, the work of Leyendecker is associated much more with the early decades of the twentieth century rather than the 1940s, but, paradoxically, it is this strange collaging together of styles from the 1920s and 1940s that lends this image its distinctively eighties feeling. The outfit depicted in this advertisement is noticeably much more conservative than that featured in the *L'Uomo Vogue* photoshoot of seven years earlier featuring garments by the same designer (Valentino a Vent'Anni, 1976).

18 Margaret Thatcher once going so far as to claim "There is no such thing as society" (1987).

19 Fifty percent of respondents believed that "sexual relations between two adults of the same sex [was] always wrong" in 1980, increasing to 64 percent by 1987.

20 Of course, the acid house/rave subculture, along with new-age travelers, grunge, and indie (with their progressive, collectivist politics) continued, in their various ways, to provide loci of resistance during the late 1980s, and 1990s. But it is notable that these subcultures—in stark contrast to those of the early 1980s—were, in general, less focused on glamor and dressingup. A notable exception to this rule was the club kid scene of early nineties New York, centered on nights like Disco 2000; there, a feeling for glamor and androgyny continued (but this aesthetic influenced mainstream men's fashion of the period very little).

Chapter 3

1 Of course, working-class women worked in factories and large-scale sites of production throughout the nineteenth and twentieth centuries, but plants and job types became increasingly gender segregated in the nineteenth century, while most heavy industries became exclusively male: for example, in the UK women were legally excluded from coal mining by an Act of Parliament in the 1840s.

2 And connectedly, danger, pollution, and decadence.

3 And in art and culture more generally.

4 Of course this is something of a generalization, and it is worth noting that conditions were radically different, at the level of economics, between the United States and the UK (in which austerity and rationing continued into the early 1950s), and even more so in devastated Germany and defeated Italy. Nevertheless, rapidly rising prosperity (aided by the Marshall Plan) transformed Western Europe as a whole, leading to the democratization of consumption, increased industrial output, and rising wages. Notwithstanding cultural differences, common themes emerge across

representations of masculinity and femininity during the period: most notably, an idealization of domesticity and the family and a return to overt femininity in women's fashion. As Cohn points out, British menswear was particularly uninspiring in the early 1950s while Italian and American men's dress was rather less dour.

5 Indeed, the UK production of the musical *Hair* was subject to a private prosecution in 1972 (Hall and Jefferson, 1993: 46). It was only possible to put on the musical at all in the UK because theater censorship was finally abolished in September 1968—the production opened the day after the law changed (News.bbc.co.uk., 2017).

6 Taking this further, one could make a link between the explicitness of films like *Satyricon* and theatrical productions like *Hair* in the late 1960s and Nijinsky's 1912 *L'Après-midi d'un faune,* which was similarly boundary-pushing (though perhaps more formally beautiful). In this sense, the greater liberty afforded the body in the 1960s and 1970s can be seen as part of a Modernist tradition that drew on mythic, folkloric and classical traditions as well as on non-Western, particularly African, art. "The 1960s and 1970s are also the decades in which dynamic men's fashions emerged in newly independent West African nations such as Mali and Nigeria. These styles combined elements of African dress with more international fashions. The Malian photographer Malick Sidibé brilliantly captures this moment of energy and flux in images of Bamako's stylish citizens.

7 American *GQ*, the British spin-off, was founded much later in 1988; for reasons of consistency I refer to the American version simply as *GQ* throughout.

8 AIDS was identified in the early 1980s and acquired its acronym in 1982. With its wasting effects upon the body and associations with gay men, AIDS acted to reinforce the primacy of an exaggerated form of muscularity connoting both heterosexuality and good health.

9 If the meaning of the built physique retained a protean quality, so too did the male body coded as feminine or androgynous: as Anya Kurennaya (2015) has described, the feminine styling of the male body common to rock and metal music genres of the 1980s simultaneously signaled an eroticized gender transgression and overt (and sometimes misogynistic) heterosexuality.

10 In this way, while advertising focused at women certainly became less sexist in the 1980s (in reaction to continued feminist agitation), advertising focused at men in some ways became increasingly normative in tone and content.

11 The adverts for C.P. Company of Spring 1994 take this disembodied aesthetic one stage further by doing away with the body entirely and presenting crumpled linen jeans in muted hues photographed lying on a flat surface. Ralph Lauren "double R" jeans in a 1994 advert also draw attention away from the male form and towards the texture of the denim, using a close-up photograph of a riveted jeans pocket and hand.

12 A similarly oversized, draping, layered silhouette is featured in multiple fashion shoots of the period not only in *Collezioni Uomo* of Autumn 1992 but also in *GQ* of January 1991 (1991: 144–145), April 1991 (1991: 186–187), January 1994 (1994: 70–73), and February 1994 (1994: 140); in *Arena Homme+* of 1994 (1994: 104–105); and in adverts for brands such as Gianfranco Ferre (Winter 1994) and Giorgio Armani (Winter 1994). This oversized layered look is already noticeable in shoots from 1989: for example, in *The Face* July 1989:30 and throughout *L'Uomo Vogue* of October 1989.

13 Though it clearly has a much longer ancestry which could be traced back to the physique magazines of the 1950s, Charles Atlas in the early twentieth century, and no doubt earlier still.

14 There is also more than a hint of classism in Martin's critique, which focuses its ire upon a largely provincial aspirational working-class or lower-middle-class demographic.

15 *Chora* is derived from the Greek word for womb (space, clearing, receptacle). For Kristeva, the *semiotic chora* represents the instinctual, bodily drives that originate from a period of early childhood development before the child is able to distinguish itself as separate from its mother (as a unique individual in the world). As such, it is a space of primal urges that exist prior to the formation of the ego, and that are subject to repression and circumscription; though, crucially, drawing on Sigmund Freud, Kristeva notes that "what is repressed cannot really be held down" (1982: 13). The *semiotic chora* relates closely to the abject, since it is a space of indeterminacy and transgression.

16 There are clear connections between Klaus Theweleit's (psycho)analysis of the White Terror and Julia Kristeva's notion of abjection since both are focused on the exclusion of "impurity," "pollution," and femininity. Theweleit, like Kristeva, underlines the importance, within the logic of patriarchy, of the suppression of both affect and the corporeal.

For Kristeva, the abject is that which challenges the wholeness and intactness of the person (the subject). It is the point at which the boundaries of personhood and the body become unclear, the point at which one is (or feels) abased, cast off, or rejected. As Kristeva describes, the abject is that which is labeled filthy and defiling, that which is prohibited, particularly that which emanates from the body (she mentions feces and menstrual blood specifically). Abjection, then, signifies the point at which the unity of the body, its boundaries and peripheries, are threatened, "the non distinctiveness of inside/outside" (1982: 61). And abjection is also associated by Kristeva with femininity in general and with motherhood (and the body of the mother) in particular.

Thus, abjection signifies not only disempowerment (and implicitly the devaluation of the feminine), but also conversely a site of desire, power, and possibility. The rejection and transgression of rules is linked to notions of transcendence (the crossing of boundaries) which in turn relates to religion and the sublime.

17 Although Capasa and Lang also used slimmer than average models by the standard of the time.

18 Though, of course, the notion that one can read off a set of values and subjectivities from any given body is rather problematic (and essentialist) one. Clearly, different sorts of identities, including gendered identities, can inhabit an almost endless variety of bodies.

19 The "twink" is both a problematic and a problematized ideal. Problematic because he is often represented essentially as a sex object, and simultaneously—particularly within North American culture—often stigmatized because of his perceived effeminacy.

Chapter 4

1 *Arena Homme+*, founded in 1994, would go on to develop a much more directional approach to fashion than the more established style magazines like *GQ, Esquire*, and *L'Uomo Vogue*. Despite this, its early editions continue to owe much to the

fashionable masculine aesthetic of the early 1990s which remained dominant on the catwalk during the period.
2. Who later was to collaborate with Raf Simons on a photobook entitled *Isolated Heroes* (1999) documenting Simons' Spring/Summer 2000 collection as photographed on street-cast models.
3. And, indeed, Simpson, unlike other commentators, sees in laddism a self-conscious performativity that connects to the notion of gender as play.
4. Of course, a number of interesting menswear designers continued to practice throughout the early and mid-1990s, including Jean Paul Gaultier, Katherine Hamnett, Yohji Yamamoto, and Dries Van Noten, who brought various non-European "ethnic" elements, indigenous subcultural influences, and some play with silhouette to the catwalk. However, looking through an issue of *Collezioni Uomo, L'Uomo Vogue,* or even supposedly "edgy" and experimental editions like *The Face* and *i-D* from the first half of the decade reveals a scarcely changing vista of unstructured jackets and uninspired jersey sportswear with prominent manufacturer's logos, season after season.
5. The English band of the late 1970s whose music gained significance for a generation of disaffected youth and whose vocalist Ian Curtis committed suicide tragically young. The members of Joy Division dressed in sober and understated suits sourced from secondhand shops in part to differentiate themselves from their punk contemporaries.
6. The label had previously been known as Christian Dior Monsieur, producing nondescript suits under an anonymous design team.
7. A provision under the 2000 EU Employment Framework Directive required member states of the European Union to ban sexual orientation discrimination in employment by the end of 2003 (Stonewall.org.uk, 2003).
8. Sander herself had been displaced by the brand's owners, with whom—having lost the rights to her own name—she was locked in bitter legal confrontation.
9. The references are to the Bauhaus, specifically, but the palette of neutrals, tints, and black (with highlights of near-primaries) prevents the aesthetic from tipping into pastiche—it is worth noting that garment design was a somewhat neglected discipline in the Bauhaus proper (though Constructivist designers in a Soviet context like Varvara Stepanova, Alexander Rodchenko, and Liubov Popova did design clothing), so Simons refers largely to furniture and graphics of the period.
10. In recent years, Simons has oscillated between more nostalgic, somber work—as in his Spring/Summer 2017 menswear collection—and a more optimistic modernizing approach, as with Spring/Summer 2013 and 2014.

Chapter 5

1. As well as in the design of Raf Simons, Demna Gvasalia, Rory Parnell Mooney, Ximon Lee, and Craig Green.
2. To say nothing of Callot Soeurs, Paul Poiret, Varvara Stepanova, Liubov Popova, Mariska Karasz, and other pioneers of women's dress.

3   It is worth noting that Connell's concept of hegemonic masculinity emerged as a way of theorizing the masculinities she observed in the empirical research she and others conducted in the 1970s and 1980s pertaining to schooling, male bodies, and Labour politics. In this sense, the qualitative/ethnographic work of the writers I cite here who have developed and built upon Connell's ideas in recent years should be seen as resulting from an evolution of her approach rather than a radical break from it.

4   This was already evident in the fieldwork of Connell, Messerschmidt, and Mac an Ghail in the 1980s.

5   Wales Bonner's resistance of these hypermasculine representations through the subversion of masculine norms, as I have intimated, may be argued to reproduce a set of less widespread but nevertheless potentially problematic images associated with exoticism, primitivism, and the "sensuality" of the black body. Nevertheless, as James Smalls (2013: 99–119) has claimed, during the early twentieth century Modernism, primitivism, and eroticism were strategies adopted by black artists, dancers, writers, and poets (such as Richmond Barthé, François Féral Benga, Josephine Baker, and Langston Hughes) as a means of inverting and resisting negative values projected onto black bodies, and as a way of situating black subjectivities at the heart of Modernism. As Smalls suggests, rather than seeing black subjects as the passive victims of various modernisms, the cultural sophistication, creativity, and agency of figures such as Benga, who adopted exoticist strategies, should be recognized. Discourses of authenticity, sensuality, spirituality, and corporeality were used by African, black French, and African American artists as a way of constructing alternative spaces of creativity, positive self-identification, and desire. This tradition of subversive, sometimes exoticizing, and frequently queered black identity has often been hidden or marginalized, and one could argue that Wales Bonner's project is focused on recuperating this tradition.

6   For all his problematic body issues.

7   And indeed more generally.

8   Breward (2016: 85) states that "historians of male dress and English politics have generally looked to the 1660s and the Restoration for evidence of the prototypical Englishman's suit," while the psychologist John Flügel (1930) argues for the French Revolution and British Industrial Revolution in the late eighteenth century as catalysts for more simple and unadorned menswear. These two positions are of course in no way irreconcilable: the moments of revolutionary change to which Flügel draws attention have deeper historical roots (as do the shifts in men's dress which accompanied them). Late Georgian/Regency menswear is particularly noteworthy because of the rapid changes that take place during this époque, and because of the sense of elegance, clarity, and modernity felt in the fashions of the period.

9   Of course, British and American fashion also played a significant part in the 1980s; I describe the innovative nature of British subcultural fashion in detail in Chapter 2. The creativity of American subcultural fashion centered upon proto and early hip-hop culture in the 1980s has been documented by Jamel Shabazz's (2002) book *Back in the Day* as well as in Sacha Jenkins' documentary *Fresh Dressed* (2015). Nevertheless, the most commercially important and innovative labels (fashion qua fashion) tended to show either in Paris or in Milan during this period.

10 Whatever that might be: as I describe in the chapter Disciplinary Discourses, texts on men's style of the late 1980s and 1990s often frame menswear of the late 1930s and 1940s as "classic," as if the styles of this period had always existed (rather than being the result of a specific set of historical processes).

11 More generally, a study by the Pew Research Centre (2013) found that the amount of time American fathers spent on housework had more than doubled between 1965 and 2011 and that the amount of time fathers spent looking after children had nearly tripled.

Conclusion

1 For this reason I am highly suspicious of the work of theorists like Demetrakis Demetriou (2001) and Tristan Bridges (2013) whose accounts of "hybrid masculinity" tend to reify heterosexuality and maleness as immutable badges of privilege.

REFERENCES

Abdulrahim, A. (2016). Autumn/Winter 2016/2017. [Menswear Collection] London: Victoria House.
Abdulrahim, A. and Sels, T. (2016). Personal Interview with Mai Gidah.
Abraham, T. (2016). Justin O'Shea Exits Brioni. *Business of Fashion*. [online] Available at: www.businessoffashion.com/articles/news-analysis/justin-oshea-out-at-brioni [Accessed October 24, 2016].
Adamson, G. (2007). *Thinking through Craft*. Oxford: Berg.
Advert: His Clothes (1962). *Town* (11), p. 25.
Akomfrah, J. (2013). The *Stuart Hall Project* [film]. United Kingdom: Smoking Dogs Films.
Anderson, E. (2009). *Inclusive Masculinity*. New York: Routledge.
Anderson, P. and Godfrey, J. (1992). Man Child. *The Face*., pp. 42–45.
Anon (1971a). *Tailor & Cutter* (April 30, 1971), p. 7.
Anon. (1971b). *L'Uomo Vogue* (10), p. 129.
Anon (1988). *Gentlemen's Quarterly* (January), p. 172.
Anon (1994). Military Precision. *Arena Homme+* (1, Spring/Summer 1994), p. 64.
Anon (2010). *Hipster Casualty 100710*, HACKNEY HIPSTER HATE. Available at: hackneyhipsterhate.tumblr.com/post/793555617/hipster-casualty-100710 [Accessed June 1, 2016].
Antonioli.eu (2015). *Ximon Lee about XIMONLEE SS16*. [video] Available at: journal.antonioli.eu/2015/11/ximon-lee-about-ximonlee-ss16/ [Accessed June 22, 2016].
Anderson, P. and Godfrey, J. (1992). Man Child. , pp. 42–45.
Arena Homme+ (1997). Collections Spring/Summer 1997: Gucci. *Arena Homme+*, p. 89.
Armengol, J. (2013). Embodying the Depression: Male Bodies in 1930s American Culture and Literature. In: J. Armengol and À. Carabí, eds., *Embodying Masculinities: Towards a History of the Male Body in U.S. Culture and Literature*, 1st ed. New York: Peter Lang.
Arnault, B. (2007). *Christian Dior 2006 Annual Report: Combined Ordinary and Extraordinary Shareholders' Meeting*. Paris.
Arrowsmith, C. (1963). The Thin End of the Wedge. *Town* (12), pp. 84–85.
Avedon, R. (2001). Advertisement for Dior Homme Autumn/Winter 2001–2002– Solitaire. *Arena Homme+* (18, autumn/winter), p. 62.
Backes, N. (1983). Valentino Advertisement. *Gentlemen's Quarterly*, p. 231.
Bailey, T. (2015). Menswear Industry Keeps on Growing. [online] *European CEO*. Available at: www.europeanceo.com/home/menswear-industry-keeps-on-growing/ [Accessed March 27, 2017].
Banks, J. (1983). Advertisement. *Gentlemen's Quarterly*.
Barcelona: Antonio Miró(1991). *Collezioni Uomo* (Autumn Winter 1991/1992), p. 337.

Barneys New York (2013). Stylish Men, in Tune: A Video with Lanvin Menswear Designer Lucas Ossendrijver. [video] Available at: www.youtube.com/watch?v=VNdsuk2ETDA [Accessed April 16, 2014].

Barnsley, P. (1962). Faces without Shadows. *Town*, 1(9), pp. 48–53.

Barry, B. and Phillips, B. (2016). Destabilizing the Gaze towards Male Fashion Models: Expanding Men's Gender and Sexuality Identities. *Critical Studies in Men's Fashion*, 3(1), pp. 17–35. doi: 10.1386/csmf.3.1.17_1.

Barthes, R. and Lavers, A. (1972). *Mythologies*. 1st ed. New York: Hill and Wang.

Bartky, S. (1990). *Femininity and Domination*. New York: Routledge.

Baudrillard, J. (1981). *For a Critique of the Political Economy of the Sign*. Candor, NY: Telos Press.

Baudrillard, J. (1994). *Simulacra and Simulation*. Ann Arbor: University of Michigan Press.

Baudrillard, J. (1998). *The Consumer Society*. London: Sage.

Baudrillard, J. and Glaser, S. (2010). *Simulacra and Simulation*. 1st ed. Ann Arbor: Michigan University of Michigan Press.

Baumol, W. J. (1986). Productivity Growth, Convergence, and Welfare: What the Long-Run Data Show. *The American Economic Review*, 76(5), pp. 1072–1085.

Behnke, C. and Meuser, M. (2012). "Look Here Mate! I'm Taking Parental Leave for a Year"—Involved Fatherhood and Images of Masculinity. In: M. Oechsle, U. Müller, and S. Hess, eds., *Fatherhood in Late Modernity: Cultural Images, Social Practices, Structural Frames*. 1st ed. Opladen, Berlin and Toronto: Verlag Barbara Budrich, pp. 129–142.

Ben Sherman Advertisement (1999). *The Face* (35), p. 27.

Berger, J., Blomberg, S., Fox, C., Dibb, M. and Hollis, R. (1977). *Ways of Seeing*. 2nd ed. London: British Broadcasting Corporation/Penguin.

Beynon, J. (2002).*Masculinities and Culture*. 1st ed. Philadelphia, PA: Open University Press.

Birch, H. (1994). Triumph of the New Lad; Stylish? Clever? Sophisticated? Don't Be Silly: The Men's Magazine of the Moment is about Football, Booze and Babes. And It's Laughing all the Way to the Bank, *The Independent*, (8th September), p. 26.

Bitterman, A. (2016). Getting beyond the Fear of Queer: The Transition from Gender-Specific Fashion to Inclusive Style. *Critical Studies in Men's Fashion*, 3(1), pp. 37–42.

Blackman, C. (2009). *100 Years of Menswear*. 1st ed. London: Laurence King.

Blanks, T. and Style.com (2012). Spring Summer 2013. [video] Available at: www.youtube.com/watch?v=EGiD8pPH77w [Accessed May 23, 2016].

Bonami, F. and Simons, R. (2003). *The Fourth Sex: Adolescent Extremes*. Milan: Charta.

Bott, D. (2007). *Chanel*. London: Thames & Hudson, p. 94.

Bourdieu, P. (1984). *Distinction*. 1st ed. Cambridge, MA: Harvard University Press.

Bourdieu, P. and Nice, R. (1984). *Distinction: A Social Critique of the Judgement of Taste*. Cambridge, MA: Harvard University Press.

Bradley, M. (1971). *Unbecoming Men: A Men's Consciousness-Raising Group Writes on Oppression and Themselves*. 1st ed. New York: Change Press.

Bradshaw, D. and Richmond, T. (1994). Overtones. *Arena Homme+*, (2, Autumn/ Winter) pp. 150, 151.

Brecht, B. (2005). Alienation Effects in Chinese Acting. In: S. Gupta and D. Johnson, eds., *A Twentieth-century Literature Reader: Texts and Debates*, 1st ed. London: Routledge.

Breward, C. (2005). Ambiguous Role Models: Fashion, Modernity and the Victorian Actress. In: C. Evans and C. Breward, eds., *Fashion and Modernity*, 1st ed. London: Berg, pp. 101–118.

Breward, C. (2016). *The Suit: Form, Function & Style*. 1st ed. London: Reaktion Books.
Bridges, T. (2013). A Very "Gay" Straight?: Hybrid Masculinities, Sexual Aesthetics, and the Changing Relationship between Masculinity and Homophobia. *Gender & Society*, 28(1), pp. 58–82.
Brigidini, Cristina Leonarduzzi (1982). Metropolitan Look. *L'Uomo Vogue* 121 (July/August), pp. 396–397.
Bryden, R. (1962). Bulge Takes Over. *Town*, 1(9), pp. 40–45.
Burdine, B. (1973). Clothes Line. *Gentlemen's Quarterly*, 4(43), p. 22.
Burman, B. (1995). The Better and Brighter Clothes: The Men's Dress Reform Party, 1929–1940. *Journal of Design History*, 8(4), pp. 275–290.
Butler, J. (1990). *Gender Trouble*. New York: Routledge.
Butler, J. (2011). Your Behavior Creates Your Gender. [video] Available at: www.youtube.com/watch?v=Bo7o2LYATDc&t=18s [Accessed March 13, 2017].
Cabasset, P. (2001). Portrait: Hedi Slimane: Le Petit Prince New-Look De Dior Homme. *L'Officiel de la Couture et de la Mode de Paris* (854), pp. 66–71.
Camara de la Moda Española Advertisement. (1976). *L'Uomo Vogue* (51, August), pp. 30–41.
Campbell, C. (2005). The Craft Consumer: Culture, Craft and Consumption in a Postmodern Society. *Journal of Consumer Culture*, 5(1), pp. 23–42. doi: 10.1177/1469540505049843.
Cancian, F. (1987). *Love in America: Gender and Self-Development*. Cambridge: Cambridge University Press.
Capasa, E. (1997). Costume National Autumn/Winter 1997–1998. *Uomo Collezioni*, pp. 32–37.
Capasa, E. (2011). Ennio Capasa, Costume National. Available at: www.costumenational.com/about/ [Accessed April 10, 2014].
Carrigan, T., Connell, B. and Lee, J. (1985). Toward a New Sociology of Masculinity. *Theory and Society*, 14(5), pp. 551–604.
Carter, A. (1979). *The Bloody Chamber and Other Stories*. 1st ed. London: Gollancz.
Casablanca. (1988). *Gentlemen's Quarterly*, pp. 164–165.
Catalano, E. (1969). La Moda a Roma si recita a Soggetto. *L'Uomo Vogue* (4), pp. 116–117.
Chandler, R. and Wales Bonner, G. (2015). Ebonics. [Menswear Collection] London: London Collections Men.
Chapman, R. (1988). The Great Pretender: Variations on the New Man Theme. In: R. Chapman and J. Rutherford, eds., *Male Order: Unwrapping Masculinity*. 1st ed. London: Lawrence & Wishart, pp. 225–248.
Charity, R. and Kelvin, J. (1994). Chill Factor. *Arena Homme+*, p. 94.
Chevignon Advertisement. (1994). *Arena Homme+*, p. 137.
Chinitz, D. (1997). Rejuvenation through Joy: Langston Hughes, Primitivism, and Jazz. *American Literary History*, 9(1), pp. 60–78.
Christensen, A. and Jensen, S. (2014). Combining Hegemonic Masculinity and Intersectionality. *NORMA: Nordic Journal For Masculinity Studies*, 9(1), pp. 60–75. doi: 10.1080/18902138.2014.892289.
Christodoulou, P. (1962). Brogues Come to Town. *Town*, (9), p. 29.
Clark, A. (1999a). 21st Century Boys; It's Spring 2000: Prepare to Ditch the Navy Jumper. Again. Adrian Clark Reports from the Multicoloured Menswear Shows in Paris and Milan. *The Guardian*, (9th July), p. 10.
Clark, A. (1999b). All about Yves: As the New Looks for Men for the New Millennium Hit the Catwalks Last Week, One Label Stood Head and Shoulders above the Rest. *The Guardian (G2 magazine)*, (9th July), p. 10.

Clark, A. (2014). Death of the Suit. [online] *ShortList Magazine*. Available at: www.shortlist.com/style/death-of-the-suit [Accessed December 21, 2016].

Clarke, J., Hall, S., Jefferson, T. and Roberts, B. (1993 [1975]). Subcultures, Cultures and Class. In: S. Hall and T. Jefferson, eds., *Resistance through Rituals: Youth Subcultures in Post-War Britain*, 2nd ed. London and New York: Routledge, pp. 3–59.

Cohn, N. (1971). *Today There are No Gentlemen*. 1st ed. London: Weidenfeld and Nicolson.

Cole, S. (2000). *Don We Now Our Gay Apparel*. 1st ed. Oxford: Berg.

Collard, J. (2016). The Death of the Suit and the Rise of "Smart Separates." *The Sunday Telegraph*, pp. 24–25.

Collins, M. (2007). *The Permissive Society and its Enemies*. 1st ed. London: Rivers Oram.

Connell, R. (1987). *Gender and Power*. Cambridge: Polity Press.

Connell, R. (2005). *Masculinities*. 2nd ed. Berkeley: University of California Press.

Connell, R., Ashden, D., Dowsett, G. and Kessler, S. (1982). *Making the Difference: Schools, Families and Social Division*. Sydney: Allen & Unwin.

Connell, R. and Messerschmidt, J. (2005). Hegemonic Masculinity. *Gender & Society*, 19(6), pp. 829–859. doi: 10.1177/0891243205278639.

Costantino, M. (1997). *Men's Fashion in the Twentieth Century*. New York: Costume & Fashion Press.

Costume National Spring/Summer 2005 (2005). *Collezioni Uomo*.

Crafts, N. and Toniolo, G. (1996). *Economic Growth in Europe since 1945*. 1st ed. Cambridge: Cambridge University Press.

Crane, T. V. (2013). Club to Catwalk: Blitz Kids. [video] Available at: www.youtube.com/watch?v=hkeM_-wVgWU [Accessed December 18, 2016].

Crewe, B. (2003). *Representing Men: Cultural Production and Producers in the Men's Magazine Market*. 1st ed. Oxford: Berg Publishers.

Cuenca, M. (2013). Invisibilizing the Male Body: Exploring the Incorporeality of Masculinity in 1950s American Culture. In: J. Armengol and À. Carabí, eds., *Embodying Masculinities: Towards a History of the Male Body in U.S. Culture and Literature*, 1st ed. New York: Peter Lang.

Cunningham, P. (2008). The Leisure Suit: Its Rise and Demise. In: A. Reilly and S. Cosbey, eds., *The Men's Fashion Reader*, 1st ed. New York: Fairchild Books, pp. 84–100.

Dahlgreen, W. (2016). YouGov | Only 2% of young men feel completely masculine (compared to 56% of over 65s). [online] *YouGov: What the World Thinks*. Available at: yougov.co.uk/news/2016/05/13/low-young-masculinity-britain/ [Accessed July 13, 2016].

Dangoor, R. (2010). Being a Dickhead's Cool. Available at: www.youtube.com/watch?v=lVmmYMwFj1I [Accessed August 2, 2016].

Davidson, L. (2015). Suits You, Sir. Menswear is Taking over Fashion World. *The Daily Telegraph* (April 1), p. 3.

Day, C. and Ward, M. (1992). Wah Wah. *The Face* 47(August), pp. 83–89.

Day, C. and Yiapanis, P. (2003). Lame. In: R. Simons and F. Bonami, eds., *The Fourth Sex: Adolescent Extremes*. Milan: Charta.

De Visser, R. (2006). Mister In-between: A Case Study of Masculine Identity and Health-related Behaviour. *Journal of Health Psychology*, 11(5), pp. 685–695.

De Visser, R. (2009). "I'm Not a Very Manly Man": Qualitative Insights into Young Men's Masculine Subjectivity. *Men and Masculinities*, 11(3), pp. 367–371.

REFERENCES

Demetriou, D. (2001). Connell's Concept of Hegemonic Masculinity: A Critique. *Theory and Society*, 30(3), pp. 337–361.
Desk Set. (1988). *Gentlemen's Quarterly*, 58(3), p. 311.
Dino Mele. (1968). *L'Uomo Vogue* (2), 142.
Dior Homme by Hedi Slimane. (2007). *Collezioni Uomo*, (60), 258–263, 262.
Drew, J. (2008). Knife Crime and Masculinity—The F-Word. [online] *Thefword*. Available at: www.thefword.org.uk/2008/07/knife_crime_and/ [Accessed August 5, 2016].
Drew, W. (2009). The Velvet Revolutionary. *Wish Magazine*, p. 46.
Drewnowski, A. and Yee, D. (1987). Men and Body Image: Are Males Satisfied with Their Body Weight? *Psychosomatic Medicine*, 49(6), pp. 626–634.
Ducat, S. (2004). *The Wimp Factor: Gender Gaps, Holy Wars and the Politics of Anxious Masculinity*. Boston, MA: Beacon Press.
Edwards, T. (1997). *Men in the Mirror*. 1st ed. London: Cassell.
Edwards, T. (2006). *Cultures of Masculinity*. London: Routledge.
Ehrenhalt, A. (2012). *The Great Inversion and the Future of the American City*. 1st ed. New York: Borzoli.
Ehrenreich, B. (1984). A Feminists' View of the New Man. *The New York Times Magazine*. Available at: www.nytimes.com/1984/05/20/magazine/a-feminists-view-of-the-new-man.html?pagewanted=all [Accessed July 26, 2016].
Elbaz, A. (2011). *Défilé Homme Printemps/Eté 2012 de Lanvin*. Paris.
Encyclopediadramatica.se. Encyclopedia Dramatica (2011). Available at: encyclopediadramatica.se/Hipsters [Accessed August 1, 2016].
Engel, B. (2004). *The 24 Hour Dress Code for Men*. Berlin: Feierabend.
Enrico Job. (1968). *L'Uomo Vogue* (3), 109.
Ervin, M. (2011). The Might of the Metrosexual: How a Mere Marketing Tool Challenges Hegemonic Masculinity. In: E. Watson and M. Shaw, eds., *Performing American Masculinities*, 1st ed. Bloomington, IN: Indiana University Press.
Etautz.com. (2017). E. Tautz. [online], Available at: etautz.com/ [Accessed January 12, 2017].
Falco, L. (1969). Modello Nativo. *L'Uomo Vogue* (5), p. 26.
Fanon, F. (1967). *Black Skins White Masks*. 2nd ed. New York: Grove Press.
Fashion TV (2011). Lanvin Runway Show, Paris Men's Fashion Week, Spring 2012. [video] Available at: www.fashiontv.com/video/lanvin-by-alber-elbaz-runway-show-at-paris-men-s-fashion-week-spring-2012-fashiontv-ftv-com_368774.html [Accessed January 20, 2014].
Fashion United (2012). Where has Menswear Growth Sprung From? [online] Available at: www.fashionunited.co.uk/fashion-news/fashion/where-has-menswear-growth-sprung-from-2012061515115 [Accessed March 21, 2014].
Fashion United (2014). The Rise of the Global "Menaissance." [online] Available at: www.fashionunited.co.uk/fashion-news/fashion/the-rise-of-the-global-menaissance-2014031920500 [Accessed March 21, 2014].
Fasteau, M. (1975). *The Male Machine*. 1st ed. New York: Dell.
Faudi, M. (2013). Givenchy Spring/Summer 2014 by Riccardo Tisci. [image] Available at: www.vogue.com/fashion-shows/spring-2014-menswear/givenchy/slideshow/collection [Accessed August 1, 2017].
Featherstone, M. (2007). *Consumer Culture and Postmodernism*. Los Angeles: SAGE Publications.
Fewings, T. (2015). Craig Green Spring/Summer 2015. [Menswear Collection] London. Image owned by Getty Images.

Filiault, S. and Drummond, M. (2007). The Hegemonic Aesthetic. *Gay & Lesbian Issues and Psychology Review*, 3(3), pp. 175–184.
Firenze: Stefano Chiassai (1991). *Collezioni Uomo* (Autumn Winter 1991/1992), p. 31.
Fiske, J. (1987). *Television Culture*. London: Routledge.
Fiske, J. (1989). *Understanding Popular Culture*. London: Routledge.
Flügel, J. (1930). *The Psychology of Clothes*. 1st ed. London: Hogarth Press and the Institute of Psycho-Analysis.
Flusser, A. (2001). *Dressing the Man: Mastering the Art of Permanent Fashion*. New York: HarperCollins.
Forster, L. and Harper, S. (2010). *British Culture and Society in the 1970s*. 1st ed. Newcastle upon Tyne: Cambridge Scholars Publishing.
Foucault, M. (1978). *The History of Sexuality, Volume I: An Introduction*. Translated by R. Hurley. New York: Pantheon Books.
Foucault, M. (1989). *The Archeology of Knowledge*. London: Routledge.
Foucault, M. (1995). *Discipline and Punish*. New York: Vintage Books.
Foucault, M. and Hurley, R. (1978). *The History of Sexuality, Volume I: An Introduction*. New York: Pantheon Books.
Foucault, M., Martin, L., Gutman, H. and Hutton, P. (1988). *Technologies of the Self*. Amherst: University of Massachusetts Press.
Fox, D. (2016). *Pretentiousness: Why It Matters*. London: Fitzcarraldo Editions.
Frayling, C. (2011). *On Craftsmanship: Towards a New Bauhaus*. London: Oberon Books.
Freeman, H. (2006a) Ask Hadley: Is it Acceptable for a Man to Wear a Vest in Warm Weather? *The Guardian*. Available at: www.theguardian.com/lifeandstyle/2006/mar/13/fashion [Accessed March 22, 2014].
Freeman, H. (2006b) Men and Jewellery. *The Guardian*. Available at: www.theguardian.com/lifeandstyle/2006/jul/03/fashion.shopping [Accessed March 22, 2014].
Freeman, H. (2010). Man Cleavage: Put It Away!. *The Guardian*. Available at: www.theguardian.com/lifeandstyle/2010/oct/31/ask-hadley-man-cleavage [Accessed March 22, 2014].
Friedan, B. (1963). *The Feminine Mystique*. New York: W. W. Norton and Co.
Friede, E. (2016). Menswear Market Showing Strong Growth. *The Gazette*, p. 3.
Friedman, S. (1994). See Me, Feel Me, Touch Me, Heal Me: Pampering, and How to Take It like a Man. *Gentlemen's Quarterly*, (January), pp. 50–52.
Friedman, R. and Downey, J. (1998). Psychoanalysis and the Model of Homosexuality as Psychopathology: A Historical Overview. *The American Journal of Psychoanalysis*, 58(3), pp. 249–270.
Furmanovsky, J. and Russell Powell, F. (1984). The New Glitterati. *The Face* (48 April), pp. 47–48.
Fuss, D. (1992). Fashion and the Homospectatorial Look. *Critical Inquiry*, 18(4), pp. 713–737.
Gahr, D. and Fish, M. (1969). *Mick Jagger and the Rolling Stones Perform at Hyde Park*. London. Image owned by Getty Images.
Galbraith, J. K. (1958). *The Affluent Society*. New York: New American Library.
Gallagher, V. (2012). Rising Menswear Sales Defy Retail Gloom. *Drapers*. Available at: www.drapersonline.com/news/multiples/rising-menswear-sales-defy-retail-gloom/5038607.article#.UyxP1a1_ty8 [Accessed March 21, 2014].
Gauntlett, D. (2011). *Making is Connecting*. Cambridge: Polity Press.
Gauze and Effect—Trunk Show (Photographer: Jerry Salvati). (1973). *Gentlemen's Quarterly*, 4(43), pp. 58–68.

REFERENCES

Gavin, F. (2014). Collier Schorr: Still Chasing the First High. [online] *Dazed Digital*. Available at: www.dazeddigital.com/fashion/article/18446/1/collier-schorrs-androgynous-youth [Accessed July 4, 2017].
Getty Images. (2016a). *E. Tautz Spring/Summer 2017*. London.
Getty Images. (2016b). *Grace Wales Bonner Spring/Summer 2017 Ezekiel*. London.
Giddens, A. (1991). *Modernity and Self-Identity*. Stanford, CA: Stanford University Press.
Gill, R., Henwood, K. and McLean, C. (2005). Body Projects and the Regulation of Normative Masculinity. *Body & Society*, 11(1), pp. 37–62.
Goffman, E. (1956). *The Presentation of the Self in Everyday Life*. Edinburgh: University of Edinburgh Social Science Research Centre.
Goffman, E. (1986). *Stigma: Notes on the Management of Spoiled Identity*. 3rd ed. New York: Simon & Schuster.
Goldrick-Jones, A. (2003). *Men Who Believe in Feminism*. 1st ed. Westport, CT: Praeger Publishers.
Gore, M. (1983). *Everything Counts*. [Vinyl] London: Mute/Sire.
Grant, P. (2016). E Tautz Spring/Summer 17. [Menswear Collection] London: 180 Strand.
Greer, G. (2003). *The Boy*. London: Thames & Hudson.
Grillo, T. (1995). Anti-Essentialism and Intersectionality: Tools to Dismantle the Master's House. *Berkeley Women's Law Journal*, [online] 10(1), pp. 16–30. Available at: scholarship.law.berkeley.edu/cgi/viewcontent.cgi?article=1093&context=bglj [Accessed July 28, 2017].
Grogan, S. (2008). *Body Image: Understanding Body Dissatisfaction in Men, Women, and Children*. New York: Routledge.
Grosz, E. (1994). *Volatile Bodies*. Bloomington: Indiana University Press.
Hackett, J. and Tang, G. (2006). *Mr Classic*. London: Thames & Hudson.
Hadis, D. (2016). Is the End of the Suit in Sight?. [online] *Vogue*. Available at: www.vogue.com/13395325/menswear-2016-suit-tailoring-comme-des-garcons [Accessed December 22, 2016].
Hall, M. (2015). *Metrosexual Masculinities*. Basingstoke: Palgrave Macmillan.
Hall, S. (1988a). Thatcher's Lessons. *Marxism Today*, March 1988, pp. 20–27.
Hall, S. (1988b). *The Hard Road to Renewal: Thatcherism and the Crisis of the Left*. London: Verso.
Hanisch, C. (1975). Men's Liberation. In: Redstockings, ed., *Feminist Revolution*. 1st ed. New York: Random House, pp. 72–76.
Harber, J. and Greene, R., eds. (1973). *Gentlemen's Quarterly*, 4(43).
Harjunen, H. (2017). *Neoliberal Bodies and the Gendered Fat Body*. Oxford: Routledge.
Harmsworth, A. (2016). Doing It Dougie Style. *Metro*, pp. 22–23.
Harpin, L. (1992). Ten Minutes in the Mind of Richey James. *The Face* (47 August), p. 55.
Harris, G. and Irvine, T. (2013). Wasted Youth. 10 Men, Winter 2013 (36).
Harrod, T. (2015). *The Real Thing*. London: Hyphen Press.
Harvey, J. (1995). *Men in Black*. 1st ed. Chicago: University of Chicago Press.
Hayward, C. and Dunn, B. (2001). *Man About Town*. London: Hamlyn.
Healy, M. (2001). Adam's Ribs. *Arena Homme+* (16, Autumn/Winter), pp. 163–164.
Healy, M. (2016). Nasir Mazhar's most honest interview ever: Murray Healy talks to the designer about his brand's new direction (and what he says will blow you away) | LOVE. [online] *LOVE*. Available at: www.thelovemagazine.co.uk/posts/6526/nasir-mazhar-s-most-honest-interview-ever-murray-healy-talks-to-the-designer-about-his-brand-s-new-direction-and-what-he-says-will-blow-you-away [Accessed August 27, 2016].

Hebdige, D. (1979). *Subculture: The Meaning of Style*. 1st ed. London: Routledge.
Hell, R. (1977). *Blank Generation*. New York: Sire Records.
Home Office, Scottish Home Department (1957). *Report of the Committee on Homosexual Offences and Prostitution*. London: Her Majesty's Stationery Office.
Homma, A., Roberts, F., Malison, M., Kissane, B., Geerts, W., Kasriel-Alexander, D., Boumphrey, S. and Homma, A. (2015) *Men's Spending on Accessories Rises in the US*, Euromonitor International Blog. Available at: blog.euromonitor.com/2015/11/accessorising-for-success-mens-spending-on-accessories-rises-in-the-us.html [Accessed January 30, 2017].
hooks, b. (1994). *Teaching to Transgress*. 1st ed. New York: Routledge.
hooks, b. (2004a). *The Will to Change*. New York: Atria Books.
hooks, b. (2004b). *We Real Cool: Black Men and Masculinity*. New York: Routledge.
Horrocks, R. (1994). *Masculinity in Crisis*. Basingstoke: Palgrave.
Hung, W. (2016). Autumn/Winter 2016/2017. [Menswear Collection] London: Victoria House.
Hustvedt, S. (2006). *A Plea For Eros*. London: Hodder & Stoughton.
Ibson, J. (2002). *Picturing Men: A Century of Male Relationships in Everyday American Photography*. Washington, D.C.: Smithsonian Institution Press.
Iida, Y. (2005). Beyond the "Feminization of Masculinity": Transforming Patriarchy with the "Feminine" in Contemporary Japanese Youth Culture. *Inter-Asia Cultural Studies*, 6(1),pp. 56–74.
J, J. (2013). UNUNIFORM Spring/Summer 2014. [Menswear Collection] Paris. Collection by Juun J. Label owned by "Samsung Everland".
Jameson, F. (1991). *Postmodernism, or, The Cultural Logic of Late Capitalism*. Durham, NC: Duke University Press.
Jeffords, S. (1994). *Hard Bodies*. New Brunswick, NJ: Rutgers University Press.
Jobling, P. (2014). *Advertising Menswear: Masculinity and Fashion in the British Media since 1945*. London: Bloomsbury Academic.
Jobling, P. (2015). *Advertising Menswear*. 1st ed. London: Bloomsbury Academic.
Johnson, D. (1984). Out Came the Freaks. *The Face*, (83), p. 3.
Juun. J (2013). UNUNIFORM. [video] Available at: www.juunj.com/collections/2014_ss/index.jsp [Accessed March 23, 2014].
Kaiser, S. (2012). *Fashion and Cultural Studies*. London: Berg.
Kane, E. (2006). "No Way My Boys Are Going to Be like That!": Parents' Responses to Children's Gender Nonconformity. *Gender & Society*, 20(2), pp. 149–176. doi: 10.1177/0891243205284276.
Kassam, F. (2013). Fall Winter Look Book. [online] *Inventory* (9). Available at: thecvrator.com/inventory-magazine-2013-fallwinter-editorial/ [Accessed July 8, 2016].
Keers, P. (1987). *A Gentleman's Wardrobe*. London: Weidenfeld & Nicolson.
Kimmel, M. (2005). *The Gender of Desire: Essays on Male Sexuality*. 1st ed. Albany: State University of New York Press.
Kristeva, J. (1982). *Powers of Horror: An Essay on Abjection*. Translated by L. Roudiez. New York: Columbia University Press.
Kristeva, J. (1986). Revolution in Poetic Language. In: T. Moi, ed., *The Kristeva Reader*, 1st ed. New York: Columbia University Press, pp. 89–136.
Kristeva, J. and Roudiez, L. (1982). *Powers of Horror: An Essay on Abjection*. New York: Columbia University Press.
Kurennaya, A. (2015). Look What the Cat Dragged in: Analysing Gender and Sexuality in the Hot Metal Centerfolds of 1980s Glam Metal. *Critical Studies in Men's Fashion*, 2(2),pp. 163–211.

REFERENCES

Kuryshchuk, O. (2012). Craig Green. [online] *1 Granary*. Available at: 1granary.com/schools/central-saint-martins/craiggreen/ [Accessed June 1, 2016].

Lagneau, N. (2011). Lanvin Spring/Summer 2012 by Lucas Ossendrijver. [image] Available at: www.vogue.co.uk/shows/spring-summer-2012-menswear/lanvin/collection/ [Accessed March 23, 2014].

La Nuova Pelle dei Nuovi Papa' (1971). *L'Uomo Vogue*, pp. 102–105.

Lang, H. and Verdy, P. (2003). *Spring/Summer 2004 Collection*. Paris. Collection by Helmut Lang Spring/Summer 2004.

Lategan, B. (1972). Sea Rig. *British. Vogue* (July), pp. 74–75.

Leach, A. (2016). The History of Stone Island | Highsnobiety. [online] Highsnobiety.com. Available at: www.highsnobiety.com/2016/03/21/stone-island-history/ [Accessed August 26, 2016].

Leitch, L. (2016). Bankers Are Selling Off Their Suits, So What's the Future of Tailoring? Giorgio Armani, Dolce & Gabbana, Thom Browne, and More Weigh In. [online] *Vogue*. Available at: www.vogue.com/13454082/armani-cucinelli-the-future-of-tailoring/ [Accessed August 17, 2016].

Lessing, D. (1962). *The Golden Notebook*. London: Michael Joseph.

Lessing, D. (1985). *The Good Terrorist*. New York: Knopf.

Levy, V. (2013). Backstage. *10 Men* (36), p. 160.

Lewis, C. and O'Brien, M. (1987). *Reassessing Fatherhood*. London: SAGE Publications.

Lighter Shades of Pale. (1973). *Gentlemen's Quarterly* 4 (43), pp. 96–99. Photographer: Jerry Salvati.

Limnander, A. (2006). Jil Sander's New Man. *Harper's Bazaar*, p. 57.

Linard, S. and McCabe, E. (1986). British Menswear Takes Flight: London Calling. *The Face* (77 September), pp. 44–51.

Long, J. (2016). *Local Heroes*. [Menwear Runway Show] London: 180 Strand.

Lorentzen, C. (2007). Why the Hipster Must Die: A Modest Proposal to Save New York Cool. *Time Out New York*. Available at: www.timeout.com/newyork/things-to-do/why-the-hipster-must-die [Accessed July 6, 2016].

Lynch, S. and Zellner, D. (1999). Figure Preferences in Two Generations of Men: The Use of Figure Drawings Illustrating Differences in Muscle Mass. *Sex Roles*, 40(9), pp. 833–843.

Mac an Ghaill, M. (1994). *The Making of Men: Masculinities, Sexualities and Schooling*. Buckingham: Open University Press.

Mackie, A. and Lloyd, B. (2010). Topman Campaign Spring 2010 (design by B Blessing). Available at: www.thefashionisto.com/topman-spring-2010-the-trench-coat/ [Accessed March 27, 2017].

Madeira, M. (2008). Jil Sander Spring/Summer 2009 by Raf Simons. Available at: www.vogue.com/fashion-shows/spring-2009-menswear/jil-sander/slideshow/collection#2 [Accessed November 19, 2012].

Madsen, S. (2015). The Designer's Poetic Take on Race and Masculinity is Breaking New Ground—But She Thinks Diversity in Fashion is More than Just a Black-and-White Issue. [online] *Dazed & Confused*. Available at: http:// The designer's poetic take on race and masculinity is breaking new ground—but she thinks diversity in fashion is more than just a black-and-white issue [Accessed July 15, 2016].

Malossi, G. (2000). *Material Man*. New York: H.N. Abrams.

Mancino, R. (1973). Front Cover. *Gentlemen's Quarterly* (Summer).

Mande, J. (2016). Look at this fucking hipster, *Lookatthisfuckinghipster.tumblr.com*. Available at: lookatthisfuckinghipster.tumblr.com/page/23 [Accessed August 1, 2016].

Maneker, M. (2002). *Dressing in the Dark*. New York: Assouline Publishing.
Margetts, M. (2011). Action not Words. In: D. Charny, ed., *Power of Making: The Importance of Being Skilled*, 1st ed. London: V&A Publishing.
Marithé et François Girbaud Advertisement. (1991). *Gentlemen's Quarterly* (February), pp. 76–77.
Marriott, H. (2015). The Age of Peacocks: British Men Get Serious at Last about Looking Good: From Leopard Print Jackets to Floral Scarves, Men are Learning to Out-glam Women in the Fashion Stakes. *The Observer*, June 14. Available at: www.theguardian.com/fashion/2015/jun/14/menswear-goes-glam-in-age-of-peacocks [Accessed June 16, 2015].
Martin, C. (2014). How Sad Young Douchebags Took over Modern Britain | VICE United Kingdom. *VICE*. Available at: www.vice.com/en_uk/read/anatomy-of-a-new-modern-douchebag [Accessed March 18, 2014].
Martin, P. (2009). *When You're a Boy: Men's Fashion Styled by Simon Foxton*. 1st ed. London: Photographer's Gallery.
Martin, R. and Koda, H. (1989). *Jocks and Nerds*. New York: Rizzoli.
The Mask You Live In (2015). [film]. Dir. Jennifer Siebel Newsom.
Mauss, M. (1973). Techniques of the Body. *Economy and Society*, 2(1), pp. 70–88.
Mayogaine Paris Advertisement. (1971). *L'Uomo Vogue* (11), 152.
Mazhar, N. (2013). London Collections Men: Spring/Summer 2014. [image] Available at: www.nasirmazhar.com/collections-season/men-ss14/ [Accessed August 3, 2016].
McCauley Bowstead, J. (2002). *Clubgoers at Trash*. London: The End.
McCauley Bowstead, J. (2015). Hedi Slimane and the Reinvention of Menswear. *Critical Studies in Men's Fashion*, 2(1), pp. 23–42. doi: 10.1386/csmf.2.1.23_1.
McCorkel, J. and Myers, K. (2003). What Difference Does Difference Make? Position and Privilege in the Field. *Qualitative Sociology*, 26(2), pp. 199–231.
McKinley, B. (1982). A Piedi Nudi sulla Sabbia. *L'Uomo Vogue* (120, June), pp. 190–192.
McKinley, J. (2002). Along the Bowery, Skid Row Is on the Skids. *The New York Times (Style Desk)*, October 13, p. 1.
McLellan, A. and Rizzo, O. (2015). Fruit Machine. *Man About Town* (Spring/Summer 2015), p. 199.
McRobbie, A. (1994). *Postmodernism and Popular Culture*. 1st ed. London: Routledge.
Menkes, S. (1998). Sharp Tailoring but With a Soft Touch/PARIS MENSWEAR: On the Straight and Narrow. *International Herald Tribune*, January 27.
Messori Autumn—Winter 1991/1992 (1991). *Collezioni Uomo*, p. 56.
Military Precision. (1994). *Arena Homme+* (1), pp. 64–65.
Milligan, L. (2011). All about The Boys. *Vogue UK*. [online] Available at: www.vogue.co.uk/news/2011/12/12/menswear-luxury-market-growth—ppr-and-lvmh [Accessed March 18, 2014].
Monden, M. (2012). The Importance of Looking Pleasant: Reading Japanese Men's Fashion Magazines. *Fashion Theory*, 16(3), pp. 297–316. doi: 10.2752/175174112x13340749707169.
Monden, M. (2015). *Japanese Fashion Cultures*. New York and London: Bloomsbury.
Mort, F. (1987). Boy's Own? Masculinity, Style and Popular Culture. In: R. Chapman and J. Rutherford, eds., *Male Order*, 1st ed. London: Lawrence & Wishart.
Mort, F. (1988). Boys Own? Masculinity, Style and Popular Culture. In: R. Chapman and J. Rutherford, eds., *Male Order: Unwrapping Masculinity*, 1st ed. London: Lawrence & Wishart, pp. 193–224.
Mort, F. (1996). *Cultures of Consumption*. 1st ed. London: Routledge.

REFERENCES

Mort, F. (2010). *Capital Affairs*. 1st ed. New Haven, CT: Yale University Press.
Mort, F. (2016). Personal Interview. British Library. September 16, 2016.
Mulas, U. (1968). Antonello Aglioti. *L'Uomo Vogue* (3), p. 77.
Mulvey, L. (1985). Visual Pleasure and Narrative Cinema. In: G. Mast, ed., *Film Theory and Criticism: Introductory Readings*, 2nd ed. New York: Oxford University Press, pp. 803–816.
The Muscle Merchant of Venice. (1991). *Gentlemen's Quarterly* (March), p. 242.
Nagel, T. (1986). *The View from Nowhere*. 1st ed. Oxford: Oxford University Press.
Navy Story. (1982). *L'Uomo Vogue* (120), June, pp. 180–189.
Needham, A. (2013). Personal Interview. The Royal College of Art. February 1, 2013.
News.bbc.co.uk. (2017). BBC ON THIS DAY | 27 | 1968: Musical Hair opens as censors withdraw. [online] Available at: http://news.bbc.co.uk/onthisday/hi/dates/stories/september/27/newsid_3107000/3107815.stm [Accessed February 15, 2017].
Newton, H. (1969a). Gérard Reinhardt. *L'Uomo Vogue* (4), p. 121.
Newton, H. (1969b). Roberto Capucci. *L'Uomo Vogue* (4), p. 77.
Nichols, J. (1975). *Men's Liberation: A New Definition of Masculinity*. 1st ed. Harmondsworth: Penguin.
Nixon, S. (1996). *Hard Looks*. New York: St. Martin's Press.
Nussbaum, M. (1995). Objectification. *Philosophy and Public Affairs*, 24(4), pp. 249–291.
Odu, M. (2017). African Menswear Goes Global. [online] *The Business of Fashion*. Available at: https://www.businessoffashion.com/articles/global-currents/african-menswear-goes-global [Accessed August 8, 2017].
Oechsle, M., Müller, U. and Hess, S. (2012). *Fatherhood in Late Modernity*. 1st ed. Opladen: Barbara Budrich.
Office for National Statistics (2013). *Full Report—Women in the Labour Market*.
Office for National Statistics (2013). Housing and Consumer Durables (General Lifestyle Survey Overview). [online] *Newport*. Available at: http://webarchive.nationalarchives.gov.uk/20160107023644/http://www.ons.gov.uk/ons/dcp171776_302199.pdf [Accessed 4 Dec. 2017].
Ormston, R. and Curtis, J. (2015). British Social Attitudes: The 32nd Report. [online] *London: NatCen Social Research*. Available at: www.bsa.natcen.ac.uk/latest-report/british-social-attitudes-30/personal-relationships/homosexuality.aspx [Accessed July 4, 2016].
Ossendrijver, L. (2011). *Défilé Homme Printemps/Eté 2012 de Lanvin*. Paris.
New Man (2017). *Oxford English Dictionary*, 1st ed. [online]. Oxford: Oxford University Press. Available at: www.oed.com/view/Entry/245763?rskey=07B9kp&result=3#eid929903000 [Accessed March 13, 2017].
Paris. (1970). *Tailor & Cutter* (1153), 794–795.
Park, A. and Rhead, R. (2013). Homosexuality. *British Social Attitudes Survey*. [online] NatCen Social Research. Available at: www.bsa.natcen.ac.uk/latest-report/british-social-attitudes-30/personal-relationships/homosexuality.aspx [Accessed April 19, 2014].
Pawley, P. (1992). *Raymond Loewy : Most Advanced Yet Acceptable*. London: Trefoil Publication Ltd.
Petri, R. and Morgan, J. (1985). Pure Prairie: London Cowboys Lay Down the Law. *The Face* (66), pp. 68, 71.
Petridis, A. (2007). Legging Lemmings. *The Guardian*. Available at: www.theguardian.com/lifeandstyle/2007/aug/04/fashion1 [Accessed March 22, 2014].
Petridis, A. (2009). Rock on with Village People. *The Guardian*. Available at: www.theguardian.com/lifeandstyle/2009/may/09/alexis-petridis-fashion [Accessed March 22, 2014].

Pew Research Centre (2013). *Modern Parenthood: Roles of Moms and Dads Converge as They Balance Work and Family*. Washington D.C.: Pew Research Centre (Social & Demographic Affairs), pp. 1–6.

Peyton, E. (2003). Leonardo DiCaprio. In: R. Simons and F. Bonami, eds., *The Fourth Sex: Adolescent Extremes*. Milan: Charta, p. 281.

Plant, S. (2011). Deconstructing Masculinity—The F-Word. [online] *Thefword*. Available at: www.thefword.org.uk/2006/02/deconstructing_masculinity/ [Accessed August 5, 2016].

Pleck, J. and Sawyer, J. (1974). *Men and Masculinity*. 1st ed. Englewood Cliffs, NJ: Prentice-Hall.

Plummer, D. (1999). *One of the Boys*. 1st ed. New York: Harrington Park Press.

Pope, H., Phillips, K. and Olivardia, R. (2000). *The Adonis Complex*. New York: Free Press.

Porter, C. (2001). Body Politic: In Menswear it Counts as a Thrilling Revolution: Hedi Slimane Tells Charlie Porter Why He's not Interested in the Musclebound Look. *The Guardian (The Weekend)*, June 30, p. 62.

Porter, C. (2016). Personal Interview. October 6, 2016.

PR Newswire Europe (2014). The Idle *Man: Former ASOS Executive Bags $1.2m in Follow on Investment and Adds ex Amazon FD to Board*. London.

Prize-winning IFC Design. (1972). *Tailor & Cutter*, February (5457), p. 11.

Pruchnie, B. (2016). Craig Green Spring/Summer 2017. [Menswear Collection] London.

Raf Simons Spring/Summer 2005 (2004). *Collezioni Uomo*.

"Real Dash for less Cash" (1991). (Editor: Arthur Cooper) *Gentlemen's Quarterly* (April), p. 242.

The Resonance of Solids in Subtle Shades Drawn from a Bold Palette, Put together in an All-New Way. (1991). (Editor Arthur Cooper). *Gentlemen's Quarterly* (January), pp. 144–146.

Ritts, H. (1992). Kate Moss and Marky Mark Calvin Klein Advertisement. [image] Available at: www.dazeddigital.com/fashion/article/20543/1/ultimate-double-denim-dreamers [Accessed November 7, 2016].

Ritts, H. (1984). Fred with Tires. [image] Available at: www.herbritts.com/#/archive/photo/fred-with-tires-hollywood-1984 [Accessed July 8, 2017].

Ritts, H. and Roberts, M. (1984). Grease Monkeys. *The Face*, (54), pp. 3, 69–73.

Roetzel, B. (1999). *Gentleman: A Timeless Guide to Fashion*. Cologne: Könemann Verlag.

Rothstein, N., Ginsburg, M., Hart, A. and Mendes, V. (1984). *Four Hundred Years of Fashion*. London: V&A and William Collins Sons & Co., Ltd.

Rust, I. (2013). Interview with Ike Rust, Head of Menswear RCA. Royal College of Art.

Sabre Helanca Advertisement. (1964). *Town* (7), 31.

Sajonas, F. (2016). Brioni's 2017 Spring/Summer Collection Is Justin O'Shea's Ode to Rock 'N' Roll Royalty. [online] *hypebeast.com*. Available at: hypebeast.com/2016/7/justin-oshea-brioni-2017-spring-summer-collection [Accessed January 12, 2017].

Salvati, J. (1973). Shirts with a View. *Gentlemen's Quarterly* 4 (43), p. 82.

Schwarz, M. and Elffers, J. (2010). *Sustainism is the New Modernism: A Cultural Manifesto for the Sustainist Era*. New York: D.A.P.

Scott, J. and Clery, E. (2013). Gender Roles. *British Social Attitudes Survey*. [online] NatCen Social Research. Available at: www.bsa.natcen.ac.uk/latest-report/british-social-attitudes-30/gender-roles/attitudes-to-gender-roles-change-over-time.aspx [Accessed April 19, 2014].

Seabrook, J. (2000). THE INVISIBLE DESIGNER: Can Helmut Lang Become a Brand Name and Still Retain His Mystique? *The New Yorker*, September 18, p. 114.

REFERENCES

Segal, L. (1987). *Is the Future Female?: Troubled Thoughts on Contemporary Feminism*. London: Virago.

Segal, L. (1994). *Straight Sex: Rethinking the Politics of Pleasure*. 1st ed. Berkeley: University of California Press.

Segal, L. (2007). *Slow Motion*. 2nd ed. New Brunswick, NJ: Rutgers University Press.

Sejersen, C. and Volkova, L. (2015). The Man Who Would be King. *Man About Town* (Spring/Summer 2015), p. 143.

Serano, J. (2007). *Whipping Girl: A Transexual Woman on Sexism and the Scapegoating of Femininity*. Berkeley: Seal Press.

Shabazz, J. (2002). *Back in the Days*. New York: PowerHouse.

Sharkey, A. (1997). STYLE: WALKING TALL; From Stilts through Velvet Slippers and Dress Shirts to Trompe l'oeil: Alix Sharkey Reports on the Paris Menswear Collections. *The Guardian*. Available at: www.nexis.com [Accessed December 1, 2012).

Sigee, R. (2015). "Men Shop More like Women Now … It's Wonderful to See Them Make an Effort"; FASHION WEEK'S DYLAN JONES ON WHY LONDON IS THE MOST EXCITING CITY IN THE WORLD. *The Evening Standard*, p. 13.

Simons, R. and Daniels, M. (1998). *Disorder Incubation Isolation*. Paris: Studio Carrère.

Simons, R. and Sims, D. (1999). *Isolated Heroes*. 1st ed. Antwerp: Raf Simons.

Simpson Guitare Beachwear Advertisement. (1966). *Town* (7), p. 14.

Simpson, M. (1994a). *Male Impersonators*. New York: Routledge.

Simpson, M. (2017). The Metrosexual is Dead. Long Live the "spornosexual." [online] Telegraph.co.uk. Available at: www.telegraph.co.uk/men/fashion-and-style/10881682/The-metrosexual-is-dead.-Long-live-the-spornosexual.html [Accessed February 22, 2017].

Simpson, M. (1994b). Here come the Mirror Men; Metrosexual Men Wear Paul Smith, Use Moisturiser, and Know that Vanity Begins at Home. *The Independent*, p. 22. Available at: www.marksimpson.com/here-come-the-mirror-men/ [Accessed March 21, 2017].

Simpson Piccadilly Advertisement—How to Cope with the Height of Summer even in the Depth of Winter. (1962). *Town* (9), p. 6.

Sims, D. and Howe, A. (1990). Snip It, Rip It, Colour It or Patch It: In Denim the Customiser is Always Right. *The Face*, (24) September, pp. 84–91.

Sims, D. and Ward, M. (1993). *i-D* (113, February), pp. 76–77.

Sinclaire, P. and Mondino, J. (1997). Hard Times. *Arena Homme+*.

Siwan, M. and Brown, P. (1984). Relax! *Blitz* (19 March), London: Jigsaw Publications, p. 35.

Slimane, H. (2000). Yves Saint Laurent Autumn/Winter 2000–2001. [video] Available at: www.youtube.com/watch?v=r-RknaCEyXo [Accessed April 28, 2013]. Paris.

Slimane, H. (2005). Dior Homme Autumn/Winter 2005 Advertisement. *Another Man*. Available at: www.hedislimane.com/fashiondiary/index.php?id=35 [Accessed April 2, 2013].

Slimane, H. (2006a).Dior Homme Autumn/Winter 2007 Campaign. Available at: www.hedislimane.com/fashiondiary/index.php?id=19 [Accessed April 15, 2014].

Slimane, H. (2006b). Dior Homme Spring/Summer 2007 Campaign. Available at: www.hedislimane.com/fashiondiary/index.php?id=28 [Accessed April 15, 2014].

Smalls, J. (2013). Féral Benga's Body. In: E. Rosenhaft and R. Aitken, eds., *Africa in Europe Studies in Transnational Practice in the Long Twentieth Century*, 1st ed. Liverpool: Liverpool University Press, pp. 99–199.

Socha, M. (2007). Today's Top Stories. *Women's Wear Daily* (November 27), p. 1.

Soloflex Advertisement. (1983). *Gentlemen's Quarterly* (July), p. 4.

Sontag, S. (2009 [1964]). Notes on Camp. In: S. Sontag (ed.) *Against Interpretation and Other Essays*. London: Penguin, pp. 275–292.

Spindler, A. (1997). Strength in Diversity at Men's Shows. *The New York Times (Late Edition)*, p. 14.

Steinman, J., Pitchford, D. and Tyler, B. (1984). *Holding Out for a Hero*. [CD] New York: Columbia Records.

Stephen, J. (1962). His Clothes Advertisement. *Town* (11), p. 25.

Stern, S. (2016). Take to the Barricades, Office Workers! And Don't Forget Your Suits. *The Guardian*. [online] Available at: www.nexis.com/search/homesubmitForm.do [Accessed December 20, 2016].

Sterne, H. (1994). Gender Gaffes: Some Enchanted Evening. *Gentlemen's Quarterly*, (February), pp. 126–128.

Suen, S. (2016). Autumn/Winter 2016/2017: Chinese Chess. [Menswear Runway Show] London: Victoria House.

Synth Britannia (2009). [TV program] BBC Four: BBC. October 16, 2009.

Tailor & Cutter (1972). The Alternative Pant. *Tailor & Cutter*, April 107 (5459), p. 3.

Takahashi, Y. (1997). *Raf Simons Spring/Summer 1998—Black Palms*. [Polaroid] Paris: Bastille.

Tan, J. (2011). Policing Boys for Masculinity in Malaysia. *The F Word*. Available at: www.thefword.org.uk/2011/04/policing_boys_f/ [Accessed December 1, 2012].

Testino, M. (1997). Gucci Advertisement Spring/Summer 1997 featuring Edward Fogg. *Arena Homme+* (7, Spring/Summer), p. 72.

Texture and pattern—New Issues in the Fashion Market. (1983). *Gentlemen's Quarterly* (September), pp. 278–279.

Thatcher, M. (1987). Speech to Conservative Party Conference. In: *Conservative Party Conference*. [online] Thatcher Archive. Available at: www.margaretthatcher.org/speeches/displaydocument.asp?docid=106941 [Accessed January 5, 2017].

The Indigo Mix (1994). *Gentlemen's Quarterly* (January), p. 70.

Theweleit, K. (1989). *Male Fantasies: Volume 2*. Cambridge: Polity Press.

Thomson, K. (1966). Ken Thomson Trying it on: 4. *Town* (9), p. 12.

Thomson, M. (2008). *Endowed*. New York: Routledge.

Topman. (2009). Topman Campaign with Model Robbie Wodge Autumn/Winter 2009. Available at: www.thefashionisto.com/topman-news-expansion-robbie-wadge/ [Accessed March 27, 2017].

Toscani, O. (1969a). Dressed-down Evening Style: Di Sera una Moda Sdrammatizzata. *L'Uomo Vogue* (6), pp. 134–135.

Toscani, O. (1969b). Peter Chatel. *L'Uomo Vogue* (6), p. 118.

Toscani, O. (1969c). With Humour, Come Day or Night: Di giorno o di sera, con ironia. *L'Uomo Vogue* (6), p. 137.

Toscani, O. (1971). The New Face of the New Dad: La Nuova Pelle dei Nuovi Papa. *L'Uomo Vogue* (10), pp. 102–104.

Toscani, O. (1976). Afro-Look. *L'Uomo Vogue* (46), pp. 133–141.

Toynbee, P. (1987). The Incredible Shrinking New Man. *The Guardian* (April 6), p. 10.

Triggs, T. (1992). Framing Masculinity: Herb Ritts, Bruce Weber & the Body Perfect. In: J. Ash and E. Wilson, eds., *Chic Thrills*, 1st ed. London: Pandora.

Tulloch, C. (2010). Style-Fashion-Dress: From Black to Post-Black. In *Fashion Theory*, 14(3), pp. 273–304.

Turner, T. (2014). German Sports Shoes, Basketball, and Hip Hop: The Consumption and Cultural Significance of the adidas "Superstar," 1966–1988. *Sport in History*, 35(1), pp. 127–155.

REFERENCES

Turra, A. (2016). Brioni Plans Job Cuts. *Women's Wear Daily*. Available at: wwd.com.arts.idm.oclc.org/business-news/business-features/brioni-job-cuts-brendan-mullane-kering-10386420/ [Accessed October 24, 2016].

Valentino at twenty: Valentino a Vent'Anni. (1976). *L'Uomo Vogue* (47), 163.

Vam.ac.uk, 1967. Pierre Cardin - Victoria and Albert Museum. Available at: www.vam.ac.uk/content/articles/p/pierre-cardin/ [Accessed March 21, 2014].

Vanderperre, W. (2014). Garments from Raf Simons' Autumn/Winter 1999–2000 Collection. *032c Magazine*.

Vanderperre, W., Rizzo, O. and Philips, P. (2003). Robbie Snelders. In: R. Simons and F. Bonami, eds., *The Fourth Sex: Adolescent Extremes*. Milan: Charta.

Venturini-Fendi, S. (2003). Fendi Autumn/Winter 2003–2004. *Collezioni Uomo* (47), pp. 115–117.

Venturini-Fendi, S. (2004). Fendi Spring/Summer 2005. *Collezioni Uomo*.

Vernon, P. (2011). How to Spot a Hipster (an easy guide for oldies). *The Times*. Available at: www.thetimes.co.uk/tto/life/fashion/article3223623.ece [Accessed June 11, 2016].

Versace Intimo Advertisement (1994). *Arena* (15), 14.

Virgile, V. (2011). Lanvin Spring/Summer 2012 by Lucas Ossendrijver. Available at: www.vogue.co.uk/shows/spring-summer-2012-menswear/lanvin/collection/ [Accessed March 23, 2014].

Virgile, V. (2013). Juun. J Spring/Summer 2014. Available at: www.juunj.com/collections/2014_ss/index.jsp [Accessed March 20, 2014].

Wales Bonner, G. (2015). Autumn/Winter 2015 Ebonics. [image] Available at: www.vam.ac.uk/content/articles/f/fashion-in-motion-grace-wales-bonner/ [Accessed January 12, 2017].

Wales Bonner, G. (2016). Ebonics—Autumn Winter 15—Grace Wales Bonner. [online] Grace Wales Bonner. Available at: www.walesbonner.net/collection/collection-2/ [Accessed July 24, 2016].

Wall, G. and Arnold, S. (2007). How Involved Is Involved Fathering?: An Exploration of the Contemporary Culture of Fatherhood. *Gender & Society*, 21(4), pp. 508–527. doi: 10.1177/0891243207304973.

Watson, E. (1984). Front Cover. *Smash Hits* (23), p. 1.

Watson, J. (2000). *Male Bodies*. Buckingham: Open University Press.

Watson, N., Bradshaw, D. and Tango Design (1989). Levi Strauss Regulation Chinos. *The Face: Pull-out Advertorial*, pp. 1–11.

Webb, I. (2015). Beautiful Freaks: Iain R Webb on Clubs, Counter Culture and Unbridled Creativity. [online] DisneyRollerGirl. Available at: www.disneyrollergirl.net/iain-webb-clubs-counter-culture/ [Accessed November 1, 2016].

Webb, I. and Lewis, M. (1986). *Blitz* (47), pp. 246–247.

Webb, I. and Owen, M. (1983). New Designers: Elmaz Huseyin. *Blitz*, p. 28.

Weber, B. (1983). Calvin Klein Advertisement. *Gentlemen's Quarterly* (October), p. 16.

Weber, B. (1991). Obsession Calvin Klein Advertisement. *Gentlemen's Quarterly* (January), p. 26.

Weber, B. (1994). Escape Calvin Klein Advertisement. *Arena* (16), pp.6–7.

Weber, B. (1982). Tom Hintnaus Models Calvin Klein Underwear. Available at: iconicphotos.org/2010/06/26/ck-tom-hintnaus/ [Accessed March 17, 2017].

Westgarth, S. and Ellis, L. (2009). Topman Campaign Autumn/Winter 2009–2010. Available at: www.thefashionisto.com/new-arrivals-topman-ltd-2/ [Accessed April 12, 2012].

WGSN (2016a). Joggers & Trackpants Spring/Summer 2017. *Commercial Update*. New York: WGSN/Ascential Group Limited, pp. 1–11.

WGSN (2016b). Tailoring: Spring/Summer 2017. *Commercial Update*. New York: WGSN/Ascential Group Limited, pp. 1–11.

WGSN (2017). *Southern Africa Menswear: Emerging Trend*. Youth, young men, trend watch. New York: WGSN/Ascential Group Limited, pp. 1–11.

White, C. (1998). Review/Fashion: Touches of Spice in a Tepid Stew. *The New York Times* January 27.

Wilchins, R. (2002). *Queer Theory, Gender Theory*. Los Angeles: Alyson Books.

Williamson, J. (1986). Male Order. *New Statesman*, 112(2901), p. 25.

Woods, J. (2013). The Unforgivable Rise of the She-man; Metrosexual Man has Gone from Tolerable Dandy to Insufferable Sissy—and Women are the Losers, says Judith Woods. *The Daily Telegraph*, May 24, p. 35.

Yahoo Style (2015). Exclusive: Hedi Slimane On Saint Laurent's Rebirth, His Relationship With Yves & the Importance of Music. *Yahoo.com*. Available at: www.yahoo.com/style/exclusive-hedi-slimane-on-saint-laurents-126446645943.html [Accessed July 20, 2016].

Yves Saint Laurent Rive Gauche Spring-Summer 2001 (2001). *Arena Homme+*.

Zweig, S. (2009 [1942]). *The World of Yesterday*. London: Pushkin Press.

INDEX

Abdulrahim, Ali xii, 1, 167–8
abjection 19, 102, 183 n.16
Africa 74, 147, 168, 174–5, 182 n.6, 185 n.5
    Southern Africa 174
    West Africa 147, 175
African-American. *See* black style
agency 4, 5, 13, 76, 177–8 n.3, 178 n.8, 185 n.5
AIDS 65–6, 88, 182 n.8
Anderson, Brett 31, 99, 120
Anderson, Eric 19–20, 106, 108, 128, 144–5, 169, 171–2
anti-semitism 72, 74, 78
Arena Homme+ (magazine) 66–9, 71, 94, 96, 103, 111–2, 182 n.12
Asia. *See also* Japan, Korea, Orientalism 1, 39, 40, 82, 110, 136, 146, 164, 170, 175

Barrett, Neil 131
Barry, Ben 4–5, 24, 173
Barthes, Roland 4, 94
black style 8, 74, 146, 147–53
Blitz Kids. *See* New Romantics
bodybuilding 89, 93
Bolan, Marc 2, 35
Bourdieu, Pierre 21–2, 52, 178 n.6
Bowie, David 2–3, 22, 52–3, 59, 116, 180 n.7
Breward, Christopher 4–5, 12, 28, 179 n.2, 185 n.8
Business Suit. *See* suit
Butler, Judith 6, 17

Capasa, Ennio 9, 20, 51, 71, 99, 104, 113–14, 117, 123–4, 126, 128, 131, 146, 183 n.17
Chanel, Coco (Gabrielle) 65, 141, 147

Clark, Adrian 4, 21–2
Cocker, Jarvis 31, 120
Cohn, Nik 3, 33, 35–9, 76–8, 181–2 n.4
Cole, Shaun xii, 4–5, 28
Connell, Raewyn 20, 144, 146, 177–8 nn.3–4, 185 nn.3–4
craft 131, 156–7

Day, Corinne 99, 111–12
Dior Homme 2, 21–2, 25, 50, 99, 102, 106, 108, 115–16, 119–21, 126, 146, 154, 169–70
discourse 5, 10–14, 17–21, 24–9, 35, 44, 55, 83–8, 93–6, 104–56, 171–4, 177 n.1, 185 n.5, 186 n.10
    discursive formation 24–5, 144–5
    reverse discourse 20, 22, 104, 171
Doma, Damir 131, 164

E. Tautz (Fashion Label) 3, 160–2
Edwards, Richey 99, 102, 120
Edwards, Tim 28, 59, 61, 64, 91, 111
effeminacy / femininity 13, 16–20, 27, 31, 33, 35–6, 72–4, 76, 89, 92, 97, 102, 106, 108, 111, 141, 144–8, 153, 174, 178 n.4, 181–2 n.4, 183 n.16
eroticism 55, 71, 92, 153, 180–1 n.16
exoticism 40, 52, 74, 78, 80, 82–3, 147–8, 158, 185 n.5

The Face (magazine) 28, 55–9, 61–2, 77, 89–91, 94, 99–102, 111, 121, 182 n.12, 184 n.4
Fanon, Franz 148
fascism 72, 74–5, 87
fatherhood 40, 44, 168–9, 177 nn.1–2, 180 n.9
Featherston, Mike 21

feminism/feminist theory 12–14, 28, 44, 72, 84, 91, 106, 109, 111–12, 124, 128, 174, 177 n.1, 177–8 n.3, 182 n.10
Ford, Tom 20–21, 104, 112–14, 117, 126, 163
Foucault, Michel 17, 22, 24–5, 27, 74, 93, 104, 106, 144

gender. *See* effeminacy/femininity, feminism, inclusive masculinity, hegemonic masculinity, performativity
gender performativity. *See* performativity
gender transgression 31, 36, 66, 74, 90, 106, 109–10, 147–8, 171, 178 n.5, 182 n.9
Green, Craig 130, 164–6, 184 n.1
Greer, Germaine 62, 106–9
Gucci 2, 71, 104, 112–13, 163
GQ/Gentlemen's Quarterly (magazine) 10, 52, 55, 62–4, 68, 80, 84–5, 87–9, 94–6, 111–12, 182 n.7, 182 n.12, 183 n.1

Hall, Stuart 6, 10, 38–9
Hebdige, Dick 28, 59
hegemonic masculinity 2–3, 13–14, 18–22, 28–9, 74–5, 88, 106, 111, 123–4, 128, 144, 146, 159, 177–8 nn.3–4, 185 n 3
heterosexuality 19, 27, 44, 68, 96, 123–4, 128, 148, 173, 180–1 n.16, 182 nn.8–9, 186 n.1
hipsters 14–19, 24–6, 123–4, 156–7
homophobia 2, 13, 19, 92, 106, 112, 123
homosexuality. *See* queer identity
Hood by Air (Fashion Label) 159
hooks, bell 6, 14
Hypebeast (website) 158

i-D (magazine) 1, 28, 55, 59, 61–2, 66, 89, 99, 102, 111, 184 n.4
inclusive Masculinity 2, 19–20, 106, 108, 128, 144–6, 169, 171–3
Indie culture 5, 9, 15, 22, 31, 99, 120, 121, 181 n.20
Inventory (magazine) 154–5
Italy 3, 32, 39, 44, 78, 120

J. W. (Jonathan) Anderson 2, 129, 132, 146, 153, 156
Japan 1, 24, 59, 110, 146, 164
Jewish designers / tailors 8, 78, 179 n.5
Juun. J 71, 129, 131, 136–41, 144, 146, 164, 166

Korea 136, 164, 170
Kristeva, Julia 102, 183 nn.15–16

Lang, Helmut 20, 99, 104, 128, 130, 166, 171
Lanvin 2, 25, 71, 119–20, 129, 132–5, 160, 163
London Collections Men 1, 24, 129, 178 n.7
London Fashion Week. *See* London Collections Men
Long, James xii, 3, 129
lounge suit. *See* suit
L'Uomo Vogue (magazine) 39–44, 53, 55, 62–3, 79, 81–2, 84–5, 87–9, 111–12, 126, 168, 177 n.1

Mai Gidah 1, 167
Mazhar, Nasir 71, 159
metrosexual, the 24, 26–7, 97, 112, 123–4, 145, 173
Michele, Alessandro 2, 71, 146
military aesthetics 3, 11, 29, 40, 65–6, 75, 88, 132, 163
misogyny 2, 19–20, 73, 178 n.4, 182 n.9
mod (subculture) 8, 28, 32, 35, 54, 77–8, 120
Modernism 59, 74, 126, 185 n.5, 185 n.8
Monocle (magazine) 154
Mort, Frank xii, 4–5, 28, 61, 64, 89
Mr Fish 2, 8, 39, 78, 180 n.7
Mulvey, Laura 72–3, 148, 153, 180 n.16
muscularity 20–1, 65, 71, 75, 85, 87–9, 91–3, 96–9, 102, 148, 182 n.8

new lad 14, 68, 70, 112, 124
New Man, the 13–14, 18–19, 44, 55, 64, 68, 89, 91, 97, 168, 173, 177 nn.1–2
New Romantics 7, 9, 59, 61, 66, 83, 89, 120, 180 n.14
Nixon, Sean 28, 64, 89

INDEX

objectification 72, 92, 99, 107–9, 148, 153, 175, 180–1 n.16
Orientalism 33, 52, 74
orthodox masculinity 2–3, 5, 12, 16, 18–19, 21, 27, 66, 73, 83, 92, 97–9, 102, 110–11, 124, 128, 144–7, 169, 171–3, 178 n.5
Ossendrijver, Lucas 2, 9, 25, 71, 119–20, 131–6, 141, 144, 146, 156, 163–4, 172

peacock revolution 2, 7, 9, 31–3, 78, 81, 128
performativity 14, 17–18, 59, 89, 96, 184 n.3
Petri, Ray 59, 61, 66, 89, 180 n.14
Petridis, Alexis 26–7
pleasure 7, 35, 52, 72, 76, 80, 88–9, 95, 97–8, 107, 114, 148, 169
Porter, Charlie xii, 4–5, 21–2, 66, 104, 115, 120
pretension 18
punk 7, 9–10, 20, 28, 32, 40, 54, 56, 59, 113–15, 119–21, 128, 154, 157, 180 n.14, 184 n.5

queer identity 22, 33, 35–6, 59, 91, 123–4, 128, 146, 148, 185 n.5

Ritts, Herb 84, 87, 90–1
Rubchinskiy, Gosha 159

Schorr, Collier 99, 108
Segal, Lynne 14, 68, 124, 128
Simms, David 99–100, 111–12, 121
Simons, Raf 1, 9, 20–2, 51, 71, 78, 99, 102–4, 106–8, 110, 113–15, 120–1, 123–6, 128, 131, 136, 141–4, 146, 153, 157, 166, 171–2
Simpson, Mark 97–8, 112, 123–4, 184 n.3
slim bodies 21, 71, 78, 83, 88, 92, 99–102, 108–10, 115, 116
Slimane, Hedi 1–2, 9, 20–2, 25, 51, 71, 78, 83, 99, 102–6, 108, 110, 113–17, 119–21, 123–4, 126, 128, 131, 146, 153, 154, 164, 166, 171, 172
socialist realism 75, 87
South Asia 39, 40, 82, 164
spornosexual 97–8, 124
sportswear 11, 55–6, 113, 116, 119, 141, 156–60, 163–4, 180 n.10, 184 n.4
Stephen, John 2, 8, 32–6, 77–8, 179 n.1
subculture. *See also* mods, punk, new romantics, teddy boy 2, 8–10, 15, 17–18, 28, 32, 35–6, 38–9, 54–5, 59, 66–8, 83, 89, 96, 99, 111–12, 114–15, 120–1, 128, 157–9, 179 n.1, 181 n.20, 185 n.9
Suen, Sean xii, 2–3, 141, 166
suit, the 3, 12, 33, 45, 62–4, 163, 179 n.2

Tailor & Cutter (journal) 45–52, 126
teddy boy 8, 28, 77
Thatcher/Thatcherism 55, 61, 64, 112, 181 n.18
Theweleit, Klaus 19, 72–4, 76, 87–9, 183 n.16
thin bodies. *See* slim bodies
Tisci, Riccardo 71, 157
Topman 1–3, 25, 119, 160, 169, 178 n.7
Town (magazine) 33–7, 44, 77–8

Vanderperre, Willy 99, 102, 115
Vetements (fashion label) 132, 156, 159
Vince's Man's Shop 32–3
violence 1–2, 5, 13, 16, 20, 70, 95, 144, 147, 159
Vionnet, Madeleine 141

waif. *See* slim bodies
Wales Bonner, Grace 2, 146–53, 169, 185 n.5
Webb, Ian, R. 59, 61, 180 n.5
Weber, Bruce 84, 87, 92–4
WGSN 163, 174